PETER MATTHIESSEN

The Tree Where Man Was Born

PICADOR

in association with Collins

Portions of the text originally appeared, in
somewhat different form, in *The New Yorker*

First published in Great Britain 1972
by William Collins Sons & Co. Ltd
This Picador edition published 1984
by Pan Books Ltd,
Cavaye Place, London SW10 9PG
in association with William Collins Sons & Co. Ltd
9 8 7 6 5 4 3
© *The New Yorker* 1972
ISBN 0 330 28196 8

Phototypeset by Input Typesetting Ltd, London SW19 8DR
Printed and bound in Great Britain by
Cox & Wyman Ltd, Reading

In Memoriam

DEBORAH
LOVE
MATTHIESSEN

in love
and
gratitude

Author's Note

The wild creatures I had come to Africa to see are exhilarating in their multitudes and colors, and I imagined for a time that this glimpse of the earth's morning might account for the anticipation that I felt, the sense of origins, of innocence and mystery, like a marvelous childhood faculty restored. Perhaps it is the consciousness that here in Africa, south of the Sahara, our kind was born. But there was also something else that, years ago, under the sky of the Sudan, had made me restless, the stillness in this ancient continent, the echo of so much that has died away, the imminence of so much as yet unknown. Something has happened here, is happening, will happen—whole landscapes seem alert.

In early 1961, on the way around the world to join an anthropological expedition into New Guinea, I traveled south through Africa, wishing to see the Egyptian temple of Abu Simbel, up the Nile, the warrior-herdsmen of the south Sudan, and the great animal herds of the Serengeti Plains, all of which, in 1961, seemed on the point of disappearance. Traveling overland from Cairo, I got as far south as the Ngorongoro Crater, in the country still known then as Tanganyika. The new Sunday air charter from Nairobi permitted a brief visit to the Serengeti, where I saw the first leopard of my life, loping along among low bushes by a stream; on the homeward journey the pilot flew over the endless companies of game animals on the plain that is the greatest wildlife spectacle left in the world. But animals seen from the air, without the dimensions of sound and feel and smell, remain remote. I had no real sense of having experienced the Serengeti, and when I was invited to return by John Owen, then director of the Tanzania National Parks, I fairly leapt at the opportunity. From late January to mid-March of 1969 I lived mostly at Seronera, where I was very hospitably received by the parks staff and the scientists of the Serengeti Research Institute, set up in 1966 for the crucial ecological studies that will certainly affect the future of man and animal in Africa. Often these men—wardens and scientists alike—took me along on air surveys, field trips, and safaris, and gave me invaluable instruction in African ecology; meanwhile I had my own Land Rover, with four-wheel drive, and the chance to investigate all and everything, as I pleased ...

Because of the chronic political disorder in East Africa in the decade since this book was published, any attempt at revising the text from a political/geographic point of view would probably be out of date before this edition could be printed; thus, Lake Turkana in Kenya's Northern Frontier District will be recognized in these pages by its former name, Lake Rudolf. The land and the wildlife problems continue in much the same pattern as before.

Peter Matthiessen

Contents

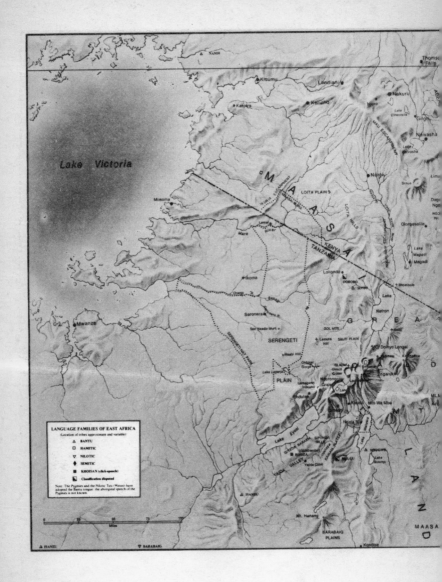

LANGUAGE FAMILIES OF EAST AFRICA
(Location of tribes approximate and variable)

△ BANTU
□ HAMITIC
▽ NILOTIC
◆ SEMITIC
■ KHOISAN (click-speech)
▣ Classification disputed

Note: The Pygmies and the Nilotic Tutsi (Watusi) have
adopted the Bantu tongue; the aboriginal speech of the
Pygmies is not known.

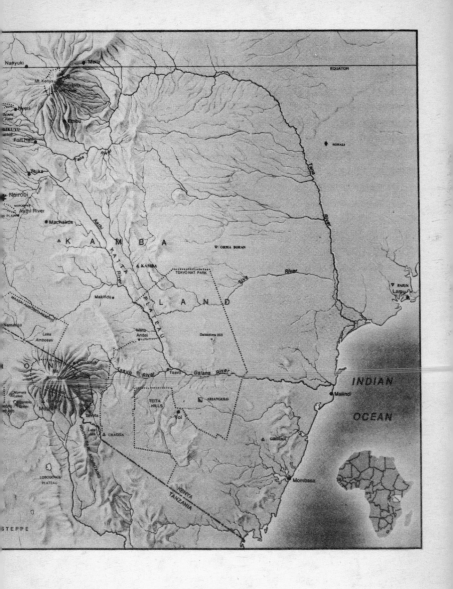

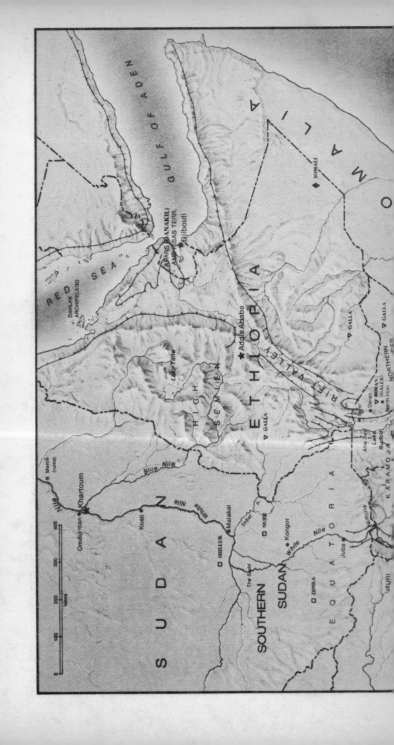

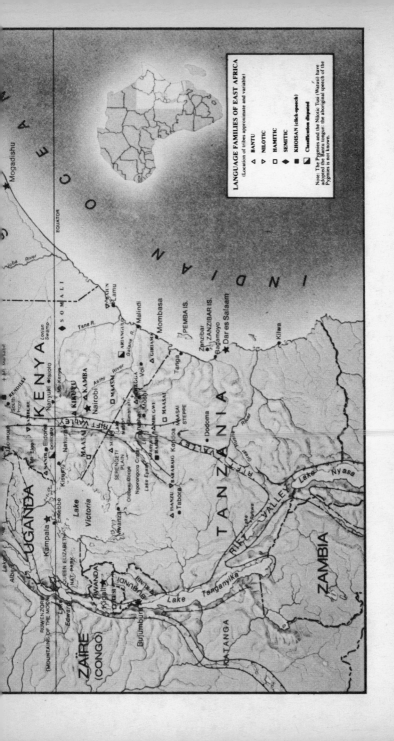

LANGUAGE FAMILIES OF EAST AFRICA
(Location of tribes approximate and variable)

△ BANTU
▽ NILOTIC
◻ HAMITIC
◆ SEMITIC
■ KHOISAN (click-speech)
▨ Classification disputed

Note: The Pygmies and the Nilotic Tusi (Watusi) have adopted the Bantu tongue; the aboriginal speech of the Pygmies is not known.

1. The Tree Where Man Was Born

In the time when Dendid created all things,
He created the sun,
And the sun is born and dies, and comes again.
He created the moon,
And the moon is born, and dies, and comes again;
He created the stars,
And the stars are born, and die, and come again;
He created man,
And man is born, and dies, and does not come again.

Old Dinka Song[1]

The tree where man was born, according to the Nuer, still stood
within man's memory in the west part of the south Sudan, and I
imagine a great baobab thrust up like an old root of life in those wild
grasses that blow forever to the horizons, and wild man in naked
silhouette against the first blue sky. That bodeful man of silence and
the past is everywhere in Africa. One hears the silence, hears one's
step, and stops . . . and he is there, in the near distance. I see him
still: a spear point glitters in the sun.

In the south Sudan, man is tall and gaunt, and black as the burnt
skeleton of a tree: Dinka, who carves his scars in shallow v's, and
Shilluk with his raised beads of skin in a string curling down toward
the ear, and Nuer with six jagged welts, temple to temple—his terrible
brows and filed front teeth, jutting like fangs, give Nuer a fixed death's
head grin that is not to be mistaken for a smile. In 1961, a few still
wandered as far north as Khartoum, where I first saw them. In mission
shorts, they stalked the Arab bazaars of Omdurman, dwarfing the
scurrying traders of the suq. Others crossed the Khartoum bridge,
near the confluence of the Blue Nile and the White. Oblivious of
bridge and rivers, ignoring the horn blare and exhaust stink and shrill
shouting of despised beings who owned no cattle, the entranced
figures forded the twentieth-century traffic in the single file that would

15

wind southward nearly a thousand miles across desert and river into Equatoria.

To most of the tribesmen, the Sudan government is a foreign power, having come into existence (in 1955) without the agreement or even the knowledge of many of its inhabitants: the desert north is a part of the Arab world while the south, a thousand miles away, lies in black Africa. In 1961, when I traveled south through Egypt and the Sudan into East Africa, these southern provinces—Upper Nile, Bahr el Ghazal, and Equatoria—had been made "closed territories," since the tribesmen would not heed their Moslem government. No foreigner could pass through without a permit, and no photographs of the naked peoples were permitted. Nor was the journey overland an easy one, for there was no road across the desert, which extends for several hundred miles south of Khartoum. In the absence of scheduled transport, I rode upon the cargo of an old trading truck sent south during the dry season by the merchants of Omdurman, and my bed of potatoes, wire tubing, tinware, and iron doors was shared with two whites met in Omdurman—a young student bound home for South Africa and a bearded American veteran of the Israeli wars with a hidden sheath knife, beret, dark glasses, and gold earring—as well as sixteen mission tribesmen, mostly Dinka and Shilluk, with a pair of Nuer. No matter how we arranged ourselves, we were never in close physical contact with less than five companions, and in the long wait and great heat, morale was low when at twilight the truck started up and set off through streets which even in the poorest towns of the north Sudan are swept clean daily by twig brooms; on a minaret, against a clear pink sky, a muezzin called the faithful to the prayers of evening.

Night had fallen by the time the truck had cleared the city, and a spray of stars froze on a blue-black sky. The vague track wandered south into a soft emptiness of cooling sand haired over thinly, here and there, by bitter thorns of drought. In the headlight's jogging beam danced ghostly gerbils, hopping and fluttering on tiptoe, like stricken birds. And farther onward, close to midnight, where the sands relented, came the birds of night—the African owl, and nightjars, and pale Senegal stone curlews whirling straight up into the dark like souls departing.

As the night passed, the way grew less distinct. Random tracks leading off into the void were followed faithfully by the driver, who

16

was no Bedouin and knew nothing of the stars. Once the truck halted, and the Moslem cabal in the cab got out their prayer rugs, washed their feet, and in the beam of the headlights, touched their foreheads to the ground. Presumably they were pointed east, toward Mecca, but this did not appear to mean that they knew which way was south, for the truck soon halted once again, having traveled for some time in rude circles; shortly thereafter it was driven remorselessly into a ditch. The passengers leapt from the tilted cargo and stood in a long respectful line while the driver spun his wheels into the earth. When the axles touched at last, he left the truck and joined the line, contemplating the work of Allah with every evidence of satisfaction. Then everybody but the two Americans, who had none, got out blankets and lay down upon the desert.

The cold of the desert night, toward four, was the cold of the dark universe descended. Dawn came at last, and an hour later, a faint warmth; nourished by dusty dates and cold sardines, we dug the truck out of the desert. Solitary figures, white shrouds blowing, wandered the landscape; the brown lumps of their habitations merged with a stony rise a mile away. Near the ditch grew a thin grass, but elsewhere, as far as the eye could see in all directions, stretched sere distances burned off to gravel.

In the old millenniums of rain during the Pleistocene and after, much of this waste had been well-watered grassland. Years later, flying at dawn from Rabat on the Atlantic coast and drifting southeast over endless red infernal reaches of gravel, windspun sand, and smoky sky, I would see the ancient rivers of the Ice Age, like fossil tracings in the sands of the Sahara. Hunters had once wandered there, and left red drawings on those rocks, but now there was no sign of life, no track. Seven millenniums ago, when men of Asia brought wheat and barley, sheep and goats, to the lower Nile, the desert was already spreading, and the work of drought was rapidly advanced by the goats of man, which ate the thorn that had sewn tight a land that soon unraveled into sand.

The Stone Age hunters found by the Asians are known as the Tasarians and Bedarians, and the Afro-Asiatics born of these encounters raised villages on the flood plains of the Nile that would become the dynasties of Egypt. Until now, Africa had known no agriculture, nor any domestic animal except possibly the dog. But in the next one thousand years native plants were domesticated in West Africa, and certain millets in the highlands of Ethiopia. By 3500 B.C., domestic stock appears to have passed into the hands of the West African Negroid peoples, perhaps by way of traders from the Mediterranean who were already opening up the great north-south caravan routes across the Sahara. Advanced cultures had rapidly developed in West Africa—the Nok culture is thought to have begun well before 2000 B.C.—but although some trade no doubt continued, the peoples of Bilad al-Sudan—Land of the Blacks—were little affected by the surge of Mediterranean civilizations. Domestic animals and a few plants had been acquired, but the age of bronze went by without their knowledge. Even the use of iron that had reached the Cush kingdom of Meröe, not far north of Khartoum, by 300 B.C., took another thousand years to reach the tribesmen of the south Sudan, for the desert between the Nile and the mountains of Ethiopia was all but impassable, and travel on the river was impeded by the vast riverain swamp known as the Sudd, which prevented the extension of Egyptian splendors into the south and marked the southern limits of the Roman Empire. The Romans were still able to graze animals on what are now the sands of Libya, and Alexandrian ivory traders, mentioned in Ptolemy, brought back reports of the great central lakes and what are thought to be the snow-capped Ruwenzoris, the Mountains of the Moon, but few Mediterranean invaders got farther than that part of the Sahara called the Nubian Desert, an hallucinatory void burned by bright winds. What was left of the North African pastures was destroyed by hordes of Bedouins who swept through the northern continent ten centuries ago; today a few Arabs and sad donkeys cling to dim sand-strangled outposts, and a rare caravan of camels navigates by the lone railroad track that comes to Khartoum across the waste from Wadi Halfa.

As the day went on, the camels vanished from the sand horizons. Close to the Nile, the desolation was offset by a haze of grass behind the river banks, but this is a land of bare subsistence where the threat of drought is made worse by the desert locust. Today the sun had become fierce, and the bare land a reflector: distant huts turned eerily in a melted sun, like igneous lumps in the lava seas of a volcano. At the huts where the truck stopped to trade and cool its tires were hordes of a non-biting fly that seeks out moisture at the eyes and mouth. The flies formed black rings on the eyes of the small children, giving them a haunted appearance, but only the very smallest fretted, the rest having learned the resignation to discomfort that was so noticeable in the tribesmen on the truck. The "Europeans," as whites are known in Africa, were much less stoic. The damp touch of the flies, in company with heat and filth and a cumulative fatigue, brought on a half-delirium of thirst and soreness. We fashioned poor turbans out of rags, but the light refracted from the burnished land seared our faces to masks of leather. The Sudanese went bare-headed without complaint, but the Israeli veteran turned a dangerous color: with his dark glasses and rag-tattered head, he glared out over the land like some sort of mad avenger. And the South African boy, the only white to demonstrate with the African students in London after the notorious Sharpeville Massacre in his own country—he spent three weeks in jail for his pains—whose nerves, giving way in the press and stench of his multicolored kind, brought forth the very phrase of the colonials that he had quoted earlier in contempt: "These bloody niggers, they're just down out of the trees!" He laughed at himself, close to tears, so shocked was he by his own outburst, and so relieved that these tribesmen spoke no English. Yet the Africans, who had learned that he came from the country of apartheid and were by no means blind to his ambivalence, plainly preferred him to the soldier, who was truly democratic in a way that few whites are, and recommended himself, besides, by an overt hatred for the Arabs in the cab, whom these tribesmen hated also: the Arab trade in slaves, which devastated the south Sudan in the nineteenth century, has never been forgotten or forgiven. But the soldier was beyond their ken, not the beret and beard and earring but because he kept no tribal distance, observed no protocol. Intensely conservative, fearful especially of the bizarre, the Africans glowered at the pantomimes and clowning that he offered as a means of communication. Caught up by the anti-white fever sweeping Africa, they felt patronized or even threatened, and were forever on the watch for foreign attempts to encroach upon native territories from the imperialist enclave set up just behind the cab, out of the desert wind. But the soldier tried and tried again, refusing to see that his friendliness gave offense, that these carved masks might have been just as suspicious, perhaps more so, of his black friends in America, who were also westerners, with a makeshift western sense of life and death.

Gradually the square huts of mud-brick were replaced by the African beehive hut, a cylinder of mud and sticks topped with straw thatch bound tight into a cone. In mid-afternoon, the truck reached Kosti, where we sat waiting in the suq for the sun to die. Kosti has what might be called a sewing-machine economy; ancient specimens of these instruments, in the smaller villages, are ordinarily the sole evidence of the machine age. We ate strange local sheep off doubtful ware, drank the black tea of the desert, and in the late twilight, started off again, traveling onward intermittently until after midnight, when once again we lay down upon the ground. The night was warmer, warm enough for the mosquitoes, and it came to an end at last. During the night, the hippos bellowed from the Nile, a distant sound, the first murmurings out of the heart of Africa.

The first light shone on a new land of long grass and small acacia, with occasional great solitary baobab. The feather-leaved, sweet-scented acacias or thorn trees, in their great variety, are the dominant vegetation in dry country south to the Cape, but the tree of Africa is the baobab, with its gigantesque bulk and primitive appearance; it is thought to reach the age of twenty-five hundred years, and may be the oldest living thing on earth. The grassland danced with antelope and birds—tropical hawks, doves, pigeons, guinea fowl and francolins, bee-eaters, rollers, hornbills, and myriad weavers, including the quelea or Sudan dioch, which breeds and travels in dense clouds and rivals the locust as an agent of destruction. At the edge of a slough stood two hundred crested cranes and a solitary ostrich, like a warder; where trees gathered in a wood were the white faces of the vervet monkey. In the afternoon, the savanna opened out on a great plain where gazelles fled to the horizons, and naked herdsmen, spear blades gleaming, observed the passage of the truck through the rushing grass with the alert languor of egrets. All the world was blue and gold, with far islands of acacia and ceremonial half circles of human huts. Toward dusk, the truck arrived at Malakal, where it would turn to go back into the north.

The two days passed in Malakal, awaiting a ride south, I spent mostly on a long peninsula which cut off a swamp along the Nile edge. There was a footpath to a point on the peninsula where a Shilluk tended a weir; from here, in crude dugout canoes, the tribesmen crossed the river to a large village in a grove of palms. Respecting crocodiles, I did not press to be taken across, for the north wind which blows from

November to March was sweeping up the river, and the canoes were desperately overcrowded; instead I watched the people come and go, and listened to the singsong of their voices. Shilluk women who passed along the path bore cargoes on their heads, swaying like cobras through the blowing grass, and bands of girls, straight-backed, high-breasted, flirted and waved. The men were painted in a gray ash or red ocher, and the oldest had several rows of beads raised on their foreheads, but scarification, which is performed at a boy's initiation into the tribe, is dying out, for few younger men had more than a single row, and some were not scarred at all.

From the village across the river, on the wind, came a chant and a thump of drums. On the peninsula, bent figures hoed small gardens, and in the swamp behind, two naked fishers, laughing and arguing, handled a cast net. Cisticolas flitted through fierce reeds, and a snake slid out across some rotted sedge into the water, and trees of the river danced with turquoise rollers. In such a setting, in the expectant sunrise, the naked men seemed archetypal: here were dark figures of prehistory. A few centuries ago, the Shilluk lived as far north as Khartoum, and perhaps these glistening fishers were descended from some of the earliest known Negroids, a community of Middle Stone Age fishermen who inhabited the Khartoum region at least seven thousand years ago. (It has been suggested that the Khartoum fishermen invented pottery, possibly through the accidental burning of the mud-lined baskets that are still in use.[2]) The early Negroids appear to have been scattered and few; perhaps they were sedentary fishermen whose modern dominance of the African population came about with the development of agriculture. Possibly they evolved in the central lakes region, and only later came to occupy those regions southwest and west of the Sahara which are now associated with the "true Negro," whoever that may be: a skull contemporaneous with the skulls found at Khartoum has been dug up northeast of Timbuktu, in a land which had not yet turned to desert, and other remains of ancient Negroids have been found in Nigeria and on Lake Edward.

That so little is known of Negroid origins is one of the enigmas of inner Africa, where history must be deduced from chipped stones, clay sherds, rock paintings, and the bones of man and prey. It is presently assumed that Bushmanoid, Pygmoid, and Negroid are races of an ancestral African who adapted over the millenniums to differing environments—the open grasslands, the equatorial forests, the river

21

basins—and would later share his continent with Caucasoids* out of the north, and that a confluence of Negroid and Caucasoid produced the long-headed, small-faced race called the Nilotes or Nilotic peoples, represented by these tall Shilluk casting their nets upon the Nile.

One morning on the Nile peninsula, in a large company of tribesmen, I met two Shilluk who had ridden on the truck. Dressed as they were in mission pants, their pagan scars and fierce filed teeth could only seem grotesque. The two candidates for civilization were glad to see me, for my acquaintance was an evidence of their worldliness. "*Ezzay-yek, ezzay-yek!*" they greeted me in Arabic—another attainment—and offered a passive rubber handshake. And staring after these new Africans as they moved off toward the river, I felt a terrific sadness. The Shilluk believe that when God set out to create man, he used light-colored clay, but toward the end his hands became dirty, and that the dark peoples were less favored than the light in such attainments as guns and a written language.[3]

There is a Nuer song that may have come from the Arab slaving raids of the last century . . .

The wind blows *wirawira*.
Where does it blow?
It blows to the river . . .
This land is overrun by strangers
Who throw our ornaments into the river
And draw their water from its bank.
Blackhair my sister,
I am bewildered.
Blackhair my sister, I am bewildered.
We are perplexed;
We gaze at the stars of God.[4]

* The term "Caucasoid" is used loosely here to signify peoples with Eurasian blood who have mixed with Africans to varying degrees over the centuries. The Caucasoids include the Hamitic-speaking Berber, Tuareg, Egyptians, and Ethiopians of northern Africa as well as more recent Semitic invaders such as the Arabs and Somali; the northern Sudanese today are a mixture of Arab, Hamite, and Negro. Since racial and linguistic groupings are still disputed by authorities, so that no two books on Africa are consistent, I have confined myself where possible to the names of the main language families (cf. Nilotic, Hamitic, Semitic) and avoided more precise and less dependable terms such as Nilo-Hamitic, Cushitic, Sudanic, Afro-Asiatic, etc. The selected references-bibliography at the end of the text will indicate where full discussion of such questions may be found.

We left Malakal in the cab of a small pickup truck whose driver was called Gabriel Babili. A cable ferry took us across the Sobat River, where a group of Dinka washed themselves, slowly and gracefully, beside a stranded metal whaleboat, a sister craft of the British boat in the museum of the Mahdi wars, at Omdurman. In the wind-blown grass along the track, men of the Nuer carried paired spears of the style used by the Dervishes, which, together with hoes, fish-hooks, and ornaments, are gotten in exchange for hides. The truck stopped everywhere to trade. Once the way was blocked by a great herd of the archaic cattle of Egyptian art, their huge horns curved inward at the tip. The herdsmen were coated from face to foot with ash; the mouths and eyes in the gray masks looked moist and hideous. Some were heedless of the truck, not understanding it, and others, panicked by the horn, fled for their lives. Across the dry plains to the east ran a faded track. "That is the road to Abyss-in-i-a," said Gabriel Babili, who had a bad smell, mission English, and an enchanted smile.

Christian missions were established in the south Sudan as early as A.D. 540, at the time of the Axumite Christianity in Ethiopia, and the Nubian kingdoms that resulted held out against the tide of Islam until the fourteenth century. But modern missions set up at the turn of this century in what had become the Anglo-Egyptian Sudan do not appear to have made a deep impression. The people are beautiful, the women modest, and the girls saucily turned out in head feathers, beads, copper bracelets, and cowries, but away from the towns the men go naked—from a narrow point of view, that is, for often those parts of their persons of no interest to moralists are superbly decorated with beads and clay—and this freedom from shame is a source of distress to missionary and Mussulman alike.

In terms of material culture, the Nilotes of the south Sudan have remained among the most primitive people in Africa, and moral dis-approval of their condition dates back at least as far as the 1860s, when the august Sir Samuel Baker, barging upriver with Mrs. Baker and a sedate avalanche of baggage in search of the headwaters of the Nile, concluded that the Dinka had less character than dogs (perhaps Sir Samuel had stern British dogs in mind) due less to this abominable nudity than to what Sir Samuel perceived as an unconscionable absence of rules and regulations in their society or for that matter of any society at all that could be recognized as such by a subject of Her Britannic Majesty. But, in fact, the Nilotic societies are based on a very elaborate set of laws and customs, including the practice among Dinka and Shilluk of their own form of ancient Egyptian divine kingship, with its custom of putting to death the failing chief. Among the Dinka, the Master of the Fishing Spear indicates by a sign of the hand that he is now to be buried alive "to avoid admitting . . . the involuntary death which is the lot of ordinary men and beasts."[5]

The Nuer and Dinka subsist chiefly on milk, cheese, and blood drawn by arrow from their animals' necks. In the rainy season, they grow millet, and in the dry season, when the cattle are herded to the rivers, they eat fish. They are poor farmers and poor hunters, which accounts for the abundance of wild creatures in their land. In effect, their dependence on cattle is total. Besides blood and milk (meat is rarely eaten except when a beast dies of its own accord) the herds furnish dung for fuel and plastering, hides for decorative leather articles, tail hairs for tassels, bones for armlets and utensils, horns for spoons and fishing spears, and scrota for pouches. The ashes of burnt dung supply hair dye and hair straightener—the hair of the Nilotes is markedly longer than that of the Bantu peoples farther south—as well as mouthwash, and the urine is valued not only for tanning but for churning and cheese-making and for bathing the face and hands. Inevitably, intertribal wars are fought over cattle and cattle land, the aggressors being the Nuer and the victims the Dinka. Originally, God gave an old cow and a calf to Dinka and to Nuer, his two sons, but Dinka stole the calf of Nuer under cover of darkness. God, enraged, ordered Nuer to seize Dinka's cow, and the Nuer have done so ever since. It remains the tradition of both tribes that the Nuer takes openly what the Dinka takes by stealth, and the Nuer adhere to an ancient custom of raiding and killing Dinka, who are resigned to their inferior role and offer small resistance; instead they prey upon the Bari, who live mostly on the islands of the Nile and, as a defense against mosquitoes, are said to array themselves each night in a coat of mud. The Nuer rarely war on the more sedentary Shilluk, who have few cattle and subsist mostly on maize meal, eked out by small animals speared in the night and by trapped birds. Alone of the three tribes, they have developed a crude snare, but they remain poor hunters, and are often hungry. The Nuer say[6] that formerly Stomach lived apart from Man, off in the bush, an unobtrusive creature glad of a few roasted insects from the bush fires. Then Man permitted it to join his body, and it has tormented him ever since. But in most tribes in the Sudan and elsewhere, hunger and all human afflictions came about with God's departure from the world. Once the sky pressed so close to the earth that the first man took care when he lifted spears or tools, lest he strike God. In those times, so the Dinka say, God had given the first man and woman one grain of millet every day, and this was plenty, until the woman took more than her share and, using a longer pestle, struck the sky. Then the sky and God withdrew out of man's reach, and ever since man has had to work hard for his food, and has been visited by pain and death, for God is remote, and rarely hears him.[7]

The savanna was still gold, still blowing. Toward sunset, the grass turned silver, and in a strange light a cheetah slipped across the track, its small head carried low. The plain changed gradually to woodland—acacias, fig, baobab, euphorbia, and palms. Soon vegetation crowded to the road, which was crossed at dusk by a band of bush-pig, neat-footed and burly, neck bristles erect, as if intent on punching holes right through the truck. They churned into the scrub. Gabriel, dire in all his thoughts, spoke darkly of encounters with night elephants, and blinded himself by keeping the lights on inside the cab "so other car not hit we," although no other car had been seen that day. He was also fearful of rebellious tribesmen, who were raiding the government posts and whose attitudes toward drivers, most of them Arab, were not to be depended on. In this district alone, he said, seven warriors had been shot down in the past month.

The road edge glittered with night eyes—jackals, a porcupine, mongoose, a squirrel, small cats, gazelles, and the small woodland antelope known as duiker. I kept an eye out for an antelope known as Mrs. Gray's lechwe, but this intriguing creature remained hidden. Toward nine, the truck surprised a pair of lionesses in the track; two males crouched down into the grass off to one side. These first wild lion I had ever seen were stirring, turning their heads without haste to regard the lights, then vanishing in matched bounds into the dark, one to each side. I stared at the dusty grass where they had gone, but the night was still. Perhaps the cats had been stalking a tiang, for moments later a band of these large blue-flanked antelope (the East African race is called the topi) fled past, eyes flashing. Panicked by

25

the truck, they seemed at the same time drawn to it, rushing the headlights, one by one, before veering away.

That night was spent on the floor of a Dinka hut, with bats chirping in the thatch above and the rhythm of chants and tom-toms in the distance. Toward four, we resumed the journey south. In a rainy mist, at dawn, a giraffe crossed the track and moved off westward toward the Sudd, pausing after a time to peer over its long shoulder. By midday, the track had come to Equatoria, the southernmost province of the Sudan, and late that afternoon it arrived at Juba, where we said good-by to Gabriel Babili.

At Juba, the sweet smells of rot on the soft air, the tin ring and squawk of radios across the bare dirt yards of open-air cafés, the insect din, the mango trees in silhouette against the southern stars, evoke all tropics of the world. In the river, a few hippos rise and sink, and a tame ostrich, property of the governor, skirts pools in the mud street, and lepers come and go like the brown kites, tattered and scavenging. In early February, 1961, it was a refuge for displaced Belgians from the Congo, who occupied every bed at the hotel, and in a lot nearby the cars abandoned by refugees already fled to Europe were gathering red dust. The hostel of sorts to which we were sent had been commandeered by fleas, and we slept outside upon the ground, departing Juba without regret the following day. Through the border town of Nimule, the Sudanese assured us, passed all manner of transport into Uganda, for was not Nimule the frontier city of the largest country in all Africa, with vehicles arriving from all corners of the world?

Our truck climbed all afternoon toward the plateaus of central Africa. But thanks to a dispute with the Arab driver incited by the soldier, who had risked our lives on more than one occasion by saluting the Moslems with hurled spit, we were thrown off in the dead of night at a silent crossroads known as Mangara. The culprit, who would clown in hell, ran after the truck down the road. "Hey, fellas, *wait* a minute! Like, there are *lions* here!" A kind citizen, attracted by his outcry, soon stood beside us in the darkness, and opened a room of the crossroads store for us to sleep in, and toward noon of the next day another truck picked us up and took us on to Nimule. There the border guards admitted that no machine of any kind had challenged their barrier in many days, though they, too, expressed confidence that Nimule was the crossroads of the world.

*

Nimule is little more than a gathering of huts to which women carried water on their heads a mile or more uphill from the river, and the fried fish, bananas, papaws, and a scrawny pullet scavenged in the village would not be enough to see us through the long hot days. But we did not know this in the beginning, and at dawn on the second day, before any vehicles that might take us south could arrive from Juba, the South African and I walked a few miles downriver, where a small tract has been set aside for wildlife.

Nimule is the only national park in the Sudan, and in the number and variety of animals to be seen in a small area, it is one of the best in Africa. It is also one of the most beautiful, a natural park between the mountains and a bend in the Albert Nile. To the south and west, early one morning, the mountains of Uganda brought the sky of Africa full circle. Somewhere in those mountains, down to the southeast, lived a light, small people called the Ik who until recently used pebble tools of the sort made in the Old Stone Age; in the Congo's Ituri Forest, to the west, lived Pygmies who still carried fire rather than make it.

Soft hills inset with outcrops of elephant-coloured boulders rose beyond a bright stretch of blue river, and elephants climbed to a sunrise ridge from a world that was still in shadow. More than a hundred moved slowly toward the sun; the landscape stirred. The small boat manned by two askaris—rangers in khaki shirts and shorts, rakish safari hats, and long puttees—pushed through reeds and scudding nympheas to the open water.

On the west bank, the askaris shook small bags of a fine dust to gauge the direction of the wind. We moved inland. Very soon there arose out of a copse a herd of buffalo, with its coterie of cattle egrets rising and settling once again on the twitching, dusty backs. To judge from the rapidity with which the askaris cocked their rifles, we were too close; the beasts took a few steps forward. Wet nostrils elevated to the wind, they wore an aggrieved, lowering expression. There were no handy trees to climb, and I wondered how to enter most promptly and least painfully the large thornbush close at hand. But the buffalo panicked before I did, wheeling away in dark commotion, leaving the white birds dangling above the dust.

To the south, on a rise that overlooks the Albert Nile where it bends away into Uganda, a herd of kob antelope stepped along the hill—some sixty female kobs and calves led by a single male with

27

sweeping horns and fine black forelegs—and the delicate oribi, bright rufous with brief straight horns, scampered away in twos and threes, tails switching. A gray duiker, more like a fat hare than an antelope, gathered its legs beneath it in low flight, and a sow wart hog with five hoglets, new sun glinting on the manes and the inelegant raised tails, rushed off in a single file at the scent of man. Here and there a stately waterbuck regarded us, alert.

Kob and waterbuck would be large animals elsewhere in the world, but here they seemed almost incidental, for to the east of them, the entire hillside surged with elephant, nearly two hundred now, including a few tuskers of enormous size. And to the north, on a small hillock, stood four rhinoceros, one of these a calf. The askaris approached the rhino gradually, keeping downwind—not always a simple matter, as the light wind was variable—and eventually brought us within stoning distance of the animals; they were astonished that we had no cameras, but simply wished to *see*. The rhinos were of the rare "white" (*weit*, or wide-mouthed) species, a grazing animal that lacks the long upper lip of the black rhino, which is a browser; mud-crusted, with their double horn, their ugliness was protean. The cow and calf having moved off, two males were left, and these, aware of an intrusion but unable to detect it, moved suspiciously toward each other, stopping short at the last second as if to contemplate the risks of battle, then retreating simultaneously. Having just come to Africa, I did not know that the white rhino is gentle and rarely makes a charge; buffalo in herds are also inoffensive, and no doubt the askaris were teasing as well as pleasing us, though they kept their laughter to themselves.

Beyond the rhino, dry trees rose toward the dusty mountains, and beyond the hills hung the blue haze of Africa, and everywhere were birds—stonechats and silver birds, cordon bleus and flycatchers, shrikes, kingfishers, and sunbirds. Overhead sailed vultures and strange eagles and the brown kite of Africa and South Asia, which had followed me overland two thousand miles from Cairo, up the Nile. Here in Equatoria, in the heart of Africa, with Ethiopia to the east, Uganda and the Congo to the south, Lake Chad and the new states of what was once French Africa to the west, one sensed what this continent must have been, when the white rhinoceros was not confined to a few pockets but wandered everywhere, like the kites, from the plains of Libya south to the Cape of Good Hope. Today

Libya is desert, and the wild things disappear. The ragged kite, with its affinity for man and carrion, will be the last to go.

2. White Highlands

> In a low and sad voice (Moga wa Kebiro) said that strangers would
> come to Gikuyuland from out of the big water, the colour of their
> body would resemble that of a small light-coloured frog (kiengere)
> which lives in water, their dress would resemble the wings of
> butterflies; that these strangers would carry magical sticks which
> would produce fire.... The strangers, he said, would later bring
> an iron snake with as many legs as monyongoro (centipede), that
> this iron snake would spit fires and would stretch from the big
> water in the east to another big water in the west of the Gikuyu
> country. Further, he said that a big famine would come and this
> would be the sign to show that the strangers with iron snake were
> near at hand.... That the nations would mingle with a merciless
> attitude towards each other, and the result would seem as though
> they were eating one another.... Many moons afterwards ... the
> strangers dressed in clothes resembling the wings of butterflies
> started to arrive in small groups; this was expected, for prior to
> their arrival a terrible disease had broken out and destroyed a great
> number of Gikuyu cattle as well as those of the neighbouring tribes,
> the Masai and Wakamba. The incident was followed by a great
> famine, which also devastated thousands of the tribesmen.

> Jomo Kenyatta, *Facing Mt. Kenya*

Those days at Nimule I recall as the longest in my life. There was
no point in trying to cross the border, as the nearest town was far
away across an arid plain. For fear of missing the stray vehicle that
might pass through, we waited forever at the guard post, and during
this period—though we never knew the reason for the crisis until days
later, when finally we got away into Uganda—Patrice Lumumba, the
firebrand of the new Africa, was murdered at Katanga in the Congo.

Overnight, the friendly Sudanese became bitterly hostile. Guards
and villagers gathered in swarms, their pointing and muttering interspersed with shouts and gestures. We could not understand what was
being said, but it seemed clear that our crime was being white—so
far as we knew, there were no members of our race closer than Juba,

a hundred miles away—and that our fate was being decided. (Numbers of whites were killed that year in Africa; a thousand died in Angola alone.[1]) Until now, the people of Nimule had been gentle and hospitable. The schoolmaster had offered us his hut, and even his own cot, and when our food ran out, the border guards shared their calabash of green murk and tripes into which three dirty white hands and seven or eight black ones dipped gray mucilaginous hunks of manioc, a low vegetable that, like maize, was brought to Africa from the Americas at the time of the Atlantic slave trade.

After a day and night of dread, peremptorily, we were summoned once more to eat from the communal bowl. Doubtless the schoolteacher had interceded for us, though he had been at pains to seem as hostile as the rest. I knew we must accept the food to avoid discourtesy, and the South African agreed; bravely he gagged down his tripe, retiring immediately behind a hut to puke it up again. But my countryman refused to feed, declaring that if he ate he would die anyway; he ignored our pleas and curses. The Africans took baleful note, and muttered, but did nothing; like the tribesmen on the truck south from Khartoum, they feared this hairy avatar, who sat inscrutable behind dark glasses, making strange ceremonial dipping motions with his hand.

In Uganda, parting company with my companions, I made my way southwest to Murchison Falls, where the upper Nile, descending from the high plateaus of the central continent, bursts through a narrow gorge. From there I went to Queen Elizabeth National Park, across Lake Edward from the Congo, which has a prospect of the Mountains of the Moon, and from there to Kampala, north of Lake Victoria. This wet and fertile country of the central lakes is a great kingdom of the Bantu peoples, who form the mass of the population throughout east, central, and south Africa. The Bantu—their own word for "people," used by scholars to describe a language family rather than an ethnic group—are made up of many tribes in many countries, most of them tillers of the soil. Banana fronds and smoke-plumed villages fill a landscape of wild sunlit colors set against purple clouds. Graceful people in white shirts and bright kangas walk everywhere along red roads to flowering markets, and the umbrella, jitney bus, and bicycle are ubiquitous—an African of Kenya tells[2] of seeing a Ugandan with a whole stove mounted on his bicycle, upon which he prepared and cooked and ate his meal while pedaling along.

For all its life, there is something about this domesticated country of rank greens and imminent rain that I found oppressive. In East Africa, most of the limited land suited to agriculture lies in the weather of great lakes and mountains, in country of heavy humid leaves and bruised thick skies, and the small farms or shambas, each with its corn patch, thatch hut, and roosters, differ little from those to be seen in tropics all around the world—this was not the East Africa of my imaginings, a remote region shut away until a century ago by deserts and mountains of north Africa, the rain forests of the Congo, the gray thorn nyika and unnavigable rivers of the Indian Ocean coast, a land of wild beasts, silence, and immensities where man was a lone herdsman with a spear or a small aborigine with bow and arrow. Also I felt ambivalent among the Bantu, or at least among acculturated Bantu, whose adoption of western dress and aspirations had been accompanied almost everywhere by rejection of western rule. Patrice Lumumba, whose murder had involved us so abruptly in the chaos of anti-colonialism, had been a Bantu, and these people share much with the black American or West Indian whose ancestors were transported out of Africa in Anglo-Saxon ships, and whose anger and unrest and hope lashes the white conscience in the cities of the West. The Bantu is the new African who is met with in Kampala and Nairobi, in streets and offices, shops, customs, roadsides, markets. I shook his hand, said, "Jambo, Bwana!" and smiled warmly. In shirt and tie, speaking good English, he seemed deceptively familiar, and only several journeys later did I see that in my ignorance and lack of curiosity I had failed to perceive him at all. Yet it is these people, not the gentle hunters, the fierce herdsmen, whose history is the most remarkable on the southern continent, these Bantu-speakers who overcame the stupefying obstacles of tropical climate and disease, tribal warfare and wild animals, to move and expand and found cities and kingdoms far in the interior of what the western world, until a century ago, had dismissed as Darkest Africa.

In January, 1961—perhaps during the days that I spent at Nimule—Patrice Lumumba wrote a last letter to his wife.

I am writing these words not knowing whether they will reach you, when they will reach you, and whether I shall still be alive when you read them. . . . History will one day have its say, but it will not be the history that is taught in Brussels, Paris, Washington or in the United Nations. . . . Africa will write her own history, and to the north and south of the Sahara, it will be a glorious and dignified history.... Do not weep for me, my dear wife.... Long live the Congo! Long live Africa![3]

The earliest record[4] of East Africa, from an Alexandrian trading voyage of the first century A.D., makes no mention of any black men, and it is probable that none were there; east and south Africa were still the province of Bushmanoid hunter-gatherers and the Caucasoid herdsmen who were drifting down the continent along the grassy high plateaus of the interior. Derived from the Caucasoids, it appears, were the "Azanians" found along the coast of "Zinj"—tall bearded men, "red" in color, a piratical tribe of fishers who traded tortoise shell, soft ivory, and aromatic gums for iron blades and beads and cloth. Perhaps by this time the Azanians had mixed with those early Indonesians who brought the outrigger canoe and the marimba to the Indian Ocean coast and were to colonize Madagascar. Then, in the first centuries of the Christian era, waves of black peoples appeared out of the interior, bearing iron tools and weapons of their own.

The knowledge of iron that had spread from Meröe on the Nile, traveling to West Africa, perhaps, by way of old trade routes to Lake Chad, then south and east again through equatorial forest that metal tools and domestic plants had made less formidable, had encouraged a surge in population. Among the peoples set in motion were the ancestors of the Bantu-speakers, who are thought to derive from Negroid stocks in the Cameroon Highlands region of the Niger River. Wherever they came from, it appears that the great Bantu increase that impelled a geographic spread took place in middle Africa, in the Katanga region between the headwaters of the Congo and Zambezi, where an advanced and very wealthy civilization that mined and traded in copper had developed at Lake Kisale by the eighth century. By that time, Bantu peoples had occupied both coasts and settled the fertile lands around Lake Victoria, and within a few centuries, with remarkably small divergence in the Bantu tongue, they had spread throughout the subcontinent as far south as the Cape, then north again into present-day East Africa, and along the coast to the Juba River and Somalia. From the Caucasoids, perhaps, they acquired the Ethiopian millets and domestic animals that permitted them to settle the dry countries of south Africa, where many became herdsmen. On the southeast coast, they had access to such tropical Asian crops as the banana, yam, and taro, the coconut and mango. The implement

33

of Bantu prosperity was the iron blade, in ax and hoe and spear, which insured their dominance and the adoption of their language almost everywhere. Older Negroid stocks found living along the rivers as well as certain herdsmen and hunter-gatherers were absorbed—hence the variety of Bantu physical types, which are mostly lighter and less prognathous than the Negroids of West Africa. Even today, as far south as Natal, non-Negroid features are discernible in certain Zulu who interbred with the Xam Bushmen, and adopted a Khoisan language, whereas the Pygmies of the Congo and the pygmoid Twa of the central lakes are clearly of the Old People in origin, despite their adoption of Bantu speech.

In most of East Africa, the Middle Stone Age gave way abruptly to the Iron Age, without that intervening stage of New Stone Age settlement that came about elsewhere with the domestication of plants and animals. Yet here and there the remains of Neolithic earthworks, terraces, dams, wells, and irrigation ditches have been found, together with stone "hut circles" or pit dwellings dug into wet hill regions suitable for farming. These are thought to be the work of northern peoples, the Caucasoid "Proto-Hamites," precursors of the modern Hamites of north Kenya and Ethiopia. The great kingdoms of the interior—the mining civilization at Katanga, the stone city of Great Zimbabwe in Rhodesia, the lake kingdoms of Uganda and Ruanda-Urundi—were all Bantu domains, but Zimbabwe, at least, may have been influenced in its construction by the northerners, who are known to have worked in stone.

On the east coast, the Azanians soon vanished among the eastern Mediterraneans and the Asians—Persians, Indians, Chinese—whose brown sails, on the winds of the monsoon, were drawn like kites to a growing trade in tortoise shell, gold, ivory, amber, leopard skins, myrrh, frankincense, and slaves. Traditionally the Bajun fishers that one sees today at Lamu, on the Kenya coast, are descended in part from the Persians. By the tenth century Moslem Arabs were dominant, and long before medieval times the trading forts that have since become the small cities of the coast had been established. Meanwhile, the Bantu were beset by waves of Nilotic and Hamitic peoples moving south, and their political systems disrupted everywhere by feverish tribal wars set loose by the slave trade, which was intensified, in the sixteenth century, by the arrival on the east coast of Portuguese navigators, first among the Europeans. Though they established trade with the people of the Zimbabwe region, the Portuguese knew nothing of the interior. The slaving caravans not run by local tribes—for the tribes were encouraged to prey upon one another—were managed by Arabs or Swahili Bantu, a coastal people that intermixed with the Arabs (could the Swahili have derived from the Azanians?) and whose tongue, with its elements of Arabic, was to become the trading language of East Africa.

In south Africa, at the Cape, the Dutch East India Company established a supply port for its fleet in the seventeenth century, and later the Dutch South Africans known as the Boers, trekking inland, helped to set off a great northward expansion of Ngoni Zulu, who were to overrun Zimbabwe and settle finally in the region of Lakes Nyasa and Tanganyika. Elsewhere the Europeans had no territorial ambitions nor even curiosity about the hinterland, with its fierce heat, tsetse fly, beasts, spears, disease, and pillage. Such missionary-explorers as David Livingstone who penetrated into central Africa in the mid-nineteenth century were astonished to find elaborate civilizations based on concepts that apparently had filtered southward by way of Meröe and the Sudanic civilizations, and certain baroque and cruel customs of these kingdoms laid a firm base for the belief in African barbarism that has been used ever since to excuse the more refined atrocities of the pale peoples from the north, but much of this despotism arose out of the anarchy brought by the slave trade and the advent of firearms. It may be that at the time of the white man's coming the great Bantu kingdoms were already in decline, leaving few traces of the past, for in the tropics, a city of thatch and timber—not necessarily more primitive than one of stone—would subside into the earth with the turn of seasons.

In the late nineteenth century, for political reasons having little to do with Africa, the nations of Europe had embarked on colonial conquest. Less than twenty-five years after Speke and Grant had discovered the Nile headwaters, in 1864, East Africa had been divided into British and German spheres of influence, and by the turn of the century, a railroad had been built from Mombasa, on the Kenya coast, into Uganda. In the next decades, plantations of cotton, coffee, tea, pyrethrum, sisal, and pineapple drew more and more white settlers to East Africa, and modern medicine, like the iron hoe two thousand years before, brought on a renewed increase in the African population. Now, however, there was nowhere left for these Africans to go.

*

35

The Kikuyu of Kenya who occupied the highland forests when the first Europeans appeared in the late nineteenth century had not been there for more than a few centuries. Tradition and the evidence agree that they came from Juba Land, north of the Tana River, toward the coast, having been displaced in the fifteenth or sixteenth centuries by invasions of Galla nomads from the Horn of Africa, who had been displaced in their turn by waves of Somali crossing the Red Sea from Arabia. At the headwaters of the Tana on Mt. Kenya and the Aberdares, the Kikuyu came upon a small, pit-dwelling people known as the Gumba who presently vanished into hiding places underground and failed to reappear. Broken pots of a people resumed to be Gumba have been found high in the Aberdares, on the cold moors to which the remnant aborigines retreated. Jomo Kenyatta, who in the Thirties won a degree in anthropology as a student of the eminent Malinowski, at the University of London, suggests that these Old People absorbed the first Kikuyu wanderers into the region, and made hunters of them, and that the resultant race was that hunting tribe of obscure origin whose remnants are known today as the Dorobo: "There is strong reason to support the latter theory, for soon after the Gumba had disappeared as a race, there came into being another race of hunters known as the Ndorobo or Aathi, who seemed to have grown like mushrooms in the forests. Unlike their predecessors they were not short in stature, but something between the Gumba and the Gikuyu." In any case, the Kikuyu interbred extensively with other peoples, for at the turn of the century, at least, certain Kikuyu clans claimed blood relationship with tribes as various as the Maasai, Kamba, and Dorobo, as well as the Chagga of Kilimanjaro.[5]*

From the beginning, the aboriginal hunters, small and few, and the primitive herdsmen, who drifted with the seasons and remained isolated in their own customs, were more agreeable to Europeans than the Bantu cultivators, who were not only ambitious but occupied the most desirable land. A prejudice that still continues was set down as early as 1883, in the region of what is now Nairobi:

At Ngongo we had reached the southern boundary of the country of

* "Masai" is properly "Maasai" and "Kikuyu" is more accurately "Gikuyu," but in the latter case I have retained the "literary" spelling, which is now favored by the tribe; also, I have dropped the Wa— prefix (signifying "people"), which is used so inconsistently throughout the literature (one finds Wakamba but not Wakikuyu, Wandorobo but not Wamaasai).

Kikuyu, the natives of which have the reputation of being the most trouble-some and intractable in this region. No caravan has yet been able to penetrate into the heart of the country, so dense are the forests, and so murderous and thievish are its inhabitants. They are anxious for coast ornaments and cloth, and yet defeat their own desires by their utter inability to resist stealing, or the fun of planting a poisoned arrow in the traders. These things they can do with impunity, sheltered as they are by their forests, which are impenetrable to all but themselves.[6]

But within a few years another explorer had perceived that this tribe "was destined to play an important part in the future of East Africa,"[7] and the young engineer who became famous for killing the man-eaters of Tsavo, two great maneless lions that terrorized the railroad construction crews for months, considered the Kikuyu intel-ligent and industrious.[8] So did an official of the Imperial British East Africa Company—later Lord Lugard, greatest of all African administrators—who had to fight them at what is now the Nairobi suburb of Dagoretti. "Kikuyu promised to be the most progressive station between the coast and the lake," Lugard wrote in *The Rise of Our East African Empire.* "The natives were very friendly, and even enlisted as porters to go to the coast, but these good relations received a disastrous check. Owing largely to the want of discipline in the passing caravans, whose men robbed the crops and otherwise made themselves troublesome, the people became estranged, and presently murdered several porters." The East Africa Company, obsessed with the promise of Uganda, was inefficient and undercapitalized in Kenya, and its agents ravaged the villages of both the Kamba and Kikuyu in an effort to make the Machakos and Dagoretti stations self-supporting. As the British Commissioner at Zanzibar had written to his wife in 1893, "By refusing to pay for things, by raiding, looting, swash-buckling, and shooting natives, the Company have turned the whole country against the white man."[9]

In the first years of the twentieth century the Maasai herdsmen still engaged in cattle raids across the country, and Arab-Swahili caravans continued a murderous slaving trade throughout the hinterlands. In western Kenya the Nandi fought the railroad, tearing up rails and spearing Europeans. A railroad trader named John Boyes, "King of the Kikuyu," was the only white settler in the region of Nairobi, which as late as 1907 was little more than a tent city and rail depot called Mile 326, near the swampy springs known to the Maasai as N'erobi, "place of cold waters," at the south end of the fertile Kikuyu hills. These hills, well watered and free of tsetse fly, already supported a prosperous Kikuyu population, and to help justify the immense expense of the Uganda railroad, land schemes were developed to encourage settlement by Britons. Plagued by strange soils and a violent climate, dangerous animals, sullen natives, and disease, these first settlers earned every bit of the progress they had made by World War I, and not unnaturally, they tended to resist the League of Nations mandate, reaffirmed by the British government in 1923, that African economic welfare and advancement took precedence over their own. As their control of the colonial legislature increased, so did their resistance to the historical and moral truth behind "the sacred trust of civilization" that their development of Africa was supposed to represent: hadn't they already done enough, in bringing "the native" medicines and peace? (And it is true that white rule was accompanied by an enforced peace among the tribes, without which transition to the modern world, not to speak of independence, would have been impossible.) The coming of white women to the colonies had led to a strict separation of the races, and meanwhile, the British government, proceeding stolidly with the "betterment of the native," succeeded mainly in increasing his population and dissatisfaction. In the Nairobi region, the numerous and accessible Kikuyu were encouraged to emulate the white man in his values and religion, to serve him and advance his commerce as apprentice Europeans, but their reward was increasing servitude and contempt. The hunter or herdsman, off in the bush, might be considered picturesque—at the least, he retained a certain dignity—whereas the mission African, ill-smelling in his single set of cast-off clothes, was a parody of the white man. Judged by values that were not his own, he was much patronized and derided, even as his own resentment grew.

The assumption of knowing the African's mind has been very often heard in the usual phraseology: "I have lived for many years amongst the Africans and I know them very well." Yet this is far from the actual fact, for there is a great difference between "living" among a people and "knowing" them. While a European can learn something of the externals of African life, its system of kinship and classification, its peculiar arts and picturesque ceremonial, he may still have not yet reached the heart of the problem. . . . With his preconceived ideas, mingled with prejudices, he fails to achieve a more sympathetic and imaginative knowledge, a more human and inward appreciation of the living people, the pupils he teaches, the people he meets on the roads and watches in the gardens. In a word he fails to understand the African with his instinctive tendencies (no doubt very like his own), but trained from his earliest days to habitual ideas, inhibitions and forms of self-expression which have been handed down from one generation to another and which are foreign, if not absurd, to the European in Africa.[10]

Jomo Kenyatta's *Facing Mt. Kenya*, written in the 1930's, is essential to an understanding of the conflicts that were to give rise to the Mau-Mau Rebellion, 1952–1956; though never a terrorist himself, Kenyatta spent seven years in a detention camp as an early advocate of land reform and a symbol of Kikuyu resistance. A great source of Kikuyu bitterness was the conviction that the tribe had been tricked out of its land, for every foot of Kikuyu land was owned by individual tribesmen, not only the pieces for which token sums were paid but also the fallow land that was appropriated by the government, then dispensed to the colonials on the grounds that African farming techniques would be the ruin of it. Much high-minded legislation for the benefit of whites was bulled through by Hugh Cholmondeley, Lord Delamere, whose memorial was an order of the British Crown, in 1939, that no African or Asian was permitted to own land in what had already become known as the White Highlands. Four-fifths of this best land in Kenya was now the province of perhaps four thousand whites; a million Kikuyu were to make do with the one-fifth set aside as the Kikuyu Reserves. The tribe's exposure to missions and clinics had led to a fatal population increase, and their growing poverty and frustration were all the more onerous for the education that numerous Kikuyu had struggled to obtain. Those who had fought in the British Army in Burma, then returned to inferior status in their own land, had an additional cause for bitterness, and many of these soldiers joined the Land Freedom Army movement, which was armed mostly with the cane-cutting machete called the panga. A half century of resentment was set aflame by the winds of pan-Africanism sweeping the continent, and the rebellion fell into the hands not of men like Kenyatta but of fanatic malcontents such as Dedan Kimathi, who made the name Mau-Mau, as the colonials called the movement, a symbol of the alleged barbarism, bestialities, and black magic that gave its oathing ceremonies such evil repute. But in the opinion of most Africans, Kimathi has been much maligned and the Mau-Mau atrocities exag-

39

gerated to excuse the savagery of the repression, and veterans of the Kenya Regiment acknowledge that atrocities were committed by both sides.

Until recent years, most Africans clung to the hope of a fair accommodation with the white man, and Mau-Mau received only limited support from other tribes. The last of the guerrillas, led by the strange Kimathi, retreated into the high Aberdares, and at the end they wore animal skins, like the vanished Gumba who had fled there from the Kikuyu centuries before. In the dense forests of bamboo, on the moorlands of black trees and tussock from which torrents plunge into the stagnant clouds in the ravines, one can envision the human figures in their scraps of reeking hide, the remnant aborigines and the Kikuyu outlaws, hunched at their covert fires. At Gura Falls, red gladioli shiver in the mountain wind, and far below, in the greening mist, three bushbuck, kin of those whose meat and skins sustained life in the fugitives, stand listening to the rush of rains off Kingankop.

In Nairobi, in 1961, Mau-Mau was still fresh in people's minds, and in the streets and pubs, a colonial tone of voice prevailed. Yet Independence was already underway in Kenya, and change everywhere seemed imminent, even in South Africa, where the student who had come south with me from Khartoum had gone to warn his parents to flee that medieval region before the inevitable uprising. The Mau-Mau Rebellion, though defeated, had led within a very few years to victory, and Jomo Kenyatta, released from prison a few months after my arrival, was to become Kenya's first president. The Old Man or Mzee, as he is known to black and white alike, decreed that the past must be put aside in the interests of Kenya's future, and even appointed the police officer who had led the hunt for Kimathi as his private bodyguard. Those whites who would not work with blacks left quickly, and others left, too, who despaired of their prospects and security. "I reckon I'll go south," one man told me. "Rhodesia, or South Africa." He shook his head. "I was raised in the White Highlands, you know. We never thought we'd lose it. Never."

A number of remarkable civil servants stayed on in Kenya (and Uganda and Tanzania) to help the new country get a start, although a main purpose of their jobs was the training of Africans to replace them. For their part, most black Kenyans shared their president's good-humored attitude; there is still a "Lord Delamere Room" at the

Hotel Norfolk, and few of the visitors walking Kimathi Street in front of the New Stanley know or care that it was named in memory of the desperate Mau-Mau leader who was hung.

With the collapse of colonial governments, the destruction of wildlife by rampaging Africans had been widely predicted, and a glimpse of the last great companies of wild animals on earth was the main object of my trip to Africa in 1961. Since then (though their future remains uncertain) the East African parks and game reserves have actually increased in size and numbers. Even the Congo's great Albert Park (now Kivu National Park), for which the worst had been foreseen, escaped serious damage. The one park destroyed by political unrest is the beautiful small park at Nimule, where civil rebellions, already begun when I passed through, have broken down all order. Blaming the revolt of the Nilotic tribesmen on mission efforts to discourage Moslem influence and resurrect the bitter memories of the slave trade, the Sudanese government has expelled the missionaries, and it is feared that the repression of the wild peoples has neared the stage of systematic genocide. A large shipment of ivory and white rhino horn that turned up in Mombasa a few years ago was apparently intended to buy arms for the desperate tribesmen, and almost certainly it came from Nimule. John Owen, a District Commissioner in that region of the former Anglo-Egyptian Sudan who later became director of the Tanzania National Parks, flew over Nimule in a light plane in 1969. "A careful search," he told me, "produced nothing but one buffalo." Very likely the vanishing white rhino is gone forever from the Sudan.

Mr. Owen had invited me to return that year to Africa, and I came by way of Entebbe, in Uganda, flying out of the raining reaches of Lake Victoria into western Kenya. A clearing sky laid bare the high plateaus that extend southward the entire length of eastern Africa; the plane's shadow crossed the Nandi hills, the Mau Range, and Maasai Land. Soon the circles of beehive huts, like scars on the crusty skin of the Rift Valley, drew together in the tin-roofed Kikuyu accumulations that surround Nairobi.

In 1961, Nairobi was still a frontier town where travelers to wilder parts were served and outfitted. Gazelle and zebra crossed the road at Embakasi Airport, and the Aathi Plain and the Ngong Hills, bringing Maasai Land to the very edges of the city, made it credible that the first six people to be buried in Nairobi's cemetery had been killed by lions.[11] The National Museum was still called the Coryndon, the British Director of the National Parks wore a monocle, and the Norfolk and New Stanley were the only presentable hotels. Eight years later, hotels of international pretensions soared out of the polyglot byways of Nairobi, Delamere Avenue had become Kenyatta Avenue, and processional boulevards with names like Uhuru (Independence) and Harambee (All Together—!) carried visitors too rapidly from one end of this small city to the other. But beneath an enlarged and shining surface, Nairobi was the same hot curry of bazaars and colonial architecture, curio shops, mosques, noise, and reeking slums, where crippled beggars were the envy of the swarms of unemployed. Once I had acquired the sunburn and old Land Rover that permitted me to be taken for a settler, I was beset by young Kenyans in the street who were anxious to find work of any kind.

Unemployment, not to speak of street theft and corruption, permits diehard colonials to point at the inefficiency of the Kikuyu, who are too able and ambitious to be borne: "They all have degrees, these bloody Kyukes, but they can't do a bloody thing." But it would be more fair to say, ". . . but there isn't a bloody thing for them to do," for the new nation has few places for all these aspirant accountants, pharmacists, lawyers, and white collar workers, and few people trained in the skilled labor—carpentry, mechanics, and the like—that was formerly done by Asians. Even more so than the whites, the Asians were resented: the common man feels he was exploited by the shopkeepers, while the educated speak of an Asian practice of sending their money out of the country. Those who have lost their jobs seek desperately to emigrate almost anywhere, but they are quiet, and their plight, wherever possible, has been ignored. In an Asian shop on Hardinge Street (now Kimathi Street), African help has replaced the sallow children who were so cheap and efficient, and a pair of strong safari shorts, tailored for pennies in a few hours in 1961, cannot be copied in inferior material at three times the price in less than fifteen days.

Whites are needed but not wanted—hence the undercurrent of rudeness beneath the precarious civilities. A black man abusing his authority, less in malice than in lack of confidence, is a daily trial for those not shepherded past such hazards by the tour companies (though one is startled just as often by a magical courtesy and gentleness). I remember one day in the Highlands, when the car had broken down.

42

An African who yelled, "What's wrong!" from the back of a passing truck was showing off his English, not expressing concern, and perhaps he was jeering—the red-faced settler beside me was quick to assume so. "Mind your bloody business!" this man fumed, under his breath. For the new African, such confrontation is a way of forcing the white to look at him at last, to perceive him as a man, an individual, on equal terms and face to face. Or so I assume, without much confidence; the episode occurred in 1970, when after several stays in Africa, having read much and heard more, I knew less than ever about the essential nature of the African.

> The discovery of Bantu philosophy must trouble those of us who are concerned with the education of Africans. . . . we have thought we were educating children, "big children", and this seemed an easy task. But now, suddenly, we see that we are dealing with a humanity that is adult, conscious of its own wisdom, penetrated by its own universalist philosophy. And we feel the ground slipping from beneath our feet.[12]

The first night of my return was spent at the New Stanley, since the old-fashioned Norfolk was full. After dark there was a light failure for two hours, most of which I passed contented in a huge white colonial tub, watching weird flickers of faraway torches in the bath-room airshaft and listening to the cries of the staff below, the sound of breakage and feet pounding. In front of the hotel, next day, African guests from the new nations were mingling with travelers of all tongues; tourists of limited income are now common in Nairobi, and the old dark green safari wagons make way for zebra-striped tour buses in herds. Inside at the Long Bar, the settlers in town from the White Highlands, from Nyeri and Eldoret and Rumuruti, exchanged gossip, news, and exasperation with the African that before Independence would certainly have been expressed in the hearing of the barman. The Long Bar is a last redoubt of the old-style wardens and white hunters—now called "professional hunters"—and the talk turned inevitably to the great days when the native knew his place. But others present understood that Independence had to come. As one such man remarked to me after a game warden had decried the "bloody Kyukes," "the end of the game," and all the rest, "Those old boys oughtn't to take on like that—after all, they had the best of it."

Much has been written of the colorful decades when the Kenya

Colony could be spoken of as "white man's country," and there seems no point in adding to it here. I wasn't there, and anyway, the patterns of colonialism do not differ very much from one place to another. For me, the least fascinating aspect of East Africa is the period of technocracy and politics that began under white rule, which lasted little more than half a century among the millenniums that man has been in Africa. Jomo Kenyatta, born Kamau wa Ngengi, whose lifetime easily spans the entire colonial period, never laid eyes on a white at all, so it is said, until after the turn of the century, when he was already ten. And one of Livingstone's bearers was still living in the 1930s, when Karen Blixen, in her splendid *Out of Africa*, began the lament for the end of the great days. In 1970 I chanced to meet the Kikuyu hero of that book, her servant "Kamante." Kamande Gatora is a contained person with the watchfulness of the near-blind; he had taken the Mau-Mau oath, and been imprisoned, in the years after his mistress had gone home to Denmark, despite "the kind deeds I was receiving from her untold and the old life we stayed with her, like black and white keys of a piano how they are played and produce melodious verses."[13] It was idle to address him, and I stood silent, for my words could not be understood, and my face was but a blur in his blind eyes, though the eyes were cold and clear.

It is not easy to get to know the Natives. They were quick of hearing and evanescent; if you frightened them, they could withdraw into a world of their own, in a second, like the wild animals which at an abrupt movement from you are gone—simply not there. . . . When we really did break into the Natives' existence, they behaved like ants, when you poke a stick into their ant-hill; they wiped out the damage with unwearied energy, swiftly and silently—as if obliterating an unseemly action.[14]

In a letter dictated a few years ago, Kamande gave a "description of my mind concerning the old life and the new. Simply I can see just like the same. We were enjoying what we had, and until now we are enjoying what we have, so I don't see any different. And the times were not so old for the history begins in our lifetimes. When Baroness leave for England the Mr. Matthew Wellington leave in Mombasa. Mr. Wellington help carried Dead Bwana Livingstone to the sea, so the history is now."[15]

A half century after he had come to work for the "everlasting dear Baroness," as a sickly boy responsible for her dogs, Kamande stood there in the Langata dusk in the last light from the Ngong Hills and the Maasai Plain. In this old African's remote unsqueamish gaze one saw that reasons were beside the point, that such events as Mau-Mau and the passage of his mistress had causes not apprehended by the stranger, who must fail in a logical comprehension of the African, yet may hope to intuit his more mysterious, more universal sense of existence. Life begins before a soul is born and commences once again with the act of dying, and as in the Afro-Asian symbol of the snake of eternity swallowing its tail, all is in flux, all comes full circle, with no beginning and no end.

3. Northwest Frontier

Somewhere the Sky touches the Earth,
and the name of that place is the End.

—a Kamba saying[1]

Of all roads in East Africa, the road north from Nairobi toward Mt. Kenya will hold most associations for the traveler with any acquaintance with the brief history of the region. One soon comes to Thika and the Blue Post Hotel, a relic of the days not long after the turn of the century when the first planters of coffee and flax and pyrethrum were clearing Kikuyu Land, and continues to Nyeri, named in 1903 by Colonel Richard Meinertzhagen, the hero of the Nandi wars, who witnessed a procession of some seven hundred elephant through its village street. Crossing the equator at Nanyuki, the high road begins a slow descent over the ranching country west of Mt. Kenya—Kere-Nyaga, named for Nyaga or Ngai, which is the Maasai word for God used also by the Kamba and Kikuyu—a formidable mountain, dark and looming, jagged and malign, rising to snow fields that the Africans avoided, for the bright whiteness was a kingdom of Ngai.

Before World War I, when Elspeth Huxley was a child on a Thika farm, a few Dorobo still wandered in these highlands:

A brown furry figure stepped forth into a shaft of sunlight, which awoke in his fur pelt a rich, rufous glow, and twinkled on his copper ornaments.

He was a small man: not a dwarf exactly, or a pygmy, but one who stood about half-way between a pygmy and an ordinary human. His limbs were light in colour and he wore a cloak of bushbuck skin, a little leather cap, and ear-rings, and carried a long bow and a quiver of arrows. He stood stock-still and looked at me just as the dikdik had done, and I wondered whether he, too, would vanish if I moved. . . . I knew him for a Dorobo, one of that race of hunters living in the forest on game they trapped or shot with poisoned arrows. They did not cultivate, they existed on meat and roots and wild honey, and were the relics of an old, old people who had once had sole possession of all these lands—the true aborigines. Then had come others like the Kikuyu and Masai, and the Dorobo had taken refuge in the forests. Now they lived in peace, or at least neutrality,

46

with the herdsmen and cultivators, and sometimes bartered skins and honey for beads, and for spears and knives made by native smiths. They knew all the ways of the forest animals, even of the bongo, the shyest and most beautiful, and their greatest delight was to feast for three days upon a raw elephant.[2]

Like the Bushmen of south Africa, who were hunted down or driven into swamps and deserts by black men and white alike when they struck at domestic stock that threatened their hunting lands, the Dorobo were threatened by the clearing of their forests, and doubtless there were skirmishes and killings before they attached themselves to the Nandi and Maasai as rainmakers and tricksters, circumcisers and attendants of the dead. Probably it is too late to discover the true origins of this outcast people, who have lost their own language and whose name (from the Maasai il-torrobo, meaning "poor man," or "person without cattle"—thus, any hunter-gatherer) is now used to describe almost any man who has reverted to subsistence in the bush, or "turned Dorobo." Still, it interests me that the Muisi Dorobo who once inhabited Mt. Kenya's bamboo forests were said[3] to have been very small, and that one of the two main clans of the Dorobo was known as the Agumba—the other was the Okiek—who lived in covered pits and were said to have gone away toward the region of Kismayu after failing to stop the clearing of their forests by the Kikuyu; I like to think that the Agumba and the vanished Gumba may be one. Perhaps the Dorobo are related to such remnant hunting groups as the Ik of northeastern Uganda, who were also hunters until recent years, and are also described as lighter-skinned and smaller than their neighbors, and conceivably both groups may derive from the same ancestral stock as the larger Khoisan or click-speaking peoples (such as the modern Bushman relatives known as the Khoi or Hottentots) whose traces have been found as far north as the Blue Nile and Ethiopia. (Both Bushman and Pygmy, where unmixed with other groups, are slight and small and yellow-brown in color, and while differences in other physical character appear to justify a racial separation, their Bantu-speaking neighbors, from Uganda to South Africa, know both groups as the Small People—the Abatwa or Twa.)

In Africa, for all its space and emptiness, there is no place any longer for the Small People, most of whom have been described by those who found them as gentle and quiet, in harmony with the land and the changing seasons, with none of the aggressiveness and greed that the domestication of plants and animals, with its illusion of security and permanence, brought to mankind. In former times, the Bushmen say, wild animals spoke with men, and all were friends. They had a reverence for the life and death of the animals they hunted—what the Nandi, in reference to the wilderness instinct of the Dorobo, call *comiet*, "affinity"[4]—and their legends have the ring of all creation. The Small People, the Old People, still quick with instinct, knew the secret of the silence, and I wanted a glimpse of the vanishing hunters above all.

In Nairobi one heard of bands of hunters that were said to derive from the Old People, including one group "somewhere" in the hills east of Mt. Kenya that were described as a remnant of the Gumba, but those for whom good information was available had long since adopted both language and ways of the stronger tribes around them (even the Ovajimba of southwest Africa, the last tribe known that makes and uses crude stone tools, have adopted the speech of the Herero Bantu who pass through their country). The only hunter-gatherers in Kenya said to be living more or less as they had always done were a few primitive fishermen of Lake Rudolf, the El Molo, considered by some authorities[5] to be a relict group of the Dorobo.

In June, 1970, I accompanied the photographer Eliot Porter, his two sons, and a daughter-in-law on a journey to Lake Rudolf by way of Mt. Marsabit, a well-organized safari into remote country with scant water that I could not attempt alone in my old Land Rover. Until recently, this Northern Frontier, or NFD, a waste of desert and near-desert scrub and thorn extending north and east to Ethiopia and Somalia, has been closed to travel, being under control of Somali shifta who claim it for their country. Shifta, or "wanderer," is a name for tribesmen without property, but the term has come to signify guerrillas or bandits; the Somali guerrillas and the true bandits, who may be Somali or Boran, are lumped together under this same term. The Boran are also the chief victims of the shifta operations; their villages are burned and livestock stolen by bandits of all persuasions, and those left standing may be reduced to rubble by Kenya's security police, who often conclude that those Boran settlements not actually composed of shifta give shelter to the raiders. In consequence, numbers of Boran must turn to banditry in order to survive, and others subsist as refugees at Isiolo, where they mix with Somali traders, Bantu laborers from the south, and a few Samburu and Turkana.

Beyond the sentry barrier at Isiolo, the road disintegrates to dirt, and fences end. Traditionally this frontier region between the highlands and the NFD has been a province of the Samburu, and a tract of high plains by the Uaso Nyiro River has been set aside as a game reserve named in their honor. Here the safari truck had set up camp in a grove of umbrella thorn with a westward prospect of the Laikipia Plateau; the Uaso Nyiro comes down out of Laikipia and dies eventually in the Lorian Swamp, east of Mado Gashi. With water so close, it came as a surprise, each day at daylight, to see a flight of white egrets undulating southward over the dry scrub, bound for waters unknown under Mt. Kenya.

The plains and hills that surround the Uaso Nyiro are inhabited by striking animals such as the reticulated giraffe and Grevy's zebra (seen here in mixed herds with the more common Burchell's zebra) that are absent farther south; the fringe-eared oryx and the blue-legged Somali ostrich have replaced the more southerly races of their species, and the gerenuk is the most conspicuous of the gazelles. This extraordinary creature, stylized even to the carved eyeline and the bronzy gloss that gives its form the look of well-oiled wood, browses habitually on its hind legs, tail switching, fan ears batting, delicate hooves propped on the swaying branches. When I came to Samburu previously, in winter, the long-necked animals had been nibbling on florets of a gum acacia that filled the air with its sweet scent, but now the long dry season had begun, and the high plains had reverted to near-desert.

Samburu has been a game reserve since 1966, but most of its life it has been closed due to the shifta; bandits on a poaching raid killed two of its African game scouts only this year. Such tracks, fords, dams, and bridges as it can claim are largely the work of Terence Adamson, who in February was living in a thatched banda of his own construction by the river, and had been kind enough to lend me the only complete map of Samburu's tracks. A strong old man with a white head, in floppy hat, huge floppy shorts, and heavy shoes, Mr. Adamson is a bachelor and hardened recluse who in the seven years he was stationed at Marsabit, one hundred miles off to the north, went to Nairobi just once, for a bad toothache; he loathes Nairobi and what it represents of the change in Africa, and will never go again if he can help it.

Although a veteran of shifta raids on Isiolo, where an African district commissioner has been assassinated, Adamson is sympathetic with the guerrillas. "Why should these Somali be under Kenya? Somalis don't think of themselves as African at all, and of course they're right." He sighed. "They have odd ways, granted, like all Arabs, but they stick to their word, and they stick to their code, like it or not—once I saw half a Samburu in the fork of a tree here; he'd been dragged up by a leopard after the Somali had caught up to him for cattle stealing."

In the old days—for Mr. Adamson's generation, their own youth and the great days of the Kenya Colony are the same—Adamson used to sleep outside on the ground wherever he went. "Rhinos could be a nuisance sometimes—just as blind at night as they are in the day. Chough, chough, chough," he said, making a rhino face. "Never two or four snorts, always three." He shook his heavy head. "In ten years the game will be up in Kenya. I just hate to think what will happen when the Old Man goes—I just hope they let me see it out."

Winds of the southeast monsoon blew up from the hot nyika, and a haze of desert dust obscured the mountains. But the Uaso Nyiro flows all year, and along its green banks the seasons are the same. A dark lioness with a shining coat lay on a rise, intent on the place where game came down to water. At a shady bend, on sunlit sand bars, baboon and elephant consorted, and a small crocodile, gray-green and gleaming at the edge of the thick river, evoked a childhood dream of darkest Africa. Alone on the plain, waiting for his time to come full circle, stood an ancient elephant, tusks broken and worn, hairs fallen from his tail; over his monumental brow, poised for the insects started up by the great trunk, a lilac-breasted roller hung suspended, spinning turquoise lights in the dry air.

On a plateau that climbs in steps from the south bank of the river, three stone pools in a grove of doum palms form an oasis in the elephant-twisted thorn scrub and dry stone. The lower spring, where the water spreads into a swampy stream, has a margin of high reeds and sedge; here the birds and animals come to water. One afternoon I swam in the steep-sided middle pool, which had been, in winter, as clear as the desert wind; now the huge gangs building the road north to Ethiopia were washing here with detergent soaps that bred a heavy film, and I soon got out, letting the sun dry me. A turtle's shadow vanished between ledges of the pool, and dragonflies, one fire-colored and the other cobalt blue, zipped dry-winged through the heat. Despite the wind, there was a stillness in the air, expectancy: at the lower spring a pair of spurwing plover stood immobile, watching man grow older.

In the dusty flat west of the spring, ears alert, oryx and zebra waited. Perhaps one had been killed the night before, for jackals came and went in their hangdog way east of the springs and vultures sat like huge galls in the trees. With a shift in the wind, a cloud across the sun, the rush of fronds in the dry palms took on an imminence. Beyond the springs oryx were moving at full run, kicking up dust as they streamed onto the upper plateau. Nagged by the wind, I put my clothes on and set off for camp.

Climbing from the springs onto the plain, I crossed a stone ridge where, in winter, a fine lion had made way for my Land Rover; I stared about me. In every distance the plain was sparse and bare. Strange pale shimmers were far oryx and gazelle, and an eagle crossed the sky, and a giraffe walked by itself under the mountains. A Grevy's zebra stallion (why not "gray" and "common" zebra?) charged with a harsh barking, veered away, then circled me, unreconciled, for the next two miles, unable to place a man on foot in its long brain.

Northward, over pinnacles and desert buttes, the sky was clear, but directly ahead as I walked south, dark rain arose over Mt. Kenya, fifty miles away. Coming fast, the weather cast a storm light on the plain, illuminating the white shells of perished land snails, a lone white flower, the white skull and vertebrae of a killed oryx.

I wanted to look at the species of larks that had the dry plain to themselves, but the sun, overtaken by the clouds, was sinking rapidly toward the Laikipia Plateau, and there were still four miles to go through country increasingly wooded; I hurried on. Awareness of animals brought with it an awareness of details—a shard of rose quartz, a candy-colored pierid butterfly, white with red trim, the gleam of a scarlet-chested sunbird in the black lace of an acacia. Set against the sun at dawn or evening, its hanging weaver nests like sun-scorched fruit, its myriad points etched on the sky, there is nothing so black in Africa as the thorn tree.

In the open wood all senses were attuned to lion, hyenas, elephant, and especially elephant, as in the unlikely event of trouble there is little to be done about lion or hyenas besides climb a tree. The antelope were very shy, yet at one point a string of impala passed

51

close at full speed, bouncing high; I hoped that no lion, having missed its kill, now sat disgruntled by the trail. At the edge of the woodland, fresh elephant spoor was everywhere, and inevitably there came the *crack* of a split tree that is often the first sign of elephant presence. None was in sight, however, and I hurried past. The red sun, in a narrow band of sky between clouds and mountains, had set fire to spider webs in the grass that while the sun was high had been invisible; where I had come from, flights of sand grouse were sailing down to the Buffalo Springs for their evening water. Then the sun was gone, and across the world, a full moon rose to take its place.

The earth was still, in twilight shape and shadow. In the wake of the wind came the low hooting of a dove, and one solitary bell note of a boubou. I met no animals but the giraffe, a herd of eleven set about a glade, waiting for night. The giraffe were alert to my intrusion but in their polite way gave no sign that they had been disturbed.

Night had come to camp before me. Already the Africans had built a fire and set lanterns before each tent; they formed a line and murmured in astonishment as I came in alone out of the trees. These men are Kamba from the dry thorn scrub on the east slope of the highlands; they are more accustomed to the bush than the Kikuyu, and more willing to sleep upon the ground. The name Kamba means "traveler," for they were always ivory traders, and participated in the slave trade, journeying south beyond Kilimanjaro and as far north as Samburu. As bush people who held little land that was coveted by settlers—except in the region of Machakos, their arable land is marginal—they are considered more dependable than the Kikuyu, who are said to be "spoiled" by their exposure to the missions and civilizing influences of Nairobi. In Kenya, most safari staff are Kamba, who are noted for filed teeth, dancing, hunting, and a frank, open character.

In the days of the raiding Maasai, the Kamba gave a better account of themselves than most, being more expert at bush craft than the gaunt herdsmen and defending themselves skillfully with poisoned arrows. As early as 1889, they were warring successfully against both Maasai and Galla, and even made cattle raids on their old enemies; the Kamba bow, used with good effect on elephant, was strong enough to drive an arrow through the buffalo-hide shield of a Maasai, killing the man behind it.[6] More recently, the Kamba have resisted the ravages of bush-clearing (for tsetse control) by lying down in front of bulldozers. Wilderness people, they speak softly, even among themselves; the white man, in the presence of such people, lowers his voice.

The Land Rovers, driven by Jock Anderson and Adrian Luckhurst, had not yet returned with the Porter family from the north bank of the river; Adrian's wife had also gone along. I would have liked to talk to the Africans, but I spoke no Kamba and very poor Swahili, and even if my Swahili had been excellent, there was no reason to talk that they would understand: I was full of good will but had nothing at all to say. Feeling above all impolite, I sat down by the fire with a drink, and listened to crickets and soft African voices and the hum of the kerosene lamp, there was a moon in the acacias and a dying wind. Even in camp, wild things were going on about their business—tiny red pepper ticks with bites that itch for days, and a small scorpion, stepping edgily, pincers extended, over the bark bits by the camp table, and ant lions (the larvae of the lacewing fly) with their countersunk traps like big rain pocks in the fire ash and sandy soil. Unable to find footing in these soft holes, the ant slides down into the crater where the buried ant lion awaits. A faint flurry is visible—the ant lion is whisking sand from beneath the ant to hurry it along—and then the victim, seized by its hidden host, is dragged inexorably into the earth.

This morning the sun rising in the thorns looked silver and wintry in a haze and wind that made black rooks shift restlessly on the dead limbs. The silver sun was where the moon had been, in eerie light of day. The coarse bark of a grey zebra woke the plain, and the egrets went undulating southward, and oryx fled in all directions, cold dust blowing.

To the wood edge along the track where I had walked, a white-haired man had come the night before. He sat in a canvas chair beside his Land Rover, facing west over the Samburu Plain; an old black man, twenty yards away, sat on his heels against a tree trunk, facing south. There was a camp cot but no sign of a tent. Both figures were motionless, transfixed. Adrian recognized George Adamson, who for many years had been senior game warden of the NFD: "Has to be somebody like Adamson who knows what he's doing in the bush, I reckon, sleeping out like that, without a tent." I thought of this man's brother who had slept upon the ground, and the old days gone, and

53

the future unforgiven: "I do hope they let me see it out here—forty years, that's a long time, you know. They say Botswana—Bechuanaland, really—is all right, but I don't know."*

The Adamson brothers have worked in wild parts of East Africa for nearly a half century, and with Louis and Mary Leakey, who continue their monumental excavations at Olduvai Gorge, are among the last of their generation still active in the bush. Other veterans of the great days such as the white hunter J. A. Hunter, and C. P. J. Ionides, "old Iodine," of Tanzania, the acerbic ivory poacher turned game warden turned herpetologist, and Colonel Ewart Grogan, who made a famous walk from the Cape to Cairo at the turn of the century, and "T. B.," Major Lyn Temple-Boreham, game warden of the Maasai Mara and one of the few white men the Maasai have ever been able to respect (T. B. once remarked to Adrian, "The Maasai care for nothing but cattle, water, and women, in that order") had all died since Independence came.

Adrian waved to the figure in the chair, who did not wave back; white man and black, at right angles to each other, remained motionless, as if cast in stone. Like old buffalo, these old men like their solitude, gazing out over the Africa that was.

At Archer's Post, the new road crosses the Uaso Nyiro and runs north toward Ethiopia. One day it may actually arrive at Addis Ababa, but as yet it has not reached Marsabit, and none of it is surfaced. The work crews are mostly Kamba and Kikuyu brought up from the south, with a few Turkana mixed among them. The Samburu herdsmen will not work upon the roads. They share the attitudes of true Maasai, whose lands in Laikipia they occupied after the great Maasai civil wars of the 1880s, and to whom they are so similar that they are often called northern Maasai: the Samburu call themselves il-oikop—"the fierce ones," but to the Maasai are known as il-sampurrum pur (literally, the white butterflies often found around sheep and goat dung) due to their constant movement in search of water.[7] "Our customs are the same as theirs," says an old Samburu picked up along the way. The Samburu and the road laborers gaze at one another, mutually distrustful and contemptuous.

* I have since been told that the African was Stanley, Mr. Adamson's camp cook of many years, who was seized not long thereafter by an adopted lion known as Boy. Hearing a scream, Mr. Adamson came running and killed Boy, but the old man died.

54

The herdsmen are driving their cattle north, humped Asian zebu with a few long-horned Ankole, and each carries his short sword and club and two leaf-bladed spears of the style used by the Maasai until this century, when the javelin-bladed spear came into fashion; also, a leather water bottle and a small leather pouch. One has an elegant wood headrest, bartered, perhaps, from a Turkana. As a morani, or young warrior, he is painted in red ocher, and his greased braids are pulled up from the nape of his neck, jutting out over his forehead like the bill of a cap. The Samburu regard themselves as "the world's top people,"[8] and certainly they are more handsome and aristocratic than most other beings, but perhaps because their territories are surrounded by fierce nomads such as the Boran and the Turkana, the Samburu are not so arrogant as the Maasai.

To the north, odd pyramids and balanced rocks take form in the blue dust haze of the desert. Low thorn scrub is interspersed with toothbrush bush, combretum,* and the desert rose (*Adenium*), with its pink fleshy flowers, rubber limbs, and poison sap, a source of arrow poison. Eliot is struck by desert patterns and details, and we stop here and there to record them. From under a bush darts an elephant shrew; it sits on a dry leaf, twitches, sniffs, and vanishes with a dry scatter. At a hole in the red desert is a ring of grain chaff several inches deep; harvester ants gather kernels from the thin grasses and discard the husks. Farther on, where dark ramparts of the Matthews Range rise in the west, the isolated bushes shelter pairs of dik-dik from the heat: this is Guenther's dik-dik, grayer, larger, and longer in the nose than the common or Kirk's dik-dik, which is found south of the Uaso Nyiro. (As with the zebras, "common" and "gray" dik-dik seems much simpler: Messrs. Kirk and Guenther, with Burchell, Grevy, and the estimable Mrs. Gray of Mrs. Gray's lechwe, should be confined to the taxonomic nomenclature, cf. *Equus Burchelli*, where they belong. And for that matter, why should these ancient rocks of Africa commemorate the unmemorable General Matthews? Why not restore the Samburu name, Ol Doinyo Lenkiyio?)

* Because few plants in Africa have common names (except in the language of the local tribes—these names should eventually be given preference over European ones), generic names such as "acacia" (*Acacia* ssp.) and "euphorbia" (*Euphorbia* ssp.) are used ordinarily instead; I have extended this unscientific but inevitable practice to other prominent genera, cf. Commiphora, Grewia, Dombeya, Terminalia, Combretum, and the like, to avoid burdening the text with italics and capital letters.

From the mountains, which are said to shelter a few Dorobo, comes the Merille River. Samburu are digging water points in the dry river bed, and huge leather bottles, some of them three or four feet high, stand like amphoras near the holes. Other tribesmen squat beneath a big tree on the bank. The young boys, naked but for thin beads and earrings of river shell, have a scalp lock of hair on their plucked heads; the girls wear calfskin aprons and a cotton cloth tied at one shoulder that parts their pretty breasts. Unmarried girls are painted red, and some have lines of raised tattoos on their fair bellies; an infant in a sling wears a small necklace of green beads. The married women carry a heavy collar of doum palm fiber decorated with large dark red beads, and arms coils of silver steel and golden copper, the gold on the lower arm and the silver above, or the reverse. Men or women may wear metal anklets, bead headbands, copper earrings; one morani has ivory ear plugs and a string of beads that runs beneath his lip and back over his ears. At a little distance, he leans carelessly upon his spear, ankles crossed in a stance that is emblematic among warrior herdsmen from the Sudan south into Maasai Land.

North of the Merille the first dromedaries appear, a small herd in the shelter of the thorns; their keeper is nowhere to be seen. Far cones jut out of the desert, and a group of peaks has a shark-fin appearance, as if swept back by ancient winds off the High Semien, in Ethiopa. This is called the Kaisut Desert, but in June, just after the rains, the black outcroppings of lava are bedded in a haze of green.

Tin shacks of the road gangs gleam in the merciless sun at Loku-loko, in compounds enclosed by high barbed wire. Outside are the dung huts of parasitic Samburu attracted to the settlement, and a few cowled Somali women come and go. Some of the huts have rusty tin sheets stuck onto the roof, in emulation of the tin ovens of the workers; the traditional Samburu village compound is reduced here to a litter of loose hovels. Nowhere on the wind-whipped ground is there a tree or a blade of grass; the thorn scrub has been bulldozed into piles. Dust, rusting oil drums, blowing papers, black requiem birds, a scent of human poverty: in temperate climates, poverty smells sour, but in hot regions it is sickeningly sweet.

Mt. Marsabit rises from the desert haze like a discolored cloud. Grassy foothills climb in steps toward isolated cones, and the air cools. In a meadow, like a lump from the volcanoes, stands a bull elephant with great lopsided tusks curved in upon each other, the ivory burnished bronze with age like a stone font worn smooth by human hands. This high oasis far from the old trade routes and new tourist tracks, and cut off in recent years by shifta raids, is the realm of the last company of great-tusked elephants in Africa. Many have tusks of a hundred pounds or better on each side, and those of a bull known as Ahmed are estimated at 150 and 170 pounds, and may soon cross, as in the extinct mammoth.

Marsabit in June: great elephants and volcanoes, lark song and bright butterflies, and far below, pale desert wastes that vanish in the sands. On Marsabit are fields of flowers, nodding in the copper-colored grass: blue thistle, acanth, madder, morning glory, vetch and pea, and a magnificent insect-simulating verbena, its flowers fashioned like blue butterflies, even to the long curling antennae. The blossoms of the different families are all of mountain blue, as if born of the same mountain minerals, mountain rain. One cow pea has a large curled blossom, and to each blossom comes a gold-banded black beetle that consumes the petals, and each beetle is attended by one or more black ants that seem to nip at its hind legs, as if to speed the produce of its thorax. Next day I came back to investigate more closely, but the flowering was over and the beetles gone.

The roads of Marsabit are patrolled by the Kenya Rifles, there to protect the tribesmen from the shifta, and also an anti-poaching force whose quarry is often the same. They waved us to a halt. A vast elephant had been located not far from the road; they imagined it was Ahmed, who had not been seen for several weeks. All was invisible but a granite dome that rose out of the bush, and black men and white ones, creeping up, stood in a line before the gray eminence as before an oracle, awaiting enlightenment. Eventually the dome stirred, a curled trunk appeared, and modest tusks were elevated from the foliage that brought a jeer from the disappointed Africans, though they laughed gleefully at their own mistake.

Ahmed eluded us, as did the greater kudu. In size, this striped antelope is only exceeded by the eland, but the animals are not easily seen, having retreated into the retreating forest, restricted now to high Mt. Marsabit. "*Moja moja tu,*" said the Boran ranger who led us to its haunts—one sees one here and there. The Samburu crowd them with their herds, and so do the Galla—the Boran, Gabbra, and Rendille. (The Galla tribes, found mostly in Ethiopia, are modern Hamites, related to the Egyptians, desert Tuareg, and Berbers of the north.) Boran men wear the Moslem dress of the Somali, though most are pagan; the women dress also like Somali, but their faces lack the oriental cast that make the Somali what some consider the most beautiful women on this continent.

Three of the dead volcanoes on Mt. Marsabit contain crater lakes, of which the largest is Gof Bongole. From the high rim of Bongole, looking south, one sees the shark-fin moutains of Losai; eastward, the desert stretches away into Somalia. Of late, it was said, the mighty Ahmed, formerly unassailable in his serenity, had become vexed by the attentions of mankind, and perhaps he was bothered also by the roar of the machines that were bringing the new road from the south, for now he remained mostly in these forests behind Bongole, where he came to water. I awaited him one morning by an olive tree, sheltered from the monsoon wind by the crater rim. From the desert all around came a great silence, as on an island where the sea has fallen still. An amethyst sunbird pierced my eye, and a butterfly breathed upon my arm; I smelled wild jasmine, heard the grass seeds fall. From the crater lake hundreds of feet below rose the pipe of coots, and the scattering slap of their runs across the surface. But no great elephant came down the animal trails on the crater side, only a buffalo that plodded from the crater woods at noon and subsided in a shower of white egrets into the shallows.

Sun and grass: in my shelter, the air was hot. Mosque swallows, swifts, a hawk, two vultures coursed the crater thermals, and from overhead came a small boom, like the sound of a stooping falcon. But the bird hurtling around the crater rim was a large long-tailed swift of a uniform dull brown. This bird, described as "extremely uncommon and local ... a highlands species which flies high, seen only when thunderstorms or clouds force them to fly lower than usual"[9] is the scarce swift. Though not the first record at Marsabit, the sighting of a bird called the scarce swift gave me great pleasure.

Our camp was in the mountain forest, a true forest of great holy trees—the African olive, with its silver gray-green shimmering leaves and hoary twisted trunk—of wildflowers and shafts of light, cool shadows and deep humus smells, moss, ferns, glades, and the ring of unseen birds from the green clerestories. Lying back against one tree,

58

staring up into another, I could watch the olive pigeon and the olive thrush share the black fruit for which neither bird is named; to a forest stream nearby came the paradise flycatcher, perhaps the most striking of all birds in East Africa. Few forests are so beautiful, so silent, and here the silence is intensified by the apprehended presence of wild beasts—buffalo and elephant, rhino, lion, leopard. Because these creatures are so scarce and shy, the forest paths can be walked in peace; the only fierce animal I saw was a small squirrel pinned to a dead log by a shaft of sun, feet wide, defiant, twitching its tail in time to thin pure squeakings.

The Game Department people say that we should not travel beyond Marsabit without armed escort, but to carry more people is not possible: the two Land Rovers and the truck are full. We drove out from beneath the mountain clouds, descending the north side of Marsabit into the Dida Gilgalu Desert, where a raven flapped along a famished gully and pocked lava spread like a black crust across the waste.

Ahead, volcanic cones rose from the sand haze like peaks out of low clouds; the day was overcast with heavy heat. Larks and ground squirrels, camel flies and ticks; the camel fly is so flat and rubbery that it flies off after a hard slap. Occasional dry dongas support bunch grass and the nests of weavers; in this landscape, the red rump of the white-headed buffalo weaver is the only color. Though animals other than snakes are not a problem here, a lone traveler had made a small thorn shelter at the side of the road, to ward off the great emptiness. Round lava boulders, shined by manganese and iron oxides, and burnished by wind and sand, looked greased in the dry light—a country of dragons.

To the north, the Huri Mountains rose and fell away again into Ethiopia. We took a poor track westward. In the wall of an old river bed was a cave of swifts and small brown bats where man had lived, and from the dust of the cave floor I dug an ancient digging stick with a hacked point. Not far away, on the bare rock of a ridge, were tattered habitations of dung and straw where silhouettes of goats and man came together in a knot to watch us pass. Here where nothing grows, these primitive Gabbra subsist on blood and milk, in a way that cannot be very different from the way of the first pastoralists who came here many centuries ago.

The Gabbra mission at the Maikona oasis is a litter of huts patched with tin and paper, on a barren ground stalked by rooks and curs. Here children gnaw on the thin bitter skins of borassus palm nuts from the foul oasis. The nuts lie mixed with withered livestock turds around the huts, and they will be here when man has gone; such nuts are found in Old Stone Age sites that are fifty-five thousand years old. The people go barefoot on the stones, rags blowing, and they are idle, all but the smith, who pumped his fires with twin bellows made of goat skin: from scavenged car springs and an angle iron, he was beating a lean spear. As in all the Galla tribes, the smith has been despised and feared since the advent of the Iron Age brought this strange element to man, yet he seemed more cheerful than the aristocratic idlers who stared away over the desert.

Maikona lies at the south end of a black lava field that stretches north a hundred miles into Ethiopia; the lava ends in an abrupt wall where the wave of stone, thirty feet high, came to a stop. The lava flow forms the north wall of an ancient lake bed called the Chalbi Desert, a vast reach of ash and dead white soda that gives off the heat waves of mirage: for fifty miles, brown columns of dust pursued our caravan westward. Gazelle in quest of salt moved slow as ghosts across white fields of alkali, and a jackal overtaken by the heat lay with sick calm in the ash and watched men pass. The sun turned orange in a tawny sky, then luminous in the strange way of desert suns; it melted the Bura Galadi Hills on the horizon.

At dark, in the northwest corner of the desert, the cars reached the oasis at North Horr, where a police post protects the Gabbra of the region from shifta and from bands of nomad raiders out of Ethiopia. The women here have strong desert faces in black shrouds, metal arm coils and cobra-head bracelets, piled trading beads hand-fashioned from aluminum, ancient amulets; one necklace has a Victoria coin, worn thin by intent hands across a century of desert cooking fires. Perhaps it had come from the Sudan, snatched from the torn pockets of dead English at Khartoum.

Children come, with fireflies in their tight hair; the lights dance through the blowing palms. Far from the world, they play at being airplanes, which they know only from the lights that pass over in the dark, north out of Africa. Tonight there were no airplanes, but an earth satellite of unknown origin arched over the Southern Cross, followed toward midnight by a shooting star that died in a shower of ethereal blue light over the High Semien, in Ethiopia.

I slept under the desert stars, content to be somewhere called North Horr, between the Chalbi Desert and the Bura Galadi Hills: the lean sinister names evoked medieval legends, desert bandits, and the fierce grotesque old Coptic kingdoms of Abyssinia.

By morning the wind was blowing up in sandstorms. Flights of sand grouse, seeking water, hurtled back and forth over the cracking palms, and a train of camels etched a slow crack into the desert to the south.

Beyond North Horr, the track is too poor for the truck, which lacks four-wheel drive; it would meet us some days hence at the El Molo village, Loiyengalani, near the south end of Lake Rudolph. The eight white people in the party, with the Kamba cook, Kimunginye, would travel light in the two Land Rovers, since the plan was to arrive that night at Richard Leakey's archeological camp at Koobi Fora, some one hundred ten miles beyond North Horr. We carried our own food and bedding, and Richard, who expected us, would furnish the gasoline and water that would carry us back south again to Loiyengalani.

In the gravel beds of a dead river one car, towing a small trailer, had to be unhitched and pushed: beyond the river, the track made by Leakey's annual caravan was indistinct. The region is less hostile than the deserts farther east, and less monotonous. Dry river beds intersect broad dry grass plains broken here and there by sand dunes, brimstone outcrops, and ridges of dark volcanic rock scattered with bits of chert and gypsum, and the animals are tame and common, for there is no one here to hunt them. But farther on all creatures vanish, and the arid plain under a gray blowing sky seems more oppressive than bare desert, as if life had been here and had gone. In this wind is the echo of cataclysm: this is how the world will look when man brings all life to an end.

The land east of Lake Rudolf appears to have been a main migration route of early peoples, for here and there upon the landscape are strange stone heaps four or five feet high, ten feet across, encircled at the base by a ring of larger stones that gives them form. Some of these cairns or graves, most common near the water points to which the old track winds, have been identified as Galla. Others, like the tracks themselves, may be thousands of years old, growing gently in size from pebbles cast on them out of respect by passing nomads. In such silence one still hears the echo of those pebbles, tinkling to rest on the side of the mute heap.

African prehistory is an edifice of probabilities, and its dates are continually set back as new archeological sites emerge: it is now thought that Caucasoid wanderers came south into East Africa at least as early as ten thousand years ago, perhaps much earlier,[10] when all men on earth were still hunters and gatherers. These "Kenya Capsians" or "Proto-Hamites" whose remains have been found near the Rift Valley lakes used obsidian tools for working wood, bone, and hides, and were among the first people known to have possessed the bow and arrow, but essentially they were sedentary fishermen, like their contemporaries, the Negroid fishermen of Khartoum. Strangely, although one group was clearly Negroid and the other Caucasoid, both had the same barbed bone harpoons and curved arrowheads called lunates, made open pottery incised with wavy lines, and removed the two central incisors from the lower jaw, as all peoples of Nilotic origin, including the Samburu and Maasai, do to this day. A later people living near Lake Elmenteita[11] used two-edged stone blades and more symmetrical lunates, and made fine pottery before the Egyptians had learned to do so, but there is still no real evidence of a Neolithic culture based on domestic plants and animals before 1000 B.C., at least a millennium after the red cattle people of the rock paintings had left their traces in the Sahara.

South of the Sahara, Neolithic civilization was confined to certain hillsides of East Africa, and the evidence suggests that its peoples brought their animals and cereals out of southwest Ethiopia. Although the stone bowls and pestles that symbolize their culture might have been used for the grinding of red ocher and wild cereals, the Proto-Hamites surely had domestic grains as well. Meanwhile related peoples, discovering that they could live on milk and blood, were moving into a nomadic cattle culture of the sort still seen today: a Greco-Roman account of 200 B.C. tells of herdsmen south of the Sahara who worshipped their cattle, fed on blood and milk, practiced circumcision, and buried their dead in a contracted position "to the accompaniment of laughter."[12] (The "worship" of the cattle by the herdsmen, then as now, is better understood as deep affection—expressed in odes and lullabies, pet names and the like—for a life-giving force that is seen as the people's special gift from God; in the

62

same way, the Pygmies sing to the forest and the Bushmen to the desert that gives them sustenance, not in worship but in gratitude.) The nomad herdsmen, like the Bedouin Arabs who would later sweep across the northern continent, were the true barbarians of Africa, preying on others and ravaging the land. Very likely they obtained their animals and spears from the tillers they came to despise, but the prestige attached to the ownership of the precious animals that came south under their sticks was everywhere extended to their customs, which still survive in the great cattle kingdoms from the Sudan south into Tanzania, and are imitated by many tilling tribes as well.

The descendants of these "Proto-Hamites" have persisted into recent times. The Meru (Bantu) of Mt. Kenya have a tradition of a cattle people called the Mwoko with whom they warred only a few centuries ago, and who buried their dead in a contracted position under stone cairns, as the Galla do today. Farther south, the Gogo (Bantu) know of cattle keepers who preceded the Maasai onto the steppes of Tanzania.[13] This people dug wells and built reservoirs, carved holes in the rocks for the game of bao, built clay-lined huts that were fired like pottery and were red and white in color, suggesting the use of clays: probably red ocher can account for the color of the mysterious Azanians and the "red people" of the Saharan rock paintings, as well.

Ruins left by the Neolithic tillers are found almost invariably in hill country suitable to terracing and irrigation, and eventually these hills were surrounded and absorbed by the successive waves of Bantu-speakers who came after. Then, in the late Middle Ages, the black pastoral Nilotes came down out of the Sudan, while to the eastward, the so-called "Nilo-Hamites"—the Karomojong tribes, the Nandi peoples, the Maasai—swept southward from a region beyond Lake Rudolf. Traditionally, these people have been considered hybrid between the Nilotes and the Hamites, but some of their words are neither Nilotic nor Hamitic, and recently it has been suggested[14] that their Hamitic strain, at least, derives from a separate ancestral stock entirely. The term "Nilo-Hamitic" might be useful in distinguishing these brown, thin-featured herders from the darker Nilotes farther west, but even here it is not dependable: the Turkana, a tribe of the Karomojong, are coarse-featured and black. In Africa, after millenniums of human migrations, random physical traits are poor evidence of racial origin, and language is not always very much better. Most of these people are more Nilote than not in both language and customs, but the southernmost tribes, the Nandi and Maasai, have such distinctive Hamite practices as circumcision and clitoridectomy in initiation rites, the age-grade system of young warriors, despised clans of blacksmiths, and a taboo against fish. Conceivably all these practices were acquired from the Galla, who are known to have wandered the region north of Lake Rudolf in the fifteenth and sixteenth centuries, but more likely they are the heritage of earlier Hamites absorbed in the southward migrations, who may be responsible for the lighter skin as well. These vanished peoples left their traces in the terracing and irrigation techniques of the Negroids, both Bantu and Nilote, who cultivate those hillsides where their remains have been found, and who have adopted—in these regions but nowhere else—all the Hamite customs noted above.[15] The Galla tribes are the only modern Hamites in East Africa, but four hundred miles to the south, in the region of the Crater Highlands of Tanzania, peoples persist whose origins appear to be Hamitic. If so, they derive not from the Galla but from older stocks that have been isolated for many centuries, perhaps since the time of the earliest invaders out of the north.

Lake Rudolf glimmered in the west, a silver sliver down among dark mountains. Still fifteen miles inland from Allia Bay, the track turned north toward Koobi Fora. This cauterized region, in wetter climates of the Pleistocene, attracted huge companies of animals, including early hominids whose stone tools, dated at 2.6 million years, are the oldest known. Last year near Ileret, a frontier post just south of the Ethiopian border, Leakey's expedition found a skull of *Australopithecus boisei* which he believes to be 850,000 years older than the celebrated cranium of this man-ape uncovered by his parents at Olduvai Gorge. In Richard's opinion, this land east of Lake Rudolf is the world's most important archeological site, not excluding Olduvai, though others say that finds of comparable significance are being made by a French expedition to the Omo River, at the north end of the lake, in Ethiopia, which has come upon remains of *Homo sapiens* that have been dated at two hundred thousand years, or about twice the age of former estimate.

At twilight the track passed an oasis of borassus palms known as Derati that was the water source for Leakey's base camp at Allia Bay in 1968 and 1969. Beyond Derati, gray zebra and oryx clattered across stone ridges, and a black-bellied bustard rose in courtship, collapsing its wings on the twilight sky like a great cinder in the wind. Then a striped hyena rose out of the rock, a spirit of the gaunt mountain: it turned its head to fix us with its eye before it withdrew into the shadows. This maned animal of the night, with its cadaverous flanks and hungry head, is the werewolf of legend come to life.

The striped hyena is less uncommon than unseen. Even Jock Anderson, who was born in Kenya and has traveled the bush country all his life, had only glimpsed one once before, at Amboseli. But the pleasure we took in it was shadowed by the knowledge that the estimated distance to Koobi Fora was long past, with dark upon us. We stopped for a conference. At midday, I had felt uneasy about travel in desert country with two gallons of water for nine people—what would happen in the event of an engine breakdown, a wrong turning, one car separated from the other? But Leakey had made things sound so simple that Anderson had not anticipated the slightest trouble. Not that we were in trouble now, but we were down to two quarts of water and a ration of beer and fruit juice, and could not be sure that the eight gallons of spare gasoline would carry both vehicles back to North Horr, much less Loiyengalani, even if we turned around right on the spot. Presumably we were close to the Koobi Fora track, but side tracks are no more than shadows on this stony ground, and if the search failed, our only course was to go north to Ileret and radio for help. "We'd have to get in contact with somebody," Jock said shortly. "Assuming we make it," Adrian added, "past the bloody shifta." In the frustrating knowledge that Richard's camp was within fifteen miles of where we stood, it was decided to make camp at Derati and retreat to North Horr or Loiyengalani the next day.

Jock Anderson was grim and quiet; he is a man who dislikes turning back. But Jock had more to worry about than gas and water. We had been warned at Marsabit that an armed escort was desirable in this country, and at North Horr the police had described a gun battle that had taken place in the past month at Derati, where Leakey's supply caravan, with its armed guard, had come upon camped shifta, and five shifta had been killed. For the moment, Jock spared the party this ominous news. He was amazed at Leakey's claim that he had traveled from Marsabit to Koobi Fora in a single day, and annoyed that Richard had been so casual in his directions.

In the dark, at Derati, lacking a decent lantern, we could find no

65

water, only foul-smelling pits of algal murk under the roots of the borassus. We rationed out the beer. Everyone was hot and dirty, and Eliot Porter cut his leg badly in the darkness, and nobody looked happy. There was more discomfort than emergency, but trouble, once started, has a way of unraveling until it is out of control, and when Stephen Porter said, "It's not a game, we could die of thirst out here," his wife told him to hush up, but nobody contradicted him.

Derati is a gloomy place in the shadow of a mountain, and the one bright element in that evening there was the old Kamba cook, Kimunginye, who made supper without benefit of lamp or pot. With a panga he cut neat sticks by shearing palm sections from the central stalk of a fallen frond, and these he laid crossways on paired logs to make a grill; in the wood ash, deftly, one by one, he laid potatoes. Strips of meat were broiled upon the sticks and a can of string beans heated in the fire. For lack of liquid we ate lightly, but the food was good. Kimunginye is a calm old African who at midday had not asked for water, even in the 100-degree heat: the Kamba are tough—tough as the hyena's sinew, as the Maasai say. Perhaps Kimunginye recalled how, in his parents' time, these "red people," ugly as raw meat, had caused the great locust famine by running a railroad through his country (the man-eaters of Tsavo were seen by the Kamba as the spirits of dead chiefs protesting the encroachment on Kamba Land) and brought an end to the ivory trade by forbidding the Kamba to hunt elephant. If so, he gave no sign. This day was no different from another, and he went on about his work, as one felt certain that he would even if the next day were his last, his movements slow and gentle because so sure, without waste motion. The Kamba know that man dies "like the roots of the aloe," and dying was serious enough, so said his manner, without putting oneself to extra trouble over it. Kimunginye was the embodiment of what the Samburu call *nkanyit*,[6] or "sense of respect"—that quiet that comes from true awareness of the world around, with all its transience and strange significations. And I was filled with admiration, knowing, too, that Kimunginye was not exceptional, that his qualities are shared by many Africans who, seeing no need to emulate the white man, have remained in touch with the old ways.

Overhead, the crashing palms lashed wildly at the stars. In this bleak land the wind seems constant, with gusts that come as suddenly as avalanche. Grimy from a long day in the heat, we put our cots down in the fire smoke to discourage lions and mosquitoes; we would travel after midnight, to avoid the desert heat of day and its demands upon the water. Wind, discomfort, apprehension made sleep difficult for everyone except Adrian, who was so tired from the long day's drive that he went to sleep without his supper. Jock and I scarcely slept at all. He had confided to me the news of shifta, and my mind kept turning on the fact that there were two women to look out for in the event of trouble.

The wind still blew at 3:30 a.m. when we rose and broke camp and drove southward without breakfast. No water could be spared for tea, but if anyone was thirsty, he did not say so. Progress on the stony track was very slow, and it was near daylight when we passed the track down to Allia Bay, barely discernible in the cinder waste. From a visit by air last year to Allia Bay, Anderson knew of a rock pool inland, at the head of a rocky gorge; here, just after sunrise, we found water. In celebration, washing and drinking, we remained at the place two hours, then went on southeastward toward North Horr. The lonely sea, still silver, still remote, vanished behind its somber walls. Twenty-five miles from North Horr, just past the well called Hurran Hurra, a track turned off toward Loiyengalani, and as the spare gasoline was still intact, we took it; it was better to walk the last miles into Loiyengalani and send the truck back to the Land Rovers with fuel than to be stuck indefinitely at North Horr, where no fuel was available, nor transport out. The track went south along the Bura Galadi Hills, then west again, and at mid-afternoon Lake Rudolf reappeared, some seventy miles south of where we had last seen it.

Lake Rudolf, one hundred and fifty miles in length, was once connected to the Nile, and still contains the great Nile perch, two hundred pounds or better, as well as Kenya's last significant population of the Nile crocodile. Today the brackish lake is six hundred feet below the former channel to the Nile, and still subsiding, its only important source being the Omo River, which flows in the Rift fracture that crosses Ethiopia from the Red Sea. The prevailing winds of the southeast monsoon drive waves onto the west shore, in Turkana Land, 23,000 square miles of near-desert wilderness extending west to the Uganda Escarpment, which forms the divide between the Rift Valley and the Valley of the Nile.

In the western light, the lake was a sea blue, choppy with wind. The foreshore was littered with water birds—flamingos, pelicans, cormorant, geese, ducks, sandpipers and plover, gulls and terns, ibis, egrets, and the Goliath heron, largest of all wading birds in Africa. Behind them ran herds of feral ass, big-headed and wild as any zebra. At one time, the Turkana say, this shore had wild animals and good grassland, but generations of domestic stock have eaten it down to thorny stubble.

The first human beings seen since leaving North Horr were Turkana nomads, camped in a dry stream bed. To the south rose a forest of borassus palms that was sign of a large oasis; the two vehicles rolled into Loiyengalani with three gallons of gasoline between them. Word had come by radio to the police post that a truck from Koobi Fora had been shot at the day before in the region of Derati, and neither the North Horr police post nor the people at Koobi Fora had any idea where we might be. Subsequently Leakey told me that the killing of five shifta had occurred, not at Derati, but at the spring a few miles south where we had found water.

Loiyengalani is composed of a police post and a small Asian duka that serves the nomad herdsmen and El Molo; often these Indian shopkeepers were the first to penetrate unsettled regions, and few urban Africans with the training to replace them would care for the loneliness of their life. At the source of the spring, not far away, a safari lodge had been constructed, but in 1965 three men were killed here by the shifta, including the lodge manager and a priest who had come here to set up a mission. Since then, a mission has been established, but the Loiyengalani lodge subsides into the weeds. An old African sweeps the fading paths in the hope of a future, and hastened to fill the swimming pool in honor of our arrival. One of his tasks, as he conceives it, is to keep the lodge grounds clear of Samburu, Turkana, and Rendille, whose grass huts, like clusters of small haystacks, litter the oasis. None of these people of bare open spaces takes shelter from the sun and wind among the trees, preferring to build their thatch ovens on the round black stones between the oasis and the shore. The region abounds with a small venomous snake known as the carpet viper, and palm fronds left lying even for a day or two are sure to harbor one—hence the preference for the bare stones. Anyway, as one man says, the wind keeps the huts cool enough, and with one hand, one can make a window anywhere one likes.

The man who said this was an El Molo, or, more precisely, in their own pronunciation, Llo-molo; the name, he said, came from the Samburu Loo Molo Osinkirri,[17] the People Who Eat Fish. The main village of the Llo-molo, perhaps twenty huts in all, is situated still farther from the oasis than the huts of the herdsmen, on a bare black gravel slope above the lake. Stuck onto the rocks like swallows' nests, the huts have triangular mouths protected from the heavy wind by a screen of palm fronds. The black gravel all around is littered with tattered fronds and livestock dung, fish bones, old hearths, bits of rope and netting, rags. Fish dry on the thatch roofs, and on the rocks above wait rooks and gulls. Below, a smaller village stands outlined on the inland sea.

The Llo-molo, who pride themselves on honesty and hospitality, accommodate the nomads in their village even though they do not like them. The Samburu and Turkana here are forever pilfering and fighting, and a few may linger for weeks at a time as guests of the Llo-molo, who have plenty of fish and cannot bear to eat with all these strangers hanging around looking so hungry. Other tribes, the Llo-molo say, know how to eat fish better than they know how to catch them, although the Turkana fishermen on the west shore, who use set nets and fishing baskets, would dispute this. "We have to feed them," one Llo-molo says, "so that they will feel strong enough to go away."

The Llo-molo are mostly smaller than the Samburu, and many have bow legs, apparently as a result of rickets caused by their specialized diet. The men have white earrings carved from the vertebrae of cattle or Nile perch, and the women wear skirts of braided doum-palm fiber under the red trading cloth, but otherwise they imitate the Samburu, to whom they claim relationship: their moran are indistinguishable from the Samburu moran who joined them in a dance to honor the strangers. The faces of both were outlined in red masks of livid ocher, the dress and ornamentation were identical, and both carried paired spears with cowhide sheaths on the honed edges.

The dance, essentially similar in all the cattle tribes, was joined by a few Turkana warriors and women; no other women danced. Alone in East Africa, the women of the Turkana are treated as individuals worthy of respect. Though less elegant than the Samburu women, they have a bold stride and gay manner, and great character in dark, strong faces set off by beadwork and thick metal earrings. Turkana men wear black grease in their hair instead of red, and the hair is balled up in a wad of blue clay into which black ostrich feathers are inserted, and they are not circumcised. Between 1909 and 1926, the Turkana, who trade cattle into Ethiopia for rifles and to this day stage cattle raids against other Karomojong, resisted the combined authority of Kenya, Uganda, and the Sudan. But repression was less damaging to the Turkana than the drought and overgrazing in their arid lands, and today the tribe sends its men southward, seeking work.

The dancers pack together in a phalanx. As the dance begins, the moran, spears upright, step out whooping one by one, in the long, leaping Maasai trot that in time of war and cattle raids carried the herdsmen three hundred miles or more over the plains. (Adrian remarks that the Giriama of the coast, most of whom have never laid eyes on a Maasai, say to this day that there is no sense fleeing a Maasai, they have legs that can run forever.) The dancers tremble. Now two or three step out at once, and those in the main body begin to leap straight up and down, spears glinting in the sun; they shoot the chin out as they rise and stamp with the right foot as they touch the ground, and on each rise the upright spears and clubs, or rungus, are twirled all the way around. Some dancers make shrill whoops, patting their mouths; other clap hands in rhythm: "N-ga-AY!" The chant is heavy and guttural, repetitive, but one man sings a litany in counterpoint, and another orates fiercely in the background as the dance accumulates its force. The young women and old men become excited, swaying and laughing; an infant in a necklace of tiny dik-dik bones is bouncing on a girl's bare shoulders. At first these onlookers had teased the dancers but now they are caught up by the dance, eyes shining: "UM-ba-AY-uh! AH-yea-AY-y!" The old women, sullen, sit in the hot shadows of the huts, weaving palm fronds into skirts and nets and harpoon line. Perhaps they sense a condescension in the visitors, or wonder if the village will be paid.

The dance grows ever more excited, more complex, the greased red faces glistening with sweat. The moran chant in circles and then circles within circles, leaping, twirling, spears and metal arm coils shooting light, and always the chant and whooping, mournful and harmonious, the voice of man crying out to the ascending sky in exaltation and unutterable loss.

When, in 1885, Count Teleki's party reached the summit of the mountains at the south end of the lake, then made their way down to the shore, they were as stunned by the wind and sandstorms of this "valley of death"[18] as they were by its fierce beauty. At that time, the near-naked Llo-molo were all living on small islands out of fear of stronger tribes, and especially the Turkana, who made frequent raids against the Rendille of Mt. Kulal. One island village still exists and can be seen from shore, but the huts are so low and amorphous that from afar, in the sun and black sand and hard light, they look more like boulders than human habitations. The small bare island, known to the Llo-molo as Lorian, is composed of two small rises with a flat saddle in between, and the huts on the saddle are outlined on the blue mountains of Turkana Land. The Turkana say that there were formerly Llo-molo on the great South Island, far offshore, but that over the years the fires there had died out one by one.

With colonial pacification of the nomads, some Llo-molo moved to the mainland at Loiyengalani, the Place of Many Trees, and acquired a few cattle by trading fish to the herdsmen who passed through; the twenty-odd Llo-molo who still cling to Lorian have only goats. The two villages at Loiyengalani, with the remnant huts on Lorian, contain all known Llo-molo, who are scarcely more numerous today than they were in the time of Count Teleki. Their health has improved with the addition to their diet of milk and blood, meat, berries, borassus nuts, and ugali or maize meal, but the Llo-molo, being thought of as inferior, take no wives from outside the tribe, while their own young girls may be sold off to other people for a bride price.

Nguya, whose brother Nanyaluka will be next chief of the Llo-molo, says that the people who lived on Lorian subsisted entirely upon fish, which are everywhere plentiful; all the tilapia the people need can be netted a few feet away from the legs of the scrawny cattle that browse among the water weeds for want of fodder on the shore. But the fishermen of Loiyengalani go to a sand spit opposite Lorian to catch and dry fish for the village. They plant their spears in the black sand to warn off raiders, and build a fire by spinning a stick in a cleft of softer wood over a tuft of dung, taking turns with this ancient fire drill until the wood dust glows. Then more dung is laid over the spark, and the whole lifted in both hands to the wind until smoke appears and fire is created.

Lines, ropes, and nets are woven of the fiber of the doum palm. Gill nets, carried looped over the shoulder, are spiked to the lake bottom with an oryx horn, the free end being loosely overlapped with the next man's net. This process is repeated according to the number of fishermen, and meanwhile the lower mesh line is treaded into the mud, to keep the fish from fleeing out beneath. Now a boy splashes through the shallows, scaring fish into the net. The tilapia, one or two pounds each, are picked out and carried ashore, where a man squatting on his heels strips off the operculum, then draws the guts gently through the gill cavity, after which he uses the hard operculum to scale the fish. All is done deftly, without haste, and in moments the sparkling meat is rinsed off in the lake. Some of the fish are boiled and eaten, but most are split and spread onto palm matting to dry; every little while the fishermen pause to hone soft-iron knives on the glinting stones.

One morning a young man of Lorian came to the mainland on a small raft of two palm logs stabilized by log outriggers and propelled by a short pole used like a kayak paddle. On his raft, for trading purposes, he carried a black goat. After renewing his red ocher and having his hair adjusted by the fishermen, he set off with his goat for Loiyengalani.

In the old days, both crocodile and hippopotamus were taken here, and the Llo-molo harpoon, virtually identical in its design to harpoons still used in the salt waters of the world for ocean fish such as swordfish and tuna, may be a separate invention of these people. A long, straight shaft is carved from the hard root of a thorn tree, then greased and bent straight in the fire and the sun; a barbed harpoon point formerly of bone but now of iron is fastened to the harpoon line, pulling free of the shaft when the quarry has been struck. There is a light harpoon for heavy fish, a heavy one for crocodile, and for hippo the long horn of an oryx; the animal is killed by multiple spearings. For hippo, the Llo-molo must now go north to Allia Bay, where they remain a month or more eating the meat. Sometimes they dry a little to bring back for the women and children. Crocodiles, too, are hunted in the north, although some still occur near Loiyengalani.

This morning the head of a very large crocodile—"*Mkubwa sana mamba!*"—is spotted in the water off the point, a mile away. Through binoculars the surfaced snout and eyes can scarcely be made out; the fishermen cannot have seen the crocodile, only a rock that has no place along a shore that has been memorized for generations. The brute sinks slowly out of sight, to reappear some minutes later farther off; it raises the whole length of its ridged tail clear of the water before sinking away again. Everywhere else, including the Omo River, this Nile crocodile is very dangerous to man, but here it seems to be quite inoffensive. Lake Rudolf crocodiles can leap clear out of the water, and have no difficulty catching fish; mostly they hunt at night, in the lake shallows. But they also have an excellent sense of smell, and will travel a long way overland for carrion. It is said[19] that these ancient animals are unable to resist the call *im-im-im,* of a weird nasality attained by closing off one nostril of the caller, but I found no chance to put this predilection to the test.

Sometimes tilapia and Nile perch are taken with the spear, in clear water off the black stone shore south of the settlement. The fish schools are shadows in the water, and the men stalk them along the shore, moving ever more quietly until they are poised, spear shaft balanced in the left hand, butt cupped in the right, line dangling in a neat coil, the harpoon point with its hard glitter in the sun like the bill of a taut heron. Nguya and his brothers squat, knees cocked, black wet legs gleaming, until they are balanced, centered, and in time with all around them; the earth is poised, all breathe as one and hurl at the same moment. Later, Ngwinye, fishing alone, pierces a one-pound fish at least fifteen feet from shore. The stalk, the squat, the wait and rise and throw is a dance more stirring than the spear dance of the moran, which had been taken from another culture. Here was the Llo-molo hunter, the aboriginal man of Africa whose old ways fade among the colors of the people who came after; it was only a glimpse, for I was here too late. Today the three fishers wore mission shorts who only a few years ago had worn fish skins or gone naked.

Hundreds of feet above the lake is a strange old rock with two parallel lines of thirteen holes in its flat surface, carved for the ancient pebble game called bao: the land beneath the rock, eroding, is tilting it gradually into a gully. Forms of bao are still played by primitive people all over Africa, for the game comes down out of the Stone Age. Each stone represents an animal, and each hole a stock corral or boma; the point of the game, like the point of pastoral life, is to acquire more stock than one's opponent.[20] The bao rock may have lain beside a vanished stream, but more likely it lay by the old shore of the lake, which was markedly higher even in the time of Count Teleki. The gaming rock, perhaps thousands of years old, passed the time of those dim figures whose passage here is marked by the silent cairns.

On the old shore there is no sign of life, no bird, only gray shell and dusty rock and small concretions that hold fossils. All is dead but for a solitary toothbrush bush, mswaki, drawing a magic green from the spent stone. Then out of the emptiness flies a hare with a gaunt jackal in pursuit. The animals whisk back and forth and circle rises; the hare dives into the lone bush, the jackal close behind. A rigid silence is pierced by a small shriek. Soon the jackal reappears, hare in its jaws, and reverting to its furtive gait, makes off with its quarry down a gully. The rocks are still.

Inland, black boulders climb to far-off ridges that rise in turn to the Kulal Mountains, in Rendille Land. The Kulal is forested, but between the forest and the lake is desert; the only soft note in this landscape is the voice of the crested lark. Down the desert hills, early one morning, came herds of sheep and goats, like far white specks, and by midday the herds were watering at the lake shore, attended by four lithe girls bare to the waist, in red bead necklaces and golden bracelets. Leather pouches swung from their slim shoulders and in the wind their skirts wound gracefully around long legs. These Rendille were wild creatures from the eastern deserts, and when approached they ran.

The Rendille men resemble the Samburu in dress and comportment, but here they mix little with other tribes, perhaps because these despised folk eat fish. A Galla people, they wander the near-desert between Mt. Kulal and Marsabit, and others live between Lorian Swamp and the border of Somaliland. Probably they came originally from Somalia, driven out by the Somali expansion that seventy years ago carried all the way west to Mt. Kenya. The Rendille are desert nomads, and mostly they herd camels instead of cattle: when a man dies, the Rendille say, his brother mourns him with one eye and counts his camels with the others.[21]

Chewing hard twigs of mswaki, the Rendille stand like herons on one leg to contemplate our ways. One man presents himself before me: *"Kabala Rendille,"* he announces: I am of the Rendille. This is all the Swahili that he knows. He has a thorn encased in a foot that is swollen hard, and looks on with a cold smile as Eliot Porter tries in vain to remove it with a pocket knife. "He wouldn't flinch if you cut his foot in half," Adrian said, with that headshake, part condescension, part respect, that white East Africans reserve for the nomad's stoicism and endurance.

Days on this shore, though very hot, are bearable because the heat is dry, and because the wind is never still for more than a few hours. Each evening it comes howling down out of the Kulal Mountains to crash into the palms. Mounting in wild fits until after midnight, it causes the ballooning tents to lunge on their doubled moorings, and banishes all hope of sleep. Toward dawn, the winds abate, and by mid-morning may subside in vague light airs, or die with the same suddenness with which they came. The desert waits. Soon the palm fronds twitch again, and by mid-afternoon the wind is gathering toward the tumult of the night. In other seasons, said to be far worse, man takes shelter from the sandstorms in his hut, waiting dully for the months to pass.

June had turned into July; one morning we headed south. The winds and days were much the same, yet the lake has turned from a clear blue to jade, and we turned a last time to observe it from the southern mountains. From above, the inland sea is seen at its most beautiful, flowing north between two ramparts of dark mountains into the lost centuries of Abyssinia: on the desert horizon, in a desert light, the lake falls off the world into the sky. And seeing such splendor as he saw it, one regrets that Teleki named so strange a place after a Hapsburg princeling.* Before Teleki it was a lake of legend called "Samburu,"[22] but a better name still might be Anam, Great Water, a named used by the Turkana.

There is no road around the south end of the lake, only the foot trails of the few Turkana who pick their way over the lava flows to Loiyengalani. A bad track climbs out of the Rift and heads for South Horr across a region of black boulders, cairns, and strange stone circles in the sand, tracing the way of the ancient nomads toward Baragoi, and Maralal on the Laikipia Plateau, and the high savannas of East Africa.

* In early 1971, the name was debased still further when two thousand square miles of this region were set aside as the "East Rudolf" National Park.

4. Siringet

The Dorobo know the spoor of all the animals, and they like to see
the animals. The animals are not bad, for we and they all dwell
in the forest together. The intelligence of animals is not like that of
people, but it is not very different, for animals also are intelligent. All
animals of the forest are alike, though we eat some and not others,
because we the Dorobo and they the animals all live side by side
in the forest.

an anonymous Dorobo[1]

One winter dawn of 1961, looking westward from the Olbalbal Escarpment, I saw the first rays of morning sun fall on the Serengeti Plain,
in the country that was still known then as Tanganyika. Eight years
later, when I stood in the same place, in Tanzania, the mighty landscape had not stirred. No road was visible, nor any sign of man, only
a vast westward prospect spreading away to the clouds of Lake
Victoria. Off to the north rose the Gol Mountains, in Maasai Land;
in the near distance, scattered trees converged in the dark shadow of
Olduvai Gorge. Beyond the shadow, spreading away in a haze of sand
and golden grass, sun rays and cloud shadow, lay lion-colored plains
that have changed little in millions of years.

Occupation by man's ancestors of the Olduvai region at the edge
of the great grassland has probably been continuous or nearly so since
hominid creatures first emerged from the forests of central Africa.
Like the modern baboon, man's ancestors were primarily vegetarians
that turned to small game and carrion when berries and roots were
scarce, and evolved gradually as scavengers and hunters when the
stones used for splitting hides and seeds and bones were flaked into
hand-axes and missiles. The earliest hominid found at Olduvai is the
man-ape *Australopithecus*, heavy of brow and small of brain; he is
thought to have been slight and swift, with an arm fit for slinging
rocks and sticks.

In the early Pleistocene, perhaps three million years ago, crocodiles
floated in the shallow lake at Olduvai where *Australopithecus* left his

76

remains, and ever since, in response to variations in the radiation of the sun, or cyclical variations of the earth's axis, that lake has died and come again and died many times over in the long rhythms of rain and drought that characterized the Ice Age. In Africa, where these oscillations were less violent than on other continents, many great animals still survive, but tool-users such as *Homo erectus* and his contemporaries, who were large creatures themselves, hunted mastodonts, gorilla-sized baboons, wild saber-tusked pigs the size of hippopotami, and wild sheep as large as buffalo, as well as such animals as the white rhinoceros, once common on these plains. Possibly the white rhino, which is twice the weight of the black, is a giant form that has persisted into the present; although confined to the west bank of the Nile in the south Sudan and adjacent regions of Uganda and the Congo, it was once more common than its relative throughout the continent.

In the Pleistocene, the volcanoes of the Crater Highlands were still forming, and campsites of the early men who stared at the smoke-filled sky have been located beneath layers of volcanic tuff. The west foothills of the highlands, under Lemagrut Volcano, are steps made by tilting and faulting of the earth's surface that only took place some fifty thousand years ago, in the time when the Rift Valley was created. In this wet period of the Middle Stone Age, the use of fire had already spread throughout the continent, and remains found recently at the Omo River in Ethiopia together with a smooth-browed skull found earlier at Kanjera, in west Kenya, are evidence that modern man (*Homo sapiens sapiens*) existed at the time of these great tectonic movements, sharing the earth with more primitive men whose end he doubtless helped to bring about. Man the hunter had long since lost his body hair and developed sweat glands to dispel the tropic heat, and no doubt he also produced pigmentation to protect his bare skin from the tropic sun. In the next millenniums, while the heavy-browed *Homo sapiens Rhodesiensis* subsided slowly into the earth, his smooth-browed cousin modified his tools and developed language, learned to daub himself with ferruginous red clay, and suffered the first stirrings of religious consciousness, represented by the burial of his dead. *Homo sapiens sapiens*, the chimpanzee, and the gorilla are the sole survivors among the host of African apes, man-apes, and men that once competed for existence, and the gorilla, like the white rhinoceros, may soon follow the defeated ones into oblivion.

Little is known of man's evolution between the bone shards of a generalized *Homo* who used hand-axes a half-million years ago and the Kanjera skull of fifty thousand years ago, and there is a like absence of prehistory between Kanjera Man and the remains of the Negroid fishermen of Khartoum and their contemporaries, the so-called Proto-Hamites, who were the earliest invaders of East Africa from the north, some seventy centuries ago, and whose remains are the most recent found at Olduvai. Furthermore, no line of descent between these men and today's Africans has been clearly established, although many authorities see Bushmanoid characters in the Kanjera skull, and at least one[2] has suggested that the Irakw peoples of the south part of these highlands, who speak in a strange archaic tongue, may actually derive from Proto-Hamite hunters rather than from the Neolithic herdsmen and tillers who came after. In any case, hunter-gatherers have wandered this region since man evolved. The Bushmen have retreated into inhospitable parts of southern Africa, and such groups as the Gumba are entirely gone, but Dorobo hunters still turn up in the vicinity of Loliondo, trading honey and ivory to the Maasai whose ways they have adopted, and in the arid hills near Lake Eyasi to the south, where Rhodesioid Man left his remains, a few bands of Old People still persist, living much like Stone Age Man of forty thousand years ago.

The vast open space known to the Maasai as "siringet" is bordered in the east by the Crater Highlands, in the west by hills and a broken woodland that thickens as it nears the rain belt of Lake Victoria. Northward beyond Loliondo, in Maasai Land, it touches the Loita Hills and the plateaus of the Maasai Mara, in Kenya; to the south, it dies away in the arid thorn scrub west of Lake Eyasi. This eastern region of the plain lies in the rain shadow of the Crater Highlands, and is very dry. In winter, Serengeti days are made by the prevailing southeast winds, which lose their precipitation when they strike the east wall of the Highlands; even regional storms that come up over Oldeani and Endulen, on the south slope of the volcanic massif, fade at the Olbalbal Plains—hence the near-desert dust, black rock, and thorn of Olduvai Gorge, which is dry almost all the year. From Olduvai, the plain stretches west for thirty miles across short-grass prairie and long-grass plain to the riverain forests of the Seronera River, where weather from Lake Victoria becomes a factor.

The sun going north after the equinox causes a northeast monsoon, and the meeting of northeast and southeast monsoons produces rain; the winds, colliding, are driven upward, and in the cooler atmosphere, discharge their water. In summer a hard southeast monsoon comes from cool latitudes of open ocean east of Madagascar, and because the meeting of monsoons takes place over the south Sudan and Ethiopia, rain is scarce in the Crater Highlands. But distant anvil clouds and cumulo-nimbus herald the separate weathers of the lake basin, and by late spring the plains animals are already moving down the drainage lines that flow west toward the woodlands. In November, when the northeast monsoon swings southward and the Pleiades appear, white clouds rise on the eastern sky. Then the short rains fall, and the great herds, drawn by the first flush of new grass, return to the open plain in the annual movement, known as the "migration," that serves as pasture rotation for the wild animals.

In the winter of 1961, when I first visited the Serengeti, the greatest drought in memory was in progress. The short rains had failed entirely and the cow gnu or wildebeest, lacking milk, abandoned many of the calves; the following year there were no calves at all. But herd animals are adapted to calamities, and by the winter of 1969, when I returned to Seronera, their numbers had already been restored.* That January, the wildebeest were still moving eastward. The endless companies of animals, filling the sullen air with sullen blarting, are divided into cow-and-calf herds and herds of bulls; the bull gnus, especially, are wildebeests in their behavior, leaping, kicking, scampering, bucking, exploding crazy-legged in all directions as if in search of stones on which to dash their itching brains.

Often the wildebeest are accompanied by zebra. The striped horses, which foal all year instead of in a single seasonal avalanche, have less young to look out for and more intelligence to look out with; it is rare to see a zebra foal lost from its family band of stallion and mares. But among the gnu, the bony-legged calves are hard put to it to keep pace with their foolish mothers, and are often lost among the milling animals. Once separated, they are doomed, and fall to the predators in short order. The very plenty of their numbers in the few weeks of

* Droughts appear to fall in ten-year cycles: another serious drought occurred in 1971.

the calving may help preserve the species: the predators are too glutted to take advantage of all the opportunities, and many calves survive to blart another day.

Many wildebeest, streaming toward the highlands, cross the south end of Lake Lagarja, the headwaters of the Olduvai stream that cut the famous gorge; like almost all lakes of this volcanic region, it is a shallow magadi or soda lake of natron—native sodium carbonate in solution. In the low woods by the donga that drains the plateau to the west, a family of five cheetah lived that winter in the airy shadow of umbrella thorn, and greater and lesser flamingos, drawn to the soda lake's rich algal broth, rose in pink waves between the dark files of animals crossing the water. Since gnu are ever willing to stampede, the crossing is a hazard for the calves, and one morning of early winter more than six hundred drowned. Death passed among them like a windstorm, and its wake was awesome, yet the carcasses littered along the lake shore were but a third of one per cent of this antelope's annual regeneration in the Serengeti. Bloated calves had been dragged ashore by lions and hyenas, and others floated, snagged on mud reefs in the foamy shallows. In the thick heat of central Africa a stench so terrible clings to the throat; death had settled in the windless air like a foul mist. Among the carcasses, probing and sweeping, stepped elegant avocets and stilts, ignoring the taint in the stained water, and vulture and marabou in thousands had cleared the skies to accumulate at the feast. These legions of great greedy-beaked birds could soon drive off any intruder, but they are satisfied to squabble filthily among themselves; the vulture worms its long naked neck deep into the putrescence, and comes up, dripping, to drive off its kin with awful hisses. The marabou stork, waiting its turn, sulks to one side, the great black teardrop of its back the very essence of morbidity distilled. With George Schaller of the Serengeti Research Institute I made a count of the dead calves; and the vultures gave ground unwillingly, moving sideways. Vultures run like gimpy thieves, making off over the ground in cantering hops, half-turned, with a cringing air, as if clutching something shameful to the stiff stale feathers of their breast. The marabou, with its raw skull and pallid legs, is more ill-favored still: it takes to the air with a hollow wing thrash, like a blowing shroud, and a horrid hollow clacking of the great bill that can punch through tough hide and lay open carcasses that resist the hooks of the hunched vultures. Vultures fly with a more pounding beat, and the cacophony

80

of both, departing carrion, is an ancient sound of Africa, and an inspiring reminder of mortality.

Dr. Schaller, a lean, intent young man whose work on the mountain gorilla had already made his reputation, was studying the carnivores of the Serengeti. In the winter of 1969, he spent as much time as possible in the field, and often he was kind enough to take me with him. Usually we were underway before the light, when small nocturnal animals were still abroad—the spring-hares, like enormous gerbils, and the small cats and genets. The eyes of nocturnal animals have a topetum membrane that reflects ambient light, and in the headlights of the Land Rover the eyes of the topi were an eerie silver, and lion eyes were red or green or white, depending on the angle of the light. The night gaze of most animals is red, like a coal-red beacon that we once saw high in the branches of a fever tree over the Seronera River; the single cinder, shooting an impossible distance from one branch to another, was the eye of the lesser gallego, or bushbaby, a primitive small primate which may or may not resemble the arboreal creature from which mankind evolved.

In a silver dawn giraffes swayed in the feathery limbs of tall acacias, and a file of wart hog trotted away into the early shadows. Where a fork of the river crossed the road, a yellow reedbuck and a waterbuck stood juxtaposed. With its white rump and coarse gray hair, the waterbuck looks like a deer, but deer do not occur in Africa south of the Sahara; like the wildebeest, gazelles, and other deer-like ruminants, from the tiny dik-dik to the great cowlike eland, the reedbuck and waterbuck are antelope, bearing not antlers but hollow horns: the family name, Antilopinae, means "bright eyed." All antelope share the long ears, large nostrils, and protruding eyes that together with speed help protect them against predators, but non-migratory species such as topi, waterbuck, and kongoni seem more vigilant than the herd species of the green plain.[3]

At Naabi Hill, the wildebeest were moving east after the rains. In their search for new growth, wildebeest are often seen trooping steadfastly over arid country toward distant thunderstorms, which bring a flush of green to the parched landscapes. Some two hundred thousand were in sight at once, with myriad zebra and the small Thomson's gazelle. Eight wild dogs were hunting new gazelle left hidden by their mothers in the tussocks; one snatched a calf out of the grass only yards from the tires of the Land Rover, and with the two nearest dogs tore it to bits. The death of new calves is quick; they are rended and gone. But one calf older than the rest sprang away before the dog and made a brave run across the plain in stiff-legged long bounces, known as "pronking," in which all four hooves strike the ground at once. Like the electric flickering of the flank stripe, pronking is thought to be a signal of alarm. Though its endurance was astonishing, it lasted so long because most of the dogs were gorged and failed to cooperate. While the lead dog snapped vainly at the flying heels, the rest loitered and gamboled, picking up another calf that one of them ran over in the grass.

The Land Rover, dodging humps and burrows, followed the chase across the plain. Schaller clocked the young gazelle, which dodged back and forth for two and a half miles on the car's gauge and more than three in actuality; it never ran in a straight line. (The zigzag is less an evasion tactic than a way of seeing out of eyes set back on the sides of the head; in a herd, pursued animals usually run straight out.) The calf's spirit tempted us to intervene but we did not, since it was doomed whatever happened; separated from its milk when the chase began, it would have gone hungry while awaiting the first of the many beasts and giant birds that would come for it on sight. Finally, two dogs moved up to flank the leader, and in moments, the chase was over. The calf, still bouncing desperately, veered back and forth across the paths of the spurting dogs, and the dog to the eastward snatched it from the air; the other two were on it as it struck the ground.

One day, by a depression that holds water in the rains, I found a chipped flake of obsidian, much used by primitive man for his edged tools. There is no obsidian on the plain; the chip had been brought here long before. I wondered about the men who brought it—what size and color were they? Were they in hides or naked? What cries did they utter? Staring at the sun, the sky, were they aware of their own being, and if so, what did they think?

Doubtless the primitive hominids whose remains have been found at Olduvai were drawn to the edge of the great plain by the legions of grazing animals, and doubtless they were glad of a bit of carrion. The hunter Frederick Selous, in the 1870s, was appalled to see natives eat meat of an elephant eight days dead—"Truly some tribes of Kafirs and Bushmen are fouler feeders than either vultures or hyenas"4—but accounts of life on rafts and in prison camps, in plague and famine, make clear that the most civilized man will eat both carrion and his own kind when survival is at stake, as it must have been each day for low-browed figures who lacked true weapons and perhaps language, despite the physical capacity to speak. (Perhaps the earliest *Homo sapiens* of the Old Stone Age had no fire, and the gift of flame from the supreme Creator, recognized by almost all African tribes, was an earth-shaking event that is still remembered in the myths.)5

Traditional theories of the social life of earliest man are based on the behavior of non-human primates, although the apes are essentially vegetarians, and have lived very differently from man for more than a million years. Social systems, which often differ greatly among closely related creatures, tend to evolve in response to ecological conditions, and George Schaller felt that much might be guessed about early man from a comparative study of the social carnivores,6 which also pursued game in open country. While unable to run down his prey in the way of the wild dog or hyena, or even rush it swiftly as the lion does, man would have used such lion tactics as driving, ambush, and encirclement, and come upwind to the quarry, as lions have never learned to do. And as with the carnivores, a successful kill would inevitably depend on the social group that would share the food.

To judge from remains of predators found at his sites, early man was an increasingly effective creature who drove such unaggressive daylight hunters as the cheetah and the wild dog from their kills. In the dark, he was at a disadvantage and took shelter, leaving the hunt to leopard, lion, and hyena, but in the day, confronted with his sticks and stones, strange upright stance, and the shrieks, scowls, and manic jumps of primate threat display, these more dignified creatures probably gave way.

To learn how hunter-scavengers might fare, we sometimes walked some fifty yards apart for two hours or more over the plain. On most of the hunts gazelle calves were plentiful—with throwing sticks, four or five could have been killed, and with bolus stones (found at Olduvai) still more—and it was almost always possible to locate food by watching vultures in the distance. One day we came upon a Thomson's gazelle, dead of disease, that the carrion-eaters had not yet located, and also a young Grant's gazelle that must have been taken by the two huge lappet-faced vultures that we drove away, for the kill was fresh and no predators were anywhere about. Another day, when Schaller was elsewhere, I saw from a distance the white belly of a female Thomson's gazelle, fresh dead. As I approached, the first vulture, a big lappet-face, came careening in and took a swipe at her white flank. The vulture was instantly driven off by a second female gazelle; the great bird, flop-winged, chased its assailant but did not renew its assault on the dead animal.

The gazelle was still warm, and I slit open the belly to see if she had died in calving. She had milk but no calf; the wet newborn thing crouched in the grass some twenty yards away. A half hour later, her companion was still on guard, but more vultures were gathering, and finally the body was abandoned to a motley horde of griffons, white-backs, and hooded vultures that stripped it to the bones in a few minutes.

Jackals, vultures, and hyenas are alert for the defenseless moment when a new calf is born; often hyenas will attend the birth. But one day there was a mass calving of wildebeest in a shallow valley like an amphitheater between the isles of rocks, and it may or may not be significant—I simply record it—that the calving took place in the very middle of the day, when the sun was high and hot and the plain still. There was no predator in sight for miles around, nor a single vulture in the sky. Cow wildebeest were down all over the place, and a number of tottery calves less than an hour old swayed and collapsed and climbed again to their new feet. By late afternoon, when the predators become restless, raising their heads out of the grass to sniff the wind, these calves would already be running. (Wildebeest calves can usually run within ten minutes of their birth, but even this may be too slow; I have seen a lioness, still matted red from a feed elsewhere and too full to eat, walk up and swat a newborn to the ground without bothering to charge, and lie down on it without biting.)

For fear of scattering the cows, I restrained a desire to go close, for the calves will imprint on the nearest moving thing and are not to be deterred. One day, I was followed from a grazing herd by a young calf, and my efforts to head it back to safety finally resulted in putting the herd to flight. The calf did not follow, and the herd forsook it; nor would it permit itself to be caught. Finally I too left it behind. A mile away I could still see it—I can still see it to this day—a thin still thing come to a halt at last on the silent plain.

*

The unseasonal rains of late January continued into February, falling mostly in late afternoon and in the night; many days had a high windy sun. In this hard light I walked barefoot on the plain, to feel the warm hide of Africa next to my skin, and aware of my steps, I was also aware of the red oat and red flowers of indigofera, the skulls with their encrusted horns (which are devoured like everything else: a moth lays its eggs up on the horns, and the pupae, encased in crust, feed on the keratin), the lairs of wolf spiders and the white and yellow pierid butterflies, like blowing petals, the larks and wheatears (Olde English for white-arse), the elliptical hole of the pandanus scorpion and the round hole of the mole cricket, whose mighty song attracts its females from a mile away, the white turd of the bone-eating hyena, and the pyriform egg of a crowned plover in water-colored camouflage that blends the rain and earth and air and grass.

Bright flowers blowing, and small islets of manure; to the manure come shiny scarabs, beloved of Ra (god of the Sun, son of the Sky). The dung beetles, churning in over the grass, collide with the deposits of manure, or attach themselves to the slack ungulate stomachs full of half-digested grass that the carnivores have slung aside. They roll neat spheres of ordure larger than themselves and hurry them off over the plain. Here dung beetles fill the role of earthworms: the seasonal droppings of hundreds of thousands of animals, most of which is buried by the beetles, ensures that the soil will be aerated as well as fertilized.

By morning the ground is soaked again and the tracks muddy. Frogs have sprung from fleeting pools, and the trills of several species chorus in the rush to breed. Companies of storks, nowhere in evidence the day before, come down in slow spirals from the towers of the sky to eat frogs, grass-mice, and other lowlife that the rains have flooded from the earthen world under the mud-flecked flowers.

The grassland soil is built of ash blown westward from the volcanoes of the Highlands. Beyond the ash plain, in the vicinity of Seronera, the soil is derived from granitic rock and supports an open woodland vegetation. This is some of the oldest rock on earth—certain granites here are two to three billion years old—and on the plain the bone of Africa emerges in magnificent outcrops or kopjes, known to geologists as inselbergs, rising like stone gardens as the land around them settles, and topped sometimes by huge perched blocks, shaped by the wearing away of ages. The kopjes serve as water catchments, and in the clefts, where aeolian soil has mixed with eroded rock, tree seeds take root that are unable to survive the alternate soaking and dessication on the savanna, so that from afar the outcrops rise like islands on the grass horizons. In their shadows and still compositions, the harmonious stones give this world form.

When the sun has risen and the morning's hunt has slowed, the cats may resort to the rock islands. Perhaps they seek shade, or the vantage point of higher elevation—for the leopard its kopje is a hideout between raids—or perhaps, like myself, they like their back to something, for especially in summer, when the herds have withdrawn into the western woodlands and a dry wind blows in the dry grass, the granite heads are a refuge from the great emptiness of the plain. Kopjes occur in isolated companies, like archipelagoes—one group may be ten miles from the next—but most groups are related to a rising spine of rocks that emerges more or less gradually from the ash plain, from the low Gol Kopjes in the east to the majestic Morus at the edge of the western woodlands. Highest of all is Soit Naado Murt (in Maasai, the Long-necked Stone), nicknamed Big Simba Kopje, which juts straight up a hundred feet or more near the center of the spine, just off the main road from Olduvai to Seronera.

The lonely Gols are kopjes of the short-grass prairie, lying off to the north of the Olduvai-Seronera road. The shy cheetah is a creature of the Gols, its gaunt gait and sere pale coat well suited to these wind-withered stones, and one day I saw a glowing leopard stretched full length on a rim of rock, in the flickering sun shade of a fig; seeing man, it gathered itself without stirring, and flattened into the stone as it slid from view. It is said that a leopard will lie silent even when struck by stones hurled at its hiding place—an act that would bring on a charge from any lion —but should its burning gaze be met, and it realizes that it has been seen, it will charge at once. A big leopard is small by comparison to a lion, or to most men, for that matter, but its hind claws, raking downward, can gut its prey even as the jaws lock on the throat, and it strikes fast. It is one of the rare creatures besides man known to kill for the sake of killing, and cornered, can be as dangerous as any animal in Africa. Rural tribes have trouble in the night with leopards that steal into their huts to seize children by the throat and carry them off undetected—a testimony to the sleeping powers of the African as well as to the great stealth of this cat. Ordinarily, the unwounded leopard is not a menace to adults, but this past winter, a night leopard killed an African receptionist, Feragoni Kamunyere, outside his quarters at Paraa, Murchison Falls, and dragged the body, bigger than itself, a half mile or more into the bush, presumably to feed its waiting cubs. The strength of leopards is intense: I have seen one descend the trunk of a tall tree head first, a full-grown gazelle between its jaws.

There are few trees in the Gols, which are low and barren, yet in their way as stirring as the Morus, which rise like monuments in a parkland of twenty-five square miles, and have a heavy vegetation. Impala, buffalo, and elephant are attracted to the Morus from the western woods, and the elephants, which are celebrated climbers, attain the crests of the steep kopjes, to judge from the evidence heaped upon the rock. One day at noon, from this elephant crest, a leopard could be seen on the stone face of the kopje to the south, crossing the skeletal shadows of a huge candelabra euphorbia. In the stillness that attended the cat's passage, the only sound was a rattling of termites in the leaf litter beneath my feet.

Here near the woods the long grass is avoided by the herds. Lone topi and kongoni wander among these towers, and an acacia is ringed by a bright circlet of zebras, tails swishing, heavy heads alert. The wild horses are not alarmed by man, not yet; all face in another direction. Somewhere upwind, in the tawny grass, there is a lion.

I spent one February day on a small kopje, gazing out over the plain. The kopje overlooks a swampy korongo—not a true stream but a drainage line—that holds water in this season, and is bordered by dense thicket. On this rock, in recent days, I had seen a lioness and cubs swatting around the dried carcass of a gazelle that must have been scavenged from a leopard. I circled the place and studied it before committing myself, and climbing the rock, I clapped my hands to scare off dangerous inhabitants. In daylight, lions will ordinarily give way to man, and snakes are always an exaggerated danger, but care must be taken with the hands, for adders, cobras, mambas all reside here.

The hand claps echoed in a great stillness all around; the intrusion had drawn the attention of the plain. A stink of carrion mingled queerly with the perfume of wild jasmine on the rock. The birds fell still, and lizards ceased their scuttering. Then the early sun was creased by clouds. Standing in gray wind on the bare rock, I had a bad moment of apprehension—the sense of Africa that I sought through solitude seemed romantic here, unworthy. At my feet lay the reality, a litter of big lion droppings and a spat-up hair ball.

I looked and listened. From the fig tree came a whining of the flies. The sun returned, and from the sun came the soft wing snap or flappeting of the flappet lark, and the life of the plain went on again, bearing me with it.

Already the granite was growing warm, and leaves of a wild cucumber strayed on its surface. Squatted by a pool of rain that baboons had not yet found and fouled, I studied my surroundings. By the korongo spurfowl nodded through rank grass inset with a blue spiderwort, crimson hibiscus, a bindweed flower the color of bamboo. Soon a reedbuck, crouched near the stream edge until the intruder should depart, sprang away like an arrow as its nerves released it, scattering the water with high bounding silver splashes. Where it had lain, golden-backed weavers swayed and dangled from long stalks of purple amaranth. A frog chorus rose and died, and a bush shrike, chestnut-winged, climbed about in the low bushes.

A mile away to the northwest stood the great kopje that the Maasai call Soit Naado Murt. In the southern distance, toward the Morus, zebra and wildebeest passed along the ridges, and where the unseen carnivores were finishing a kill, the vultures were a black pox on the sky. To the east, under a soaring sun, ostriches ran down the grass horizon, five thousand feet above the sea. There came a start of exhilaration, as if everything had rounded into place.

Now it was man who sat completely still. In the shade of the great fig, a soft hooting of a dove—coo, co-co, co-co. The dove, too, had been waiting for me to go, blinking its dark liquid eye and shifting its pretty feet on the cool bark. Now it had calmed, and gave its quiet call. Bushes at the kopje base began to twitch where mousebirds and bee-eaters stilled by the hush were going on about their bright-eyed business, and agama lizards, stone eyes glittering, materialized upon the rock. The males were a brilliant blue and orange, heads swollen to a turgid orange-pink (kopje agamas have been so long isolated on their rock islands that color variations have evolved; those at Lemuta Kopjes, in arid country, are mostly a pale apricot), and they were doing the quick press-ups of agitation that are thought to be territorial threat display. Perhaps man lay across the courtship routes, for they seemed thwarted and leapt straight up and down, whereas the females, stone-colored, skirted the big lump that did not concern them.

As if mistrustful of the silence, a kongoni climbed to the crest of a red termite mound to look about; I focused my binoculars to observe it only to learn that it was observing me. The long-faced antelope averted its gaze first. "The kongoni has a foolish face," an African child has said, "but he is very polite."[7] Not far away, a Thomson's gazelle was walking slowly, cocking its head every little way as if to shake a burr out of its ear. It was marking out its territory by dipping its eye toward a stiff prominent blade of grass, the tip of which penetrates a gland that is visible under the eye as a black spot; the gland leaves a waxy black deposit on the grass tip, and the gazelle moves on a little way before making another sign. Once one knows it is done, the grass-dipping ceremony, performed also by the dik-dik, is readily observed, but one sees why it passed unnoticed until only a few years ago.

In the still heat that precedes rain, a skink, striped brown, raised its head out of the rock as if to sniff the flowers and putrefaction. A variable sunbird, iridescent, sipped from a fire-colored leonotis, blurred wings a tiny shadow on the sky; it vanished, and the plain lay still.

A big weather wind from the southeast came up in the late morning, and by noon it was shifting to the east, turning the dark clouds on the Crater Highlands. Once again, the herds were moving. To see the animals in storm, I abandoned my rock and went over to Soit Naado Murt, and climbed the broad open boulders on the south side, away from the road.

Soaring thunderheads, unholy light: at the summit of the rock the wind flung black leaves of twining fig trees flat against the sky, and black ravens blew among them. I straightened, taking a deep breath. From its aerie, a dog baboon reviled me with fear and fury. Puffs of cold air and a high far silent lightning; thunder rolled up and down the sky. Everywhere westward, the zebra legions fled across the plain. But dark was coming, and soon I hurried down off the high places. At the base of the rock, the suspense, the malevolence in the heavy air was shattered by a crash in the brush behind, and I whirled toward the two tawny forms that hurtled outward in a bad late light, sure that this split second was my last. But the lion-sized and lion-colored animals were a pair of reedbuck, as frightened as myself, that veered away toward the dense cover of the korongo. I stood still for a long time, staring after them as darkness fell, aware of a strange screaming in my ears. Then I came to, and moved away from the shadows of the rock. A pale band in the west, under mountains of black rain, was the last light, and against this light, on the rock pinnacles, rose the hostile cliff tribe of baboons. In silhouette they looked like early hominids, hurling wild manic howlings at my head.

5. *In Maasai Land*

The primal ancestor of the Masai was one Kidenoi, who lived at
Donyo Egere (Mount Kenia), was hairy, and had a tail. Filled with
the spirit of exploration, he left his home and wandered south. The
people of the country, seeing him shaking something in a calabash,
were so struck with admiration at the wonderful performance that
they brought him women as a present. By these he had children
who, strangely enough, were not hairy, and had no tails, and these
were the progenitors of the Masai.

Joseph Thomson, *Through Masai Land*

Like many white men that one comes across in Africa, Myles Turner
is a solitary whose job as park warden of the Serengeti keeps him in
touch with mankind more than he would like, but one day he got
away on a short safari, and was kind enough to take me with him. We
would go to the Gol Mountains, in Maasai Land, and from there
attempt to reach by Land Rover that part of the Rift Escarpment that
stands opposite a remote volcano known to the Maasai as *ol doinyo le
eng ai*, the Mountain of the God, called commonly Lengai.

The eighth of February was a day of low still clouds, waxy gray
with the weight of rain. On the plain, the herd animals were restless,
and the gnu, crazy-tailed, fled to the four winds, maddened by life.
At Naabi Hill, the eastern portal of the Serengeti Park, three lionesses
lay torpid on a zebra. Vultures nodded in the low acacias, and the
hyenas, wet hair matted like filth on their sagging bellies, dragged
themselves, tails tight between their legs, from the rain wallows in the
road.

We turned off north toward Loliondo, then east again under
Lemuta Hill. Between Lemuta and the Gols is a dry valley, in the
rain shadow of the Crater Highlands; here the hollow calls of sand
grouse resound in the still air, and an echo of wind from the stoop
of a bateleur eagle. Where we had come from and where we were
going, a pale green softened the short grass, but in the shadow of the
rain, despite massed clouds in all the distances, the flicked hoof of a
gazelle raised the soil in a spiral of thin dust.

On the far side of the desert valley is the Gol—the "Hard Country" of the Maasai—a badlands of arid thorny hills and high cold wind. The Gol is crossed by a canyon two miles wide, Ngata Kiti, that climbs gradually in a kind of arch and descends again into the Salei Plain. Ngata Kiti is the eastern range of the migrant herds, and theoretically connects the Serengeti populations with those of the Crater Highlands, but in 1959 this "Eastern Serengeti," which included Ngorongoro Crater, was returned to the Maasai. In addition, the government attempted to close off Ngata Kiti, where a few nomad Maasai kept a few cattle. Heavy posts linked with seven strands of wire were planted straight across the valley mouth. The wildebeest, faced with this fence, were undetterred; the wire held, but the whole fence went over. "Tried to interfere with what thousands of animals had done for thousands of years," said Myles, a slight wiry man with weary eyes in a weathered face and a wild shock of sandy red hair. He glared at the old fence line with satisfaction. "It's marvelous the way those animals smashed it flat. I use the posts for firewood now, out on safari."

At the mouth of Ngata Kiti is Ol Doinyo Rabi—the Cold Mountain—named for the chill wind that sweeps the Gol in summertime, when the herds have gone west to the woods, and the land is empty. This day there were small companies of wildebeest and zebra, and a secretary bird, that long-limbed aberrant eagle that stalks the open ground, but the true habitants of the Gol are the gazelles, which are the first to reach Ngata Kiti and the last to leave it. Probably the thin grass is sweet, since this soil has been enriched by the volcanos, but here in the rain shadow it is stunted for lack of water. The vehicle seemed small and lost between the walls of Ngata Kiti, winding slowly up the valley toward Naisera, the Striped Mountain, named for black streaks of blue-green algae that have formed on its granite face. Halfway up, big fig trees burst from ledges and crevasses, the bare roots feeling their way down to sustenance one hundred feet below. Behind Naisera we made camp in a grove of umbrella thorn and wildflowers; I remember a delicate apricot hibiscus. At Naisera there are highland birds: the ant-eater chat and the bronzy sunbird, crombecs, tits. . . .

Myles's Land Rover was packed with gear of all descriptions, and a truck carried tents for each of us and two tents for the staff, as well as stoves, stores, and water. Like most British East Africans, Myles

92

is extremely thorough in his safari preparations, and saw nothing strange at all in having seven pairs of hands to help us through a short trip of three days—what was strange to him was my discomfort. Not that I let it bother me for long. While the tents went up, I watched white clouds cross the black thunderhead behind Naisera; lightning came, and a drum of rain on the hard ground across the valley. On the taut skin of Africa rain can be heard two miles away. Bird calls rang against Naisera's walls, which on the north are painted white by high nests of hawk and raven. At the summit, in the changing light, the swifts and kestrels swooped and curved, and an Egyptian vulture gathered light in its white wings. Then the sky rumbled and the white bird sailed on its shaft of sun into the thunder.

The storm arrived in early afternoon. I lay content beneath the raining canvas, head propped upon my kit, and gazed through the tent flap down past Naisera into the dry valley below Lemuta where no rain fell. In the thunder, wildebeest were running. When the rain eased, I crossed the grove to a cave in Naisera's wall that had a small boma of thorn brush at the mouth, and a neat dry hearth. In a similar cave in the Moru Kopjes, shields, elephants, and abstract lines are painted on the walls in the colors that are seen on Maasai shields; the white and yellow come from clays, the black from ash of a wild caper, and the red ocher is clay mixed with juice from the wild nightshade. Presumably the artists were a band of young warriors, il-moran, who wander for several years as lovers, cattle thieves, and meat-eaters before settling down to a wife, responsibilities, and a diet based on milk and cattle blood. According to Leite, a young Maasai ranger, this cave in the Gol Mountains was also a place of meat-eating, which is forbidden in the villages, and which no woman is allowed to watch. Those women who see it are flogged, he told Myles, who nodded in approval. Leite is tall and brown, with a stretched ear lobe looped into a knot; he gazed about him with an open smile, happy to be here in Maasai Land.

Leite's people were part of the last wave of lean herdsmen to descend upon East Africa from the north. Perhaps five centuries ago the present-day Nandi tribes invaded western Kenya, driving earlier herdsmen known as the Tatog south from the region of Mt. Elgon; the Maasai tribes were farther to the east, in the grasslands and surrounding plateaus of the Rift Valley, and they, too, appear to have displaced an earlier people, known to the Dorobo as the Mokwan,[1] who had long hair and enormous herds of long-horned cattle, and who may be the same herdsmen as the Mwoko, recorded by the Meru Bantu of Mt. Kenya.

In regard to the coming of the Maasai, the Dorobo say[2] that a Dorobo hunter at the Narok River saw great companies of people coming down out of the north, and hid; he was caught by the Maasai, and guided them to water for their cattle. The Maasai are thought to have reached Nakuru and the Ngong Hills near Nairobi in the seventeenth century, and their heaven-born first laibon or medicine man was found as a youth in the Ngong at a time thought to have been about 1640. Subsequently they continued south along the Rift, and in the vicinity of the Crater Highlands held great battles with a people that their tradition calls *il Adoru*[3]—conceivably the Barabaig, a tribe of the Tatog so fierce that they are known to present-day Maasai as *il Ma-'nati* or "Mangati," the Enemy, a name reserved, so it is said, for a worthy foe.

Otherwise, the Maasai met with small resistance. By the nineteenth century, they had driven the Galla tribes northeast across the Tana, and Maasai Land extended east and west one hundred and fifty miles and five hundred miles north and south, from the region of Maralal on the Laikipia Plateau to the south end of the Maasai Steppe in Tanzania. Their raids, which spread from Ikuria Land on Lake Victoria to the Indian Ocean coast, were feared by Bantu, Arab, and European alike, so much so that Maasai Land remained unexplored until less than a century ago. Avoided by the great slave routes and trails of exploration into the interior, it was the last terra incognita in East Africa.

Linguistically the Maasai are closest to the Bari of the Sudan,[4] and the many customs that they share with other tribes of Nilotic origin include male nudity, the shaving of females, the extraction of two middle teeth from the lower jaw, the one-legged heron stance, the belief that the souls of important men turn into snakes, and the copious use of spit in benediction. Like the Nuer, the Maasai believe that all cattle on earth belong to them, and that taking cattle from others is their right. Originally it was God's intent to give all cattle to the Dorobo, but the great Maasai ancestor Le-eyo tricked the Dorobo, and God into the bargain, receiving the cattle in their place. Hence the Dorobo must live by hunting and gathering, which the

Maasai despise. Eland and buffalo may be eaten by Maasai, since these are thought of as wild cattle, but no other animal, or fish or fowl, is ever hunted except for decorative or ceremonial purposes—ostrich head plumes, monkey-skin anklets, ivory earplugs, and the great helmets of lion mane that once identified a proven warrior. (An exception, the rhino, is poached for its horn, which is bought from the Maasai by Asian traders and sold in the East as an aphrodisiac; this commerce is at least as old as the *Periplus of the Erythraean Sea*, an account of a trading voyage to the east coast in the first century A.D. In a six-month period of 1961, the Leakeys found over fifty speared rhino in the Olduvai region alone, each stripped of a horn that may be worth a few shillings a pound to the Maasai but far more to the trader. A recent increase in the trade has threatened the black rhino with extinction, all to no purpose, since despite its shape and dynamic angle, the horn—not true horn at all, but hard-packed hair—can do nothing to spur the love-bent oriental, who may pay as much as two hundred dollars per pound to ingest it as a powder.

Like the Dinka, the Maasai have a moon legend of the origin of death, which was formerly unknown among mankind, and is still thought of as unnatural: Naiteru, a deity residing on Mt. Kenya, instructed the patriarch Le-eyo that if a child of the tribe should die, he must cast away the body with the words, "Man dies, and returns again; the moon dies and remains away." But since the first child to die was not his own, Le-eyo did not bother to obey, and ever since then, man has died and the moon has been reborn. Eventually Le-eyo called his sons to his own deathbed to ask what they wished as an inheritance. The greedy elder son, who became the ancestor of all Bantu, wanted part of everything on earth; the younger said he would be content with some small remembrance of his father. This modesty was rewarded with great cattle wealth, whereas the Bantu son was given a little bit of everything, and ever since has been eking out his days with his wretched agriculture.

Within the tribes, certain Maasai became smiths, and fashioned the spear blades and the short sword known as the simi; as in Hamitic tribes, such people were inferior. When the white man appeared in the late nineteenth century, he was called l'Ojuju, the Hairy One, and lacking cattle, was despised with all the rest.

I have tried to produce an impression on the Maasai by means of forest fires, by fiery rockets, and even by a total eclipse of the sun . . . but I have found, after all, that the one thing that would make an impression on these wild sons of the Steppe was a bullet . . . and then only when employed in emphatic relation to their own bodies.[5]

At the time this was written by Karl Peters, whose perfidious treaties with unsuspecting chiefs laid the groundwork for Germany's seizure of Tanganyika, the power of the Maasai was already waning due to drought and disease and a growing resistance from such victims as the Nandi and the Kamba, as well as incessant war between their own marauding tribes; cheered on by their women, they staged great civil wars on the open plain, one consequence of which was the utter disruption of the Laikipiak Maasai, whose lands were taken over by the Samburu. In 1869, the Samburu had infected the Maasai with cholera, which raged through the tribe in epidemic, and just before the Europeans appeared in force in the 1880s, they were swept by smallpox, and their beasts struck down by waves of rinderpest, or pleuro-pneumonia, a cattle plague from Asia that also affects certain antelope (rinderpest is thought to have eliminated the greater kudu from wide areas of its former range). Kikuyu and Kamba herds, in Kenya, were also afflicted, bearing out an old Kikuyu prophecy that great famine and disaster would precede the fatal coming of pale strangers. Like the Kamba, the Maasai believe that a comet foretells the coming of disaster, and they say that a comet crossed the sky just before the appearance of l'Ojuju: the great laibon Mbatien had also prophesied the advent of the white man in a vision brought on by honey wine. On his deathbed, Mbatien bequeathed his title and attainments to his son Lenana, much to the annoyance of the elder son Sendeyo, who had reason to believe that Lenana had cheated him out of his heritage. Once again the Maasai split into hostile factions more or less separated by the boundary between what had become, in 1895, British and German East Africa. But after twelve years of rinderpest, smallpox, famine, and German harassment in the region of Kilimanjaro, Sendeyo forgave Lenana, and the Maasai were reunited. Already Lenana had made peace with the British; so weakened were the Maasai, in fact, that they needed European protection from their enemies. Because of their great misfortunes, made so much worse by their delight in fighting one another, they were unable to resist the Hairy Ones—unlike the Nandi, farther west, who were not pacified until 1905, and the Turkana, in the north, who held out for another twenty years. The Maasai wanted very much to fight against the Germans in World War I, which brought Tanganyika under British administration, but the British thought it unwise to give them arms.

In the Serengeti, according to their own tradition, the Maasai were most numerous near Lake Lagarja and in the south part of the plain, but until 1959, when their herds were banished, they lived intermittently at Moru Kopjes and elsewhere in the park, and signs of their long stay include mints and peas that thrive in the wake of overgrazing by domestic herds. Some of the kopjes have been stripped of trees, and at others the vegetation seems induced by man—certain acanths and morning glories that accompany the disruption of the soil, and thorny nightshades (*Solanum*), and an introduced legume whose spiny fruits are thought to have stuck to the old Army greatcoats gotten in trade at the Asian dukas after the last war. Today these greatcoats, regardless of temperature, are a favored article of dress throughout East Africa, though most Maasai wear the shuka or toga of broadcloth, dyed in red ocher, that is knotted on the right shoulder.

Maasai herds are still seen intermittently along the eastern boundaries of the park, and a few moran may turn up at the settlement at Seronera. One-legged or ankles crossed, leaning on their spears, they gaze impassively at the less aristocratic Africans in the service areas. Ostensibly they have put aside their warlike ways, but not long ago a dead morani was discovered on the plain—speared to death, apparently, since no predators were near. As yet, only vultures had found him. A passing Maasai might pluck some grass, which as cattle food is a symbol of good will and peace, and spit on it in benediction, and place the grass upon the skull, to protect himself from evil, but the body would be left untouched on the great siringet, under the African sky.

When the rain stopped, I climbed Naisera. Leite came with me, bringing along his muzzle-loading musket, taken from a poacher. This gun was long since defunct—it had not worked for the poacher, either. Even in the time of Livingstone, such muskets were very common in the interior—it was firearms that persuaded the Arab traders to venture inland—and with the advent of the breech-loading rifle, then the repeater, late in the nineteenth century, great numbers of muskets were inherited by the Africans. In Tanzania, thousands of muzzleloaders are still registered, and guns of the mid-nineteenth century are still carried for purposes of prestige.

Three klipspringer stood outlined on the rock's crest; by the time we reached the top, they had disappeared. We crouched in the wind and gazed up and down Ngata Kiti. To the eastward, far beyond the far end of the valley, the Mountain of God rose for a long moment in the swirling clouds, then vanished. The Maasai say that Lengai or Ngai moved to this place in the sky after a Dorobo hunter shot an arrow at him, and most of the day for most of the year his realm is hidden; now Ngai is remote, beyond their reach, and they are visited by death and famine. Leite took delight in my elation at the sight of the holy mountain. Later he exclaimed to Myles, "Lengai *must* be the Mountain of God—it is so extreme!" In 1967, this last active volcano of the Crater Highlands erupted, shrouding its slopes and all the country around with fine gray ash.

I spoke no Maasai and Leite no English; we communicated with hand signs and good will. Leite cautioned against touching a certain euphorbia whose milk was hurtful to the eyes, and showed me a small plant, ol-umigumi, taken as a stimulant with meat before a lion hunt to give warriors courage. The moran surround a big male lion, then rush in with their spears—"Fantastic!" says Myles, who has seen this twice. "Not one hangs back, they all want to be first. And when the wounded lion knows it must break out of that circle, and charges, and gets one of them down, he just curls up under that buffalo-hide shield. The others are in there so quick that he's up a second later. I saw two lions killed, and not one of those chaps ever got a scratch!"

It is said that many of the best moran died of infection in the years that followed the great rinderpest plagues, when the proliferating lions, having finished the dead cattle, turned to the live ones; even a slight mauling from a lion or leopard can be fatal, since the smears of carrion adhering to the teeth and claws make the wounds septic. Today the Maasai are forbidden to kill lions or steal cattle, much less spear their fellow Africans. In an effort to damp their warlike nature, the buffalo-hide shields, black, white, and red, have been taken away from them, although spears may be carried as a defense against wild animals, and are still used occasionally on people; a white man was killed only a few years ago in the region of Narok. The Maasai have been compared[6] to predators such as wild hunting dogs that seem strangely delicate in their adjustments to their environment, and fade quickly in the face of change. When jailed by the colonial authorities, they died so regularly that a system of fines had to be set up instead.

Turner has a high opinion of the Maasai, of their independence and their physical courage and their ferocity as warriors, and he favors a popular theory that they blocked the northward advance through East Africa of the formidable Ngoni Zulu of the South. "The Zulus were well organized, you see, none of this other Bantu lot could do a thing with them; took the Maasai to stop them. They never got farther north than the Maasai Steppe!" Myles's face is not often alight with such enthusiasm—"Oh, they're *wonderful* people!" He compared them to the Somali of Kenya's Northwest Frontier, and laughed in sympathy with those British officials who, after only a few months out in Africa, became "white Maasai" or "white Somali"—"No, no! Wouldn't hear a word said against them!" Even Lord Delamere had been a champion of the Maasai, who have an unquenchable sense of their own aristocracy, and won the admiration of the whites by looking down on them.

Myles much regrets the passing of the days when stately files of Maasai raiders in black ostrich plumes and lion headdress, spear points gleaming, crossed the plains without a sideways glance. He is proud of his library of Africana, and has read virtually all of the early accounts—the missionary-explorers like Krapf and Rebmann who first saw the snow peaks of Kenya and Kilimanjaro, and Livingstone and Speke and Burton, who explored the lakes, and Joseph Thomson, the first man to traverse Maasai Land, in 1883, and Count Teleki, who discovered Lake Rudolf, and the ivory hunters such as Frederick Selous and Arthur Neumann and Karamoja Bell, who were of necessity explorers, too. But the time of the hunter-explorers was coming to an end in 1909, when the cousins Hill who had settled on the Kapiti Plains southeast of Nairobi let Theodore Roosevelt hunt lions on their ranch and became the first of the "white hunters." Selous, who escorted Roosevelt (he died a few years later in the German wars in Tanganyika) was the last of the great hunters of the nineteenth century, and those who came after, such as John A. Hunter, began their careers as meat hunters for the Mombasa railroad, or in game control. By the 1920s, Hunter and Philip Percival, whose brother Blayney was the first game warden in the Kenya Colony, were the most renowned of the "white hunters," whose small numbers included Percival's partner, Baron Bror von Blixen, as well as his estranged

99

wife's lover, Denys Finch-Hatton, who was to become the hero of *Out of Africa*.

In East Africa, hunters have ever been great liars, and except as fuel for nostalgia, their exploits make repetitious reading, clogged as they are with stupefying lists of the carcasses left behind and encounters with death so constant as to cancel one another out. Nevertheless, a great many of the adventurers were extraordinary men, and much of the seeming exaggeration in their accounts comes less from inflamed imaginations than from the compression of the inevitable adventures into a few pages, unleavened by all the quiet days in between.

The rangers had built an enormous fire which lit up the north face of Naisera. We stood at the fire with stiff drinks. Myles was raised in the Kenya Highlands, and for many years had worked with game control, killing animals for the farmers of Mt. Kenya; he reckons that he shot seven hundred buffalo. After three years of this, he was offered a job by Ker and Downey as a white hunter, and traveled all over Africa. He recalls a mid-morning encounter outside the Norfolk Hotel with Ernest Hemingway, whose work he much admires. "Hemingway was a friend of my clients, and invited me into the bar for a drink. I told him thanks very much, but I hadn't finished up—we were going off on safari, you see." Hemingway was very offended. "Any man who doesn't drink with me fights with me," the great man told him.

Eventually Myles married a girl who worked at Ker and Downey, and in this period, like many hunters before him, he turned from hunting to protection of the game. "I was sick of killing animals," he told me. "Thought I'd try a bit of the other side." Myles was then thirty-five, which John Owen, the former director of the Tanzania parks, considers to be the age when most men outgrow shooting big animals. As a District Commissioner in the south Sudan, Owen killed a good number of elephant, and he is not sheepish about it in the least; he feels to this day that the present trend toward photographing animals instead of shooting them is like flirting instead of making it—there bloody well ought to be a certain risk involved.

Most professionals agree that a hunter who takes no risk is no hunter at all; since he lives by violence, he ought to be prepared to die that way. Yet they also agree that in the modern hunting safari there is virtually no risk to anyone but the professional, who may have less to fear from the wild animals than from his clients. A story is told of one of the Greek shipping magnates who took with him a bodyguard of three hunters, then damaged his expensive gun by dropping it when an elephant screamed; the gun's discharge sent it skidding across the rocks, and the bullet just missed one of his guards. Latin Americans, especially, think themselves unmanly if they do not pursue their own wounded animals into dangerous situations, and one hunter speaks of a Brazilian who kept firing furiously over his head as he crawled into dark bush after a wounded leopard—the hunter got it with a lucky shot at the white flare of its teeth—then refused the trophy with disdain until told that it had value, whereupon he claimed it. Another who had wounded a lion handed the hunter a movie camera, instructing him to film the inevitable charge and the destruction of the lion. "Don't shoot," he begged, "unless he has me down." The hunter refused, on the grounds that the loss of a client meant the automatic loss of his own license. (In the good old days, when hunters were not penalized in this way, one of their number obeyed such rash instructions to the letter, and the filmed record of his client's demise, together with his personal effects, was duly sent home to his loved ones.)

Myles had no use for his Latin American clients, who were notorious for killing every animal they were legally entitled to, whether they meant to take it home or not. Once he walked out on such a safari, asking the Nairobi office to send out another hunter. Whatever one may think of hunting, there is a great difference between the true hunter and the butcher, and Myles recognized it: the love of the hunter for the hunted, while scarcely of the spiritual quality attained by the Bushman or Dorobo, is no less real for having been sentimentalized and overblown. But killing without hunting, for mere souvenirs, describes most of the motorized or airborne excursions that pass today for the hunting safari. Also, the professional hunters are no longer a small band of colorful adventurers as they were in the early days when Fritz Schindelar, riding a white horse, risked and received a fatal attack from a charging lion. In Turner's time, after World War II, there were already eighteen hunters; today sixty or seventy are licensed, and their numbers increase as the animals decline.

In his days as a hunter, Myles depended heavily on his Dorobo gun bearers and trackers, who moved quietly and missed nothing: "They've incredible hearing. Not only did they know that a big animal was laying up in there, but they'd know just how far away it was, and

whether it was a buffalo or rhino. They could hear him breathing."
And it was from Myles that I first heard of the primitive Tindiga
hunters east of Lake Eyasi, some sixty miles to the south, where he
had once gone on safari. "One day we passed a small man with a
bow, sitting on a rock by a small pool. Two weeks later, when we
came back through, he was still there; he hadn't moved. He'd got one
zebra in the interim."

According to Myles, the wild Tindiga were still independent of
surrounding tribes, unlike the Pygmies and Llo-molo and Dorobo,
and had even retained their ancient tongue, which was a click-speech
like that of the Bushman. Avoiding all others, they moved in small
bands through the hills surrounding the hot arid Yaida Valley. I asked
Myles if one could visit them, and he shrugged: there might be a few
at the Yaida game post, but the wild ones would be very hard to find.

A cold night wind off the Gols whipped the steep walls of Ngata Kiti,
and this wind, by morning, had shifted into the northeast. "Dry
weather wind," Myles muttered, sipping tea at the morning fire.
"Blows the dhows south from Arabia." Though it is generally erratic,
the northeast monsoon blows from late October or November through
February; the southeast monsoon blows the rest of the year. In
summer, the land has dried to tinder, and the dry wind keeps everyone
in a bad temper: black man and white actually *grin*, says Myles, at the
first sign of the rains.

Leaving camp and the truck behind, we went eastward down the
valley, taking along a driver and two rangers. Animals were scarce,
and became scarcer. A hyena in the distance had this region to itself,
to judge from the number of ungnawed bones along the way. The
valley was much rougher than expected, and two hard hours passed
before we came onto a rise that descended to the Salei Plain. To the
south, in a kingdom of black rains, the Crater Highlands mounted
toward the rim of Ngorongoro, thirty miles away; away from the
Ngorongoro road, the Crater Highlands, girt by dead volcanoes that
rise ten thousand feet and more into their clouds, are little known.
Northeast was the rim of the escarpment, and beyond it and far below
lay the great lonely Lake Natron, stretching away to the Kenya border.
Straight ahead, lost in the clouds, Ol Doinyo Lengai rose nearly ten
thousand feet from the Rift Valley floor.

The Salei Plain, which forms a broad step between the Gols and

102

the brink of the escarpment, is a bitter place of tussock and coarse bush that rises from gray cindery ash of the volcanoes, and for a time it seemed that its creatures were all solitary—one hyena, one giraffe, a rhino—as if only here, in this land too poor to support predators, such outcast animals could survive. The big coarse grass, too high to walk through with impunity, hid stones that could gut a car, and progress, which had been slow all morning, became slower still. In eleven hours of lurching and jarring, with one half-hour stop, we were to travel less than eighty miles.

Once our route crossed an old track of the Somali traders who make their way to the Sonjo villages that overlook Lake Natron; their most popular product is Sloan's Liniment, taken internally as a beverage and nostrum. The Sonjo are a xenophobic tribe of Bantu-speakers who defend an enclave in this remote corner of Maasai Land. Like many eastern Bantu groups of hill regions, they may have a strong Caucasoid strain in their blood from the Hamitic tillers they displaced, for the average Sonjo is lighter in color than the Maasai. With the digging stick that is their only tool, they practice irrigation farming, eked out by goats and poaching. Maasai still raid their outlying camps, and the Sonjo construct fortified villages and fend off attacks with poisoned arrows. Today, the six villages still existing are built on the escarpment slopes on this west side of Lake Natron, and all overlook Ol Doinyo Lengai, which like the Maasai they consider to be the Mountain of God. It was Ngai who gave the digging stick to the Sonjo and Kikuyu, to whom the Sonjo are linguistically related, although the Sonjo themselves have a tradition of common origin with the Ikoma of Lake Victoria, with whom they still share such obscure customs as scarring infants above the left scapula and under the left breast.[7] The Ikoma and Sonjo are eighty miles and at least two centuries apart, for the tribes were probably separated by the coming of the Maasai.

The Sonjo are bad people, Leite says, teasing the Ikoma driver about Bantu fears of the Maasai and of wild animals; how could it be that people so frightened of animals could be famous poachers, like the Ikoma and the Sonjo? The driver's tribe is held in low regard by Maasai and white alike, though it must be said that the Maasai despise all Bantu tribes, known collectively as *il-meek*. The most charitable view that one hears of the Ikoma is that centuries of exposure to the tsetse fly have leached away their human virtues. "Murder *everything*,"

Myles says. The Ikoma driver, one of the rare survivors of a black mamba bite, remarked that all Maasai were cattle thieves, which of course is true.

The second ranger was Corporal Nyamahanga, an Ikuria from the Mara province at the Kenya border. Last year a poacher fired two poison arrows at Myles and the corporal, and Myles said, "Pot him," which Corporal Nyamahanga did. "Had three great whacking buckshot holes in his forehead. Bandaged him up, but I thought he was a goner. Couldn't get him to hospital that night, we were twenty miles from our vehicles, and next morning I said to Corporal Nyamahanga, 'Is he dead?' 'No sir, he's eating a good breakfast!' " Myles turned to gaze at me, disgusted. "Survived a charge of buckshot in the head, he did; took him to hospital at Musoma." He contemplated the corporal, a very strong big serious man whose black laced boots curled up sharply at the toes. "Good people, the Ikuria, and Corporal Nyamahanga is a good man—great runner, too. I'll make him sergeant as soon as there's a place."

The Land Rover groaned on through a thickening heat, but the rim of the escarpment kept retreating; each ridge disclosed new gullies and rough broken ground. Up one gully that deflected us off to the north came a lone Maasai, with a few cattle; he disdained to show surprise at meeting a vehicle in this waste where no vehicle, it seems certain, had ever been before. In his faded red toga, face a mask, the only human figure that was seen on the safari to the Gol Mountains scarcely turned to watch us pass. On a journey, the Maasai say, if a man is met who walks alone, the journey will be unsuccessful. So it proved this day, for we never reached the rim of the escarpment.

Ol Doinyo Lengai, though shrouded, was a heavy presence in the sky. Lost bands of kongoni and gazelle, wandered down out of the highland clouds, waited for everything and nothing on the edges of the cinder plain, and on a rise stood a stone oryx with one horn. The horn was long and straight and whorled; here was the unicorn. The beisa oryx is a strong gray antelope, wary and quick and spirited; oryx have been known to kill attacking lions. This one, given sudden life, went off at a fast trot. Far down the slope its herds were already moving at our approach. Myles said that in this region, where the animal is rare and wild, the hunter who killed an oryx usually earned it.

On the level ground, the game trails radiated out in cracks from the dry waterholes. Near one hole a dead zebra, still intact, had drawn a horde of griffons from the sky. The zebra did not look diseased, and we searched it for sign of Sonjo arrows, but there was nothing; it had merely died. Straightening up again, black men and white stood stunned beneath a leaden firmament, awaiting impulse: there was no sound but our own boots on the cinders. At midday Lengai loomed through the clouds and again vanished. Heat and silence became one. Adding their silence to the silence, the griffons waited.

The Land Rover retreated westward, toward the east face of the Gols. A band of green lined the bases of these cliffs, where the rare rains came down out of the mountains, and plains game stood expectant in the low still woods. Under the cliffs was a Somali track, headed south toward the mouth of Ngata Kiti, where we climbed out of the Salei in late afternoon. Soon the air was cool, and we paused on the slope, gazing back toward Lengai, which had come up out of its clouds to watch us go. The Mountain of God is a magnificent pure cone, a true mythic volcano, shrouded in pale ash so fine that it mists into the canopies of clouds, making the whole mountain an illusion.

Now the sun appeared, and the air dried; the pale tones of Ngata Kiti came to life. Round-haunched zebra stood, tails blowing, on a round curve of a hill, each wild horse in silhouette against the sky. A cheetah appeared, and then two more, moving westward up the valley; the animal survives in such dry country by lapping blood from the body cavity of its kill. The walk of lions is low-slung and easy, and leopards move like snakes, striking and coiling; the cheetah's walk looks stiff and deadly as if it were bent on revenge. The three cats were traveling, not hunting, and did not look back.

Three miles from Naisera, we got down from the Land Rover to walk home. Bouncing away, the Africans stared back at us as if we had gone mad. Then the car stink was gone, and the motor; the twilight valley rang like a great bell.

On the plain lay a tawny pipit, dead, raked by a hawk. Somewhere jackals were keening, and a restless lion roared from across the valley. Then owls emerged, and in the growing dark, the white bellies of gazelles flashed back and forth like flags in a ghostly dance. From the mouth of a burrow peered four faces of bat-eared foxes, and from Naisera came a troop of mongoose, looping out in single file over the plain; it was the time of the night hunters.

Today we were beaten, but another day we would come back. At the evening fire, we planned a foot safari that would take us southeast across the wild Loita Hills of Kenya to the Sonjo villages, and down along the western shore of Natron; we would climb Lengai, then continue south into the Crater Highlands, to Ngorongoro.

At dawn we left the Gol behind, turning north toward Loliondo. A wind from the northeast was high and cold, a wind of hawks and eagles, and beyond Lemuta, the delicate pearl-and-chestnut kestrels dipped and rose, snatching dung beetles from the hard-caked ground. Farther on, four steppe eagles in a half-circle at the mouth of a hole fed with ravenous dexterity on a hatching of termites. Africa is a place of incongruities, as if its species were still evolving—kingfishers that live in the dry woods, owls that seize fish, eagles that eat insects. And doubtless the great variety of raptors here is accounted for by their versatility of habit: nothing is overlooked, and nothing wasted.

Across the plain came a strange hyena that behaved like no hyena we had ever seen. Though unpursued, and pursuing no other creature, it ran hard, and though its head was half-averted in the manner of hyenas, its tail was raised, not tucked in the usual way between the legs, and it came straight for the car instead of fleeing it, only turning off in the final yards, still unafraid, still searching.

Myles stared after it in real surprise: he would demand a scientific explanation of such behavior from his friend Hans Kruuk. (Dr. Kruuk, the hyena specialist at Serengeti, has a high opinion of the charm, playfulness, and cleanly habits of these creatures in captivity, and keeps one as a pet). Hunters and game wardens are the traditional authorities on animal behavior, but today their opinions are regularly challenged by biologists and ecologists, and Myles, who works closely with the people at the Serengeti Research Institute, feels obsolete, "Scientists are in charge of the animals these days," he said shortly. "We just keep things going for them. But now and then we catch them out—there are still a few things they don't know."

The vehicle traversed the lonely rises, rolling a thin dust cloud toward the west. Myles wished to show me an enormous fig that stands by itself far off beyond Barafu Kopjes. These hard plains are bare and bony, with only a whisper of grass, yet the animals keep to the ridges, where the grass is shortest. In a tilted world, the wildebeest went streaming down the sky, black tail tassels hung on the wind

106

behind, all but a solitary bull, thin-ribbed and rag-tailed, old beard blowing. Perhaps he felt his death upon him, for he paid no attention to our intrusion. Soon he had the whole sky to himself.

The giant fig, which looks like a small grove in the distance, is at least as old as man's recorded history on this plain. Its spread is not less than one hundred and fifty feet, the size of six ordinary figs, and it is a tree of life. Cape rooks, kestrels, owls, and the shy brown-chested cuckoo were in residence, and none would willingly leave the tree because there are no other trees for miles around. One owl that moved onto a nearby rock was punished by the kestrels; at each blow from above, it shifted its feet and shuffled its loose feathers.

The tree has a Maasai hearth built into its thick base, and a flat stone near at hand for sharpening spear blades. One day I would like to sit under this tree that has drawn so much fat wood and fleshy leaves out of near-desert, and stare for a week or more into the emptiness. One understands why these monumental figs take on a religious aura for the Africans; they are thought to symbolize the sacred mountains, and the old ways of close kinship with the earth and rain, Nature and God. The Mau-Mau leader Kimathi used such figs for prayer as well as message depots, and his people said of one great tree that it would fall of its own accord when Kimathi was taken. In the police inspector's unsuperstitious account[8] of the hunt for Kimathi, the tree in question fell within that hour.

Even the most pragmatic narratives of life in Africa must touch on what H. M. Stanley was pleased to call "my dark companions and their strange stories"—the pervasive witchcraft and sorcery, which may be legitimate, in one's best interests, or may be used wrongfully, taking the law into one's own hands. The Kikuyu recognize nine categories of magic besides charms (protective magic) and sorcery (destructive magic), and strange powers are by no means limited to the witch doctor, but are freely applied by all. Thus his captor was awed by Kimathi's uncanny sense of impending danger, as Karen Blixen was awed by the instincts of her servants, who would always know of her return and would be at the railroad to meet her. C. P. J. Ionides, the great reptile man of southeast Tanzania, was mystified by the preventive cure administered to him by an African which appeared to have made him immune, or nearly so, to dangerous snake bites.[9] A doctor who has worked with Africans for thirty years has told me in detail of the spells and curses, especially popular among wives of unwanted husbands, that can cause a healthy person to give up and die in a few days of strange wasting diseases: he resigns himself to death because a witch has eaten his "life soul." Or a man whose wife is unfaithful while he is off hunting is subject to death or serious injury from wild animals.[10] Fetishes are in common use: certain Karomojong are cursed with drought if someone experienced in these matters places an ostrich head on a mountain top with its bill pointed at their village.

A witch has mystical resources not possessed by the mere sorcerer, and will often remain at home while his "shadow-soul" is abroad in the form of a night animal. A missionary tells[11] of an old witch doctor in a tribe plagued by lions who for years refused to be converted; then a hunter was sent in by the Game Department, and soon thereafter, the old man became a Christian. When asked why, he shook his head in resignation. "Why not?" he said. "You've shot my lions." Cults of leopard-men[12] and lion-men who kill with claws are both well known, and the lion-men, if they exist, may cloak their work behind that of a real man-eater, as was thought to have been the case in the widespread deaths in 1920 and again in 1946 among the Turu in the region of Singida, in south-central Tanzania, which came to a prompt halt when an investigation was begun: "Too many eyes are watching now," said a Turu chief.[13] Another chief in the same region predicted to a British District Officer that elephants would take care of a local man who was annoying the village by holding up an irrigation scheme, and shortly thereafter a herd of elephant came through the nearby banana groves without touching a tree and utterly destroyed the shamba of the offender.[14]

Most rural Africans have knowledge of animals controlled by gifted individuals—not always witch doctors—whose spirits inhabit them: the man-eaters of Tsavo were especially feared due to their occupancy by human spirits, and many tales are told in many parts of Africa of hyena spirits in human form who are detected by some such sign as a mouth in the back of the head.[15] A werewolf hyena is often an old witch woman, "trotting along the river now, baring her teeth in the night air,"[16] and the Bantu of Tanzania know of those who ride hyenas in the night. Peasants are more witch-ridden than hunters and nomads, and among the Mbugwe, tillers of sorghum and millet who settled on the bare mud flats south of Lake Manyara as a protection against Maasai raids, more than half the adult population are considered witches who control all the hyenas or "night cattle" in the region, and sometimes lions into the bargain; fear of black magic is so prevalent that people eat in the darkness of their huts rather than expose their food to the evil eye of others, and when in the bush hide their food with their clothes or go to eat alone behind a tree.[17] That several people in the Manyara region have been taken by lions in recent years will only affirm the beliefs of the Mbugwe.

Belief in lycanthropy involving lions and hyenas, like the summoning of beasts to carry out specific deeds, is not only widespread but in many cases very difficult to put aside as superstition; these events have a reality in the ancestral intuition of mankind that cannot be dismissed simply because it cannot be explained. The story I like best—because it is mythic and rings true, whether or not it actually took place—was told me by a lady whose husband had it from the hunter Bror von Blixen, a practical sort, so it is said, not given to flights of fancy. One day on safari Blixen was begged by natives of the locality to deal with a dangerous hyena that was raiding the village stock at night; no one dared to kill it himself for fear of reprisal from its witch. Blixen agreed, but his staff would not keep watch with him: to kill Fisi, the Hyena, would bring evil luck. Finally Blixen prevailed on his gun bearer to go along, and later this man bore witness to what happened.

The moonlight was crossed by the silhouette of a hyena, and when Blixen fired, wounding it, the creature dragged itself into a thicket. They followed the blood trail to a bush, from the far side of which the hyena soon emerged. Blixen's second shot killed it, and the two men went forward. Where the hyena had fallen, in the moonlight, lay the body of an African.

The great fig west of the Gol Mountains overlooks a dry korongo, and nearby there is a Maasai cattle well. In the well lay a drowned hyena so blue and bloated that the rotting skin shone through the wide-stretched hairs. Though it had been there many days, no scavenger had touched it. Even its eye was still in place, fixed malevolently upon the heavens.

We headed south. Miles from where it had first appeared, the lone hyena rose out of the land, and this time it came even closer, loping along beside the car, tail high and bald eye searching. We wondered then if this haunted beast was hunting for its mate, and if the mate might be the hyena in the well. But we did not know, and never would, and the mystery pleased us.

6. *Rites of Passage*

We have to share our land with wild and dangerous animals. We have to learn to give way to the elephant, the rhinoceros, the lion, etc., and this has not been our way of life. Many of us have lost children, others have lost relatives and stock to these animals which belong to the Government. The Government has value for these animals but they are of no value to us any more. The only value of these animals which we knew about is that they used to be the source of our traditionally important trophies, such as kudu horns used for war signals, lion manes worn as a sign of gallantry by the morrans (young warriors), buffalo hides for shields, elephant tusks for ornaments worn by the morrans, etc. The use of these things in our daily life is quickly becoming a thing of the past. This value of wildlife being gone, we know of no other value whatever and yet our cattle are being killed and our people either being killed or injured by these animals. We are fined or imprisoned when we kill these animals for food even in times of extreme famine despite the fact that we share our land with them. The presence of these animals in our district means loss of lives and stock every year and nothing else.

D. M. Sindiyo (*a Maasai warden,*
paraphrasing the arguments of the Samburu)[1]

At Lemai on the Mara River, eighty miles north of Seronera near the Kenya border, the Ikuria Bantu were displeased because part of their lands north of the Mara had been appropriated for the Serengeti park; they were harassing the Lemai guard post at night with threats and stones. Myles Turner flew an extra ranger to Lemai to strengthen the garrison, and I went along. We circled a concentration of six hundred buffalo near the Bangai River, then flew onward, passing east of the old Ikoma fort, built by the Germans in 1905 as a defense against rebellious Ikoma. Beyond Ikoma was another great herd of buffalo, black igneous lumps in the tsetse-ridden land. Zebra shone in the morning woods, but a rhino was as dull as stone in the early light.

To the north and west, over Lake Victoria, the cloud masses were

111

a deepening gray-black; at times the plane flew through black rain. These lake basin storms are the worst in East Africa, building all day and coming to a boil in late afternoon. But the clouds were pierced by shafts of sun, and the plane cast a hard shadow on thatch roofs, bomas, and patchwork gardens scattered along the boundary of the park. Half-naked people stood outside the huts; they did not wave. "*Wa-Ikoma*", Myles said. "Poachers." Poaching has always been a problem on park borders, all the more so because no park in East Africa is a natural ecological unit that shelters all its game animals all year round. To contain the natural wanderings of its herds, the Serengeti park, five thousand square miles in extent, would have to be doubled in size, expanding east to the Crater Highlands and northward into Kenya, through the Maasai Mara to the Mau Range. Human population increase and the lack of protein in lands which suffer from advanced protein deficiency in the poor have made the poaching of wild game a widespread industry, and an estimated twenty thousand animals are killed each year in the Serengeti area alone. Poisoned arrows, which are silent, are still preferred to rifles, but traps and steel wire snares have replaced the traditional snares woven of the bayonet aloe or bowstring hemp that gave its Maasai name to Olduvai Gorge.

The parks are the last refuge of large animals, which in most of East Africa are all but gone. The game departments are chronically bereft of funds, staff, and the technical training to protect the game, and most of their resources are devoted to destroying animals worth far more in meat and tusks and hides than the shamba being protected in the name of game control. Where animals are not shot out, poached, or harried to extinction, they are eliminated by human settlements at the only water points for miles around, or their habitat vanishes in the fires lit to bring forth new grass. Thus the survival of the animals depends on the survival of the parks, among which the Serengeti has no peer.

For purposes of efficiency when dealing with poachers and to inspire the African judiciary to impose meaningful sentences, all poachers are classed together as brutal hirelings of unscrupulous Asian interests in Nairobi or Dar es Salaam; traps, snares, and poisoned arrows maim and torture many more animals than are actually retrieved, and of late the gangs have become motorized, crossing park boundaries at will. In this official picture of the matter there is

112

considerable truth, but it is also true that the majority of "poachers" are people of the region who are seeking to eke out a subsistence diet as they have always done. The parks for which their lands have been appropriated, and which they themselves have no means to visit even if they were interested, give sanctuary to marauding animals that are a threat to domestic stock and crops, not to speak of human life, and their resentment is natural and just. It is no good telling a shamba dweller that tourist revenues are crucial to the nation when his own meagre existence remains unaffected, or affected for the worse. "The nation," the concept of national consciousness, has not penetrated very far into the bush; as in the Sudan, there are many tribesmen who have no idea that they are Kenyan or Tanzanian and would care little if they knew. Even the urban African benefits little from the tourist economy, not to speak of the revenues of the parks, which are resented as the private preserves of white foreigners and the few blacks at the top. Not long ago it was estimated that only one East African in twelve had ever seen a lion, though lions are common in the park at the very outskirts of Nairobi, but one is not allowed into the parks without a car, and very few Africans have access to a car, far less own one. The average citizen has more fear of than interest in wild animals, which most Africans regard as evidence of backwardness, a view in which they were long encouraged by European farmers and administrators. Far from being proud of the "priceless heritage" so dear to conservation literature, they are ashamed of it.

Nor is poaching a simple matter of free meat. Rural Africans in the vicinity of game reserves and parks quite naturally believe that the numbers of wild animals are inexhaustible, and see no reason why they should not be harvested as they have always been. Hunting, with its prestige for the good hunter, is a ceremony and sport as it is for westerners; its place in his economy as well as its risk to the poorly armed native hunter make it considerably less decadent. And no one can explain why killing animals is permitted to foreigners in search of trophies but not to citizens in search of food. Yet to permit random poaching by local hunters would encourage ever bolder operations directed by outsiders and carried out by professionals who do not hesitate to turn their poisoned arrows on African game rangers; arrow poisons are obtained from several plants (two Apocynaceae, an amaryllis, and two lilies), but the one used most commonly in this region comes from the shrubby dogbane (*Acokanthera*) which has no antidote, and can kill in a matter of minutes. Still, bows are no match for rifles, and ordinarily, the poacher dies instead.

Last year four poachers died in the Serengeti. One was shot down by the rangers after firing his fourth poisoned arrow. Two corpses were found under a tree, caught by a fire probably set by themselves, for grasslands near a water course are often burned to give the hunters a better view and to make sure that their poisoned arrows are not lost; also, the use of bangi (the marijuana hemp, *Cannabis*, brought to the east coast in the earliest trade with Asia) and homemade spirits is popular in the poachers' camps, and perhaps the two were taken by surprise. The fourth was mangled and decapitated by a maimed buffalo caught in his wire snare. Myles was anxious to display the poacher's head as cautionary evidence in the small museum at Seronera, but was dissuaded by John Owen, who felt that the public display of an African head might be taken amiss. The head is on view in Turner's office, over the legend (from an Italian graveyard)

> I have been where you are now,
> And you will be where I have gone

Myles Turner is sympathetic with the Ikuria, who are one of the peoples he admires. "The land is all they have," he says. But he is a traditionalist in his dealings with the Africans, and though he joked with the ranger in the plane, the jokes were firm. When his plane appeared over Lemai, a half dozen of his "Field Force" rushed to the airstrip, where they were lined up more or less smartly by their corporal. In green drill shorts, shirts, berets, and black puttees, they made a fine-looking line, and when Turner stepped down from the plane, they sprang backwards to attention, slapping rifles. "Jambo, Corporal," Turner said, by way of greeting and approval, then put the rangers at their ease. Plainly the men enjoyed these formalities as much as Myles did, and at the same time were amused. Myles gave them letters and news of their families, and they gave him messages to send back. Then we marched down to the Mara in a military manner to inspect the hippos.

Hippos can weigh twice as much as buffalo, or a ton and a half each. Like whales, they are born in the water, but ordinarily they feed on land, and their copious manure, supporting rich growths of blue-green algae, is a great boon to fish. Here they had piled up in the river rapids, where the lateritic silt had turned them the same red as the broad-backed boulders. On land, the hippopotamus exudes a red secretion, perhaps to protect its skin against the sun, and Africans say that it is sweating its own blood. With their flayed skin, cavernous raw mouths, and bulging eyes, their tuba voices splitting the wash of the Mara on its banks seemed like the uproar of the damned, as if, in the cold rain and purgatorial din, just at this moment, the great water pigs had been cast into perdition, their downfall heralded by the scream of the fish eagle that circled overhead.

East of Soit Naado Murt, on the Girtasho Plain, a burrow had been taken over and enlarged by wild hunting dogs, which differ from true dogs in having a four-toed foot. In the Girtasho pack were eleven dogs and three bitches, black with patches of dirty white and brindle, and the invariable white tip to the tattered tail. Wild dogs are mangy and bad-smelling, with bat ears and gaunt bodies, yet they are appealing creatures, pirouetting in almost constant play, and rolling and flopping about in piles. Perhaps distemper keeps their numbers low,[2] for they are faithful in the raising of their young, and the most efficient killers on the plain.

Wild dogs are nomadic most of the year, attending the migrations of the herds, but when a bitch whelps, they remain with her and bring her food. Ordinarily one dog—not necessarily the mother—remains with the pups when the pack goes out to hunt, and five dogs have been known to raise nine pups after their mother—the pack's only bitch—had died. At the den one afternoon, four pups were frolicking from dog to dog, and one of the dogs dutifully disgorged some undigested chunks of meat, but the pups were bothered by the bursts of thunder, looking up from their food to whine at the far, silent lightning. A mile to the westward, zebra herds moved steadily along the skyline. When the rain thickened, the pups tumbled down into their den, and the adults gathered in a pile of matted black and brindle hair to shed the huge tropical downpour. Toward twilight, the rain eased and the dog pile broke apart, white tail tips twirling; the animals frisked about the soggy plain, greeting anew by inserting the muzzle into the corner of another's mouth, as the pups do when begging for food. When they are old enough to follow the hunt, the pups will be given first place at the kill.

Four dogs led by a brindle male moved off a little towards the west; they stood stiff-legged, straining forward, round black ears cocked toward the zebra herds which, agitated by the storm, were moving along at a steady gallop. Then the four set off at a steady trot, and the others broke their play to watch them go. Three more moved out, though not so swiftly, and George Schaller followed the seven at a little distance. Soon the remaining animals were coming, all but one that remained to guard the den. Only the first four were intent; the rest stopping repeatedly to romp and crouch or greet the stragglers. Then these nine would run to catch the four, loping along on both sides of the moving vehicle, casting a brief look at us as they passed. Ahead, the leaders trotted steadily, and the nine stragglers, overtaking them, would again break off to romp and play.

The four lead dogs, nearing the herds, broke into an easy run; the zebras spurted. Perhaps the dogs had singled out a victim—an old or diseased horse, a pregnant mare, a foal—for now they were streaming over the wet grass. Rain swept the plain, and gray sheets blurred the swirling stripes, which burst apart to scatter in all directions. The dogs wheeled hard, intent now on a quarry, but lost it as the horses veered, then milled together in a solid phalanx. A stallion charged the dogs, ears back, and they gave way.

The chase of a mile or more had failed; the wild dogs frisked and played. But now all thirteen were intent, and in moments they were loping back past the waiting vehicle, headed west. The leaders were already in their hunting run, bounding along in silence through the growing dark like hounds of hell, and the others, close behind, made sweet puppy-like call notes, strangely audible over the motor of the car, which swerved violently to miss half-hidden burrows. All thirteen stretched cadaverous shapes in long easy leaps over the plain. In their run, the dogs are beautiful and swift, and came up with the herds in not more than a mile. Then the dark shapes were whisking in and out among the zebra, and a foal still brown with a foal's long guard hairs quit the mare's side when a dog bit at it, and was surrounded.

A six-month zebra foal, weighing perhaps three hundred pounds, is too big to be downed easily by thin animals of forty pounds apiece. The dogs chivvied it round and round. One dog had sunk its teeth into the foal's black muzzle, tugging backwards to keep the victim's head low—this is a habit of the dogs, to compensate for their light weight—and the dog was swung free of the ground as the foal reared, lost its balance, and went down. Now the mare charged, scattering the pack, and when the foal jumped up as if unhurt, the two fled for the herd. But the dogs overtook the foal again, snapping at its hams, and braying softly, it stopped short of its own accord. Again a dog seized its muzzle, legs braced, dragging the head forward, as the rest tore into it from behind and below. At the yanking of its nose, the foal's mouth fell open, and it made a last small sound. Once more the mare rushed at the dogs, and once again, but already she seemed resigned to what was happening, and did not follow up her own attacks. The foal sank to its knees, neck still stretched by the backing dog, its entrails a dim gleam in the rain. Then the dog at its nose let go and joined the rest, and the foal raised its head, ears high, gazing in silence at the mare, which stood guard over it, motionless. Between her legs, her foal was being eaten alive, and mercifully, she did nothing. Then the foal sank down, and the dogs surged at the belly, all but one that snapped an eye out as the head flopped on the grass.

Unmarked, the mare turned and walked away. Intent on her foal, the dogs had not once snapped at her. Noticing the car twenty yards off, she gave a snort and a jump sideways, then walked on. Flanks pressed together, ears alert, her band awaited her; nearby, other zebra clans were grazing. Soon the foal's family, carrying the mare with it, moved away, snatching at the grass as they ambled westward.

The foal's spread legs stuck up like sticks from the twisting black and brindle; the dogs drove into the belly, hind legs straining. They snatched a mouthful, gulped it, and tore in again, climbing the carcass, tails erect, as if every lion and hyena on the plain were coming fast to drive them from the kill. All thirteen heads snapped at the meat, so close together that inevitably one yelped, but even when two would worry the same shred, there was never a snarl, only a wet steady sound of meat-eating. When the first dog moved off, licking its chops, the foal's rib cage was already bare; not ten minutes had passed since it had died. Then the hyenas came. First there were two, rising up out of the raining grass like mud lumps given life. They shambled forward without haste, neither numerous nor hungry enough to drive away the dogs. Then there were five in a semicircle, feinting a little. A dog ran out to chase away the boldest, and then two of the five, with the strange speed that makes them deadly hunters on their own, chased off a sixth hyena—not a clan member, apparently—that had come in from the north through the twilight rain.

Six of the dogs, their feeding finished, wagged long tails as they romped and greeted; there was just enough light left to illumine the red on their white patches. The rest fed steadily, eyes turned to the hyenas as they swallowed, and as each dog got its fill and forsook the carcass, the half-circle of hyenas tightened. The last dog gave way to them without a snarl. The forequarters were left, and the head and neck, and all the bones. For the powerful jaws of the hyena, the bones of the plains animals present no problem. Hoofs, bones, and skin of what had been, ten minutes before, the fat hindquarters of a swift skittish young horse lay twisted up in a torn muddy bag; the teeth of its skull and the white eye sockets were luminous. At dark, as the tail tips of the dogs danced away eastward, the hyena shapes drew together at the remains, one great night beast sinking slowly down into the mud.

I once watched a hyena gaining on a gnu that only saved itself by plunging into the heart of a panicked herd; the hyena lost track of its quarry when the herd stampeded. The cringing bear-like lope of these strange cat relatives is deceptive: a hyena can run forty miles an hour, which is considered the top speed of the swift wild dog. Cheetah are said to attain sixty but have small endurance; I have seen one spring at a Thomson's gazelle, its usual prey, and quit within the first one hundred yards. Hyenas, on the other hand, will run their prey into the ground; there is no escape. And in darkness they are bold—a man alone on the night roads of Africa has less to fear from lions than hyena. In the Ngorongoro Crater the roles ordinarily assigned to lions and hyenas are reversed. It is the hyenas, hunting at night, that make most of the kills, and the lions seen on the carcasses in daytime are the scavengers. Hans Kruuk has discovered that the crater's hyenas are divided in great clans, and that sometimes these hyena armies war at night, filling the crater with the din of the inferno.

The natural history of even the best-known African mammals is incomplete, and such hole dwellers as the ant-bear, the aard-wolf, and the pangolin have avoided the scrutiny of man almost entirely. It is not even known which species excavate the holes, which may also be occupied by hyenas, jackals, mongooses, bat-eared foxes, aard-wolves, porcupines, ratels or honey badgers, and, in whelping season, the wild hunting dog. Often the burrows are dug in the bases of old termite hills, which stand on the plain like strange red statues of a vanished civilization, worn to anonymity by time. The termites are ancient relatives of the cockroach, and in the wake of rains they leave the termitaria in nuptial flight; soon their wings break off, and new colonies are founded where they come to earth. Were man to destroy the many creatures that prey on them, the termite mounds would cover entire landscapes. The African past lies in the belly of the termite, which has eaten all trace of past tropical civilizations and will do as much for the greater part of what now stands. At the termitaria, one may look at dawn and evening for such nocturnal creatures as the striped hyena, with its long hair and gaunt body, but in my stays in the Serengeti I never saw this wolf-sized animal that lived in the ground beneath my feet.

One day I surprised a honey badger some distance from its earth, and followed it for a while over the plain. This dark squat animal has long hair and a thick skin to protect it from bee stings, and like most of the weasel tribe, it is volatile and ferocious, with a snarl more hideous than any sound I heard in Africa. The ratel moves quickly, low to the ground, and in its dealings with man is said to direct its attack straight at the crotch.

Another day, observing hyenas with Hans Kruuk, I was lucky enough to see a pangolin, which has overlapping armor on its back and legs and tail. The pangolin has been much reduced by a Maasai notion that its curious reptilian plates will bring the wearer luck in love. At our approach it ceased its rooting in the grass and, with an audible clack, rolled up into a ball to protect its vulnerable furred stomach. We contemplated it a while, then left it where it lay, a strange mute sphere on the bare plain.

In March, renewal of the southeast monsoon brings the long rains. Rains vary from region to region, according to the winds, and since the winds are not dependable, seasons in East Africa have a general pattern but can seldom be closely predicted. The cyclical wet years and years of drought are a faint echo of the pluvials and interpluvials of the Pleistocene. In 1961 drought had destroyed thousands of animals; the next year floods killed thousands more. In the winter of 1969 rain fell in the Serengeti almost daily, and no one knew whether the short rains of late autumn had failed to end or the long rains of spring had begun too early. A somber light refracted from the water gleamed in the depressions, and the treeless distances with their

119

animal silhouettes, the glow of bright flowers underfoot, recalled the tundras of the north to which the migrant plovers on the plain would soon return.

The animals had slowed, and some stood still. In this light those without movement looked enormous, the archetypal animal cast in stone. The ostrich, too, is huge on the horizon, and the kori bustard is the heaviest of all flying birds on earth. Everywhere the clouds were crossed by giant birds in their slow circles, like winged reptiles on an antediluvian sky.

One morning the dog pile broke apart before daylight and headed off toward the herds under Naabi Hill. Unlike lions, which often go hungry, the wild dogs rarely fail to make a kill, and this time they were followed from the start by three hyenas that had waited near the den. The three humped along behind the pack, and one of the dogs paused to sniff noses with a hyena by way of greeting. In the distance, zebras yelped like dogs, and the dogs chittered quietly like birds as they loped along. As the sun rose out of the Gol Mountains, they faked an attack on a string of wildebeest and moved on.

A mile and a half east of the den, the pack cut off a herd of zebra and ran it in tight circles. There were foals in this herd, but the dogs had singled out a pregnant mare. When the herd scattered, they closed in, streaming along in the early light, and almost immediately she fell behind and then gave up, standing motionless as one dog seized her nose and others ripped at her pregnant belly and others piled up under her tail to get at her entrails at the anus, surging at her with such force that the flesh of her uplifted quarters quaked in the striped skin. Perhaps in shock, their quarry shares the detachment of the dogs, which attack it peaceably, ears forward, with no slightest sign of snapping or snarling. The mare seemed entirely docile, unafraid, as if she had run as she had been hunted, out of instinct, and without emotion: only rarely will a herd animal attempt to defend itself with the hooves and teeth used so effectively in battles with its own kind, though such resistance might well spare its life.[3] The zebra still stood a full half-minute after her guts had been snatched out, then sagged down dead. Her unborn colt was dragged into the clear and snapped apart off to one side.

The morning was silent but for the wet sound of eating; a Caspian plover and a band of sand grouse picked at the mute prairie. The three hyenas stood in wait, and two others appeared after the kill.

120

One snatched a scrap and ran with it; the meat, black with blood and mud, dragged on the ground. Chased by the rest, the hyena made a shrill sound like a pig squeal. When their spirit is up, hyenas will take on a lion, and if they chose, could bite a wild dog in half, but in daylight, they seem ill at ease; they were scattered by one tawny eagle, which took over the first piece of meat abandoned by the dogs. The last dog to leave, having finished with the fetus, drove the hyenas off the carcass of the mare on its way past, then frisked on home. In a day and a night, when lions and hyenas, vultures and marabous, jackals, eagles, ants, and beetles have all finished, there will be no sign but the stained pressed grass that a death ever took place.

All winter in the Serengeti damp scrawny calves and afterbirths are everywhere, and old or diseased animals fall in the night. Fat hyenas, having slaked their thirst, squat in the rain puddles, and gaping lions lie belly to the sun. On Naabi Hill the requiem birds, digesting carrion, hunch on the canopies of low acacia. Down to the west, a young zebra wanders listlessly by itself. Unlike topi and kongoni, which are often seen alone, the zebra and wildebeest prefer the herd; an animal by itself may be sick or wounded, and draws predators from all over the plain. This mare had a deep gash down her right flank, and a slash of claws across the stripings of her quarters; red meat gleamed on right foreleg and left fetlock. It seemed strange that an attacking lion close enough to maul so could have botched the job, but the zebra pattern makes it difficult to see at night, when it is most vulnerable to attack by lions, and zebra are strong animals; a thin lioness that I saw once at Ngorongoro had a broken incisor hanging from her jaw that must have been the work of a flying hoof.

Starvation is the greatest threat to lions, which are inefficient hunters and often fail to make a kill. Unlike wild dog packs, which sometimes overlap in their wide hunting range, lions will attack and even eat another lion that has entered their territory, snapping and snarling in the same antagonistic way with which they join their pride mates on a kill, whereas when hunting, they are silent and impassive. In winter when calves of gazelle and gnu litter the plain, the lions are well fed, but at other seasons they may be so hungry that their own cubs are driven from the kills: ordinarily, however, the lion will permit cubs to feed even when the lioness that made the kill is not permitted to approach.[4] Until it is two, the cub is a dependent, and less than

121

half of those born in the Serengeti survive the first year of life. In hard times, cubs may be eaten by hyenas, or by the leopard, which has a taste for other carnivores, including domestic cats and dogs.

A former warden of the Serengeti who feels that plains game should be killed to feed these starving cubs is opposed by George Schaller on the grounds that such artificial feeding would interfere with the balance of lion numbers as well as with the natural selection that maintains the vitality of the species. Dr. Schaller is correct, I think, and yet my sympathies are with the predator, not with the hunted, perhaps because a lion is perceived as an individual, whereas one member of a herd of thousands seems but a part of a compound organism, with little more identity than one termite in a swarm. Separated from the herd, it gains identity, like the zebra killed by the wild dogs, but even so I felt more pity for an injured lion that I saw near the Seronera River in the hungry months of summer, a walking husk of mane and bone, so weak that the dry weather wind threatened to knock it over.

The death of any predator is disturbing. I was startled one day to see a hawk in the talons of Verreaux's eagle-owl; perhaps it had been killed in the act of killing. Another day, by a korongo, I helped Schaller collect a dying lioness. She had emaciated hindquarters and the staggers, and at our approach, she reeled to her feet, then fell. In the interests of science as well as mercy, for he wished an autopsy, George shot her with an overdose of tranquilizer. Although she twitched when the needle struck, and did not rise, she got up after a few minutes and weaved a few feet more and fell again as if defeated by the obstacle of the korongo, where frogs trilled in oblivion of unfrogly things. I had the strong feeling that the lioness, sensing death, had risen to escape it, like the vultures I had heard of somewhere that flew up from the poisoned meat set out for lions, circling higher and higher into the sky, only to fall like stones as life foresook them. A moment later, her head rose up, then flopped for the last time, but she would not die. Sprinkled with hopping lion flies and the fat ticks that in lions are a sign of poor condition, she lay there in a light rain, her gaunt flanks twitching.

The episode taught me something about George Schaller, who is single-minded, not easy to know. George is a stern pragmatist, unable to muster up much grace in the face of unscientific attitudes; he takes a hard-eyed look at almost everything. Yet at this moment his boyish face was openly upset, more upset than I had ever thought to see him. The death of the lioness was painless, far better than being found by the hyenas, but it was going on too long; twice he returned to the Land Rover for additional dosage. We stood there in a kind of vigil, feeling more and more depressed, and the end, when it came at last, was shocking. The poor beast, her life going, began to twitch and tremble. With a little grunt, she turned onto her back and lifted her hind legs into the air. Still grunting, she licked passionately at the grass, and her haunches shuddered in long spasms, and this last abandon shattered the detachment I had felt until that moment. I was swept by a wave of feeling, then a pang so sharp that, for a moment, I felt sick, as if all the waste and loss in life, the harm one brings to oneself and others, had been drawn to a point in this lonely passage between light and darkness.

Mid-March when the long rains were due was a time of wind and dry days in the Serengeti, with black trees in iron silhouette on the hard sunsets and great birds turning forever on a silver sky. A full moon rose in a night rainbow, but the next day the sun was clear again, flat as a disc in the pale universe.

Two rhino and a herd of buffalo had brought up the rear of the eastward migration. Unlike the antelope, which blow with the wind and grasses, the dark animals stood earthbound on the plain. The antelope, all but a few, had drifted east under the Crater Highlands, whereas the zebra, in expectation of the rains, were turning west again towards the woods. Great herds had gathered at the Seronera River, where the local prides of lions were well fed. Twenty lions together, dozing in the golden grass, could sometimes be located by the wave of a black tail tuft or the black ear tips of a lifted head that gazed through the sun shimmer of the seed heads. Others gorged in uproar near the river crossings, tearing the fat striped flanks on fresh green beds—now daytime kills were common. Yet for all their prosperity, there was an air of doom about the lions. The males, especially, seemed too big, and they walked too slowly between feast and famine, as if in some dim intuition that the time of the great predators was running out.

Pairs of male lions, unattached to any pride, may hunt and live together in great harmony, with something like demonstrative affection. But when two strangers meet, there seems to be a waiting period,

123

while fear settles. One sinks into the grass at a little distance, and for a long time they watch each other, and their sad eyes, unblinking, never move. The gaze is the warning, and it is the same gaze, wary but unwavering, with which lions confront man. The gold cat eyes shimmer with hidden lights, eyes that see everything and betray nothing. When the lion is satisfied that the threat is past, the head is turned, as if ignoring it might speed the departure of an unwelcome and evil-smelling presence. In its torpor and detachment, the lion sometimes seems the dullest beast in Africa, but one has only to watch a file of lions setting off on the evening hunt to be awed anew by the power of this animal.

One late afternoon of March, beyond Maasai Kopjes, eleven lionesses lay on a kill, and the upraised heads, in a setting sun, were red. With their grim visages and flat glazed eyes, these twilight beasts were ominous. Then the gory heads all turned as one, ear tips alert. No animal was in sight, and their bellies were full, yet they glared steadfastly away into the emptiness of plain, as if something that no man could sense was imminent.

Not far off there was a leopard; possibly they scented it. The leopard lay on an open rise, in the shadow of a wind-worn bush, and unlike the lions, it lay gracefully. Even stretched on a tree limb, all four feet hanging, as it is seen sometimes in the fever trees, the leopard has the grace of complete awareness, with all its tensions in its pointed eyes. The lion's gaze is merely baleful; that of the leopard is malevolent, a distillation of the trapped fear that is true savagery.

Under a whistling thorn the leopard lay, gold coat on fire in the sinking sun, as if imagining that so long as it lay still it was unseen. Behind it was a solitary thorn tree, black and bony in the sunset, and from a crotch in a high branch, turning gently, torn hide matted with caked blood, the hollow form of a gazelle hung by the neck. At the insistence of the wind, the delicate black shells of the turning hoofs, on tiptoe, made a dry clicking in the silence of the plain.

7. Elephant Kingdoms

To Game Warden

Sir,

I am compelled of notifying your Excellence the ecceptional an
critical situation of my people at Tuso. Many times they called on
my praing me of adressing to your Excellence a letter for obtain a
remedy and so save they meadows from total devestation. I recused
for I thought were a passing disease, but on the contrary the invasion
took fearfully increasing so that the natives are now disturbed and
in danger in their own huts for in the night the elephants ventured
themselves amid abitation. All men are desolate and said me
sadfully, "What shall we eat this year. We shall compelled to
emigrate all. . . ."

> With my best gratefully
> and respectful regards,
> Yours sincerely,
> a Mission Boy[1]

We are the fire which burns the country.
The Calf of the Elephant is exposed on the plain.

from the Bantu[2]

One morning a great company of elephants came from the woodlands,
moving eastward toward the Togoro Plain. "It's like the old Africa,
this," Myles Turner said, coming to fetch me. "It's one of the greatest
sights a man can see."

We flew northward over the Orangi River. In the wake of the
elephant herds, stinkbark acacia were scattered like sticks, the haze
of yellow blossoms bright in the killed trees. Through the center of
the destruction, west to east, ran a great muddied thoroughfare of the
sort described by Selous in the nineteenth century. Here the center
of the herd had passed. The plane turned eastward, coming up on
the elephant armies from behind. More than four hundred animals
were pushed together in one phalanx; a smaller group of one hundred
and another of sixty were nearby. The four hundred moved in one

125

slow-stepping swaying mass, with the largest cows along the outer ranks and big bulls scattered on both sides. "Seventy and eighty pounds, some of those bulls," Myles said. (Trophy elephants are described according to the weight of a single tusk; an eighty-pound elephant would carry about twice that weight in ivory. "Saw an eighty today." "*Did* you!")

Myles said that elephants herded up after heavy rains, but that this was an enormous congregation for the Serengeti. In 1913, when the first safari came here,[3] the abounding lions and wild dogs were shot as vermin, but no elephants were seen at all. Even after 1925, when the plains were hunted regularly by such men as Philip Percival and the American, Martin Johnson, few elephants were reported. Not until after 1937, it is said, when the Serengeti was set aside as a game reserve (it was not made a national park until 1951), did harried elephants from the developing agricultural country of west Kenya move south into this region, but it seems more likely that they were always present in small numbers, and merely increased as a result of human pressures in suitable habitats outside the park.

Elephants, with their path-making and tree-splitting propensities, will alter the character of the densest bush in very short order; probably they rank with man and fire as the greatest force for habitat change in Africa.[4] In the Serengeti, the herds are destroying many of the taller trees which are thought to have risen at the beginning of the century, in a long period without grass fires that followed plague, famine, and an absence of the Maasai. Dry season fires, often set purposely by poachers and pastoral peoples, encourage grassland by suppressing new woody growth; when accompanied by drought, and fed by a woodland tinder of elephant-killed trees, they do lasting damage to the soil and the whole environment. Fires waste the dry grass that is used by certain animals, and the regrowth exhausts the energy in the grass roots that is needed for good growth in the rainy season. In the Serengeti in recent years, fire and elephants together have converted miles and miles of acacia wood to grassland, and damaged the stands of yellowbark acacia or fever tree along the water courses. The range of the plains game has increased, but the much less numerous woodland species such as the roan antelope and oribi become ever more difficult to see.

Beneath the plane, the elephant mass moved like gray lava, leaving

126

behind a ruined bog of mud and twisted trees. An elephant can eat as much as six hundred pounds of grass and browse each day, and it is a destructive feeder, breaking down many trees and shrubs along the way. The Serengeti is immense, and can absorb this damage, but one sees quickly how an elephant invasion might affect more vulnerable areas. Ordinarily the elephant herds are scattered and nomadic, but pressure from settlements, game control, and poachers sometimes confines huge herds to restricted habitats which they may destroy. Already three of Tanzania's new national parks—Serengeti, Manyara, and Ruaha—have more elephants than is good for them. The elephant problem, where and when and how to manage them, is a great controversy in East Africa, and its solution must affect the balance of animals and man throughout the continent.

Anxious to see the great herd from the ground, I picked up George Schaller at Seronera and drove northwest to Banagi, then westward on the Ikoma-Musoma track to the old northwest boundary of the park, where I headed across country. I had taken good bearings from the air, but elephants on the move can go a long way in an hour, and even for a vehicle with four-wheel drive, this rough bush of high grass, potholes, rocks, steep brushy streams, and swampy mud is very different from the hardpan of the plain. The low hot woods lacked rises or landmarks, and for a while it seemed that I had actually misplaced four hundred elephants.

Then six bulls loomed through the trees, lashing the air with their trunks, ears blowing, in a stiff-legged swinging stride; they forded a steep gully as the main herd, ahead of them, appeared on a wooded rise. Ranging up and down the gully, we found a place to lurch across, then took off eastward, hoping to find a point downwind of the herd where the elephants would pass. But their pace had slowed as the sun rose; we worked back to them, upwind. The elephants were destroying a low wood—this is not an exaggeration—with a terrible cracking of trees, but after a while they moved out onto open savanna. In a swampy stream they sprayed one another and rolled in the water and coated their hides with mud, filling the air with a thick sloughing sound like the wet meat sound made by predators on a kill. Even at rest the herd flowed in perpetual motion, the ears like delicate great petals, the ripple of the mud-caked flanks, the coiling trunks—a dream rhythm, a rhythm of wind and trees. "It's a nice life," Schaller said.

127

"Long, and without fear." A young one could be killed by a lion, but only a desperate lion would venture near a herd of elephants, which are among the few creatures that reach old age in the wild.

There has been much testimony to the silence of the elephant, and all of it is true. At one point there came a cracking sound so small that had I not been alert for the stray elephants all around, I might never have seen the mighty bull that bore down on us from behind. A hundred yards away, it came through the scrub and deadwood like a cloud shadow, dwarfing the small trees of the open woodland. I raised binoculars to watch him turn when he got our scent, but the light wind had shifted and instead the bull was coming fast, looming higher and higher, filling the field of the binoculars, forehead, ears, and back agleam with wet mud dredged up from the donga. There was no time to reach the car, nothing to do but stand transfixed. A froggish voice said, "What do you think, George?" and got no answer.

Then the bull scented us—the hot wind was shifting every moment—and the dark wings flared, filling the sky, and the air was split wide by that ultimate scream that the elephant gives in alarm or agitation, that primordial warped horn note out of oldest Africa. It altered course without missing a stride, not in flight but wary, wide-eared, passing man by. Where first aware of us, the bull had been less than one hundred feet away—I walked it off—and he was somewhat nearer where he passed. "He was pretty close," I said finally to Schaller. George cleared his throat. "You don't want them any closer than that," he said. "Not when you're on foot." Schaller, who has no taste for exaggeration, had a very respectful look upon his face.

Stalking the elephants, we were soon a half-mile from my Land Rover. What little wind there was continued shifting, and one old cow, getting our scent, flared her ears and lifted her trunk, holding it upraised for a long time like a question mark. There were new calves with the herd, and we went no closer. Then the cow lost the scent, and the sloughing sound resumed, a sound that this same animal has made for four hundred thousand years. Occasionally there came a brief scream of agitation, or the crack of a killed tree back in the wood, and always the *thuck* of mud and water, and a rumbling of elephantine guts, the deepest sound made by any animal on earth except the whale.

Africa. Noon. The hot still waiting air. A hornbill, gnats, the green hills in the distance, wearing away west toward Lake Victoria.

Until recent years, when the elephant herds have become concentrated in game reserves and parks, it has been difficult to study elephants, since one could not stay close enough to the herds to observe daily behavior. Even now, most students of the elephant are content to work with graphs, air surveys, dead animals, and the like, since behavioral studies are best done on foot, a job that few people have the heart for. An exception is Iain Douglas-Hamilton, a young Scots biologist who was doing his thesis on the elephants of Lake Manyara.

Lake Manyara, like Lake Natron, is a soda lake or magadi that lies along the base of the Rift Escarpment. The east side of the lake lies in arid plain, but the west shore, where streams emerge from the porous volcanic rock of the Crater Highlands, supports high, dark ground-water forest. The thick trees have the atmosphere of jungle, but there are no epiphytes or mosses, for the air is dry. On the road south into Lake Manyara Park, this forest gives way to an open wood of that airiest of all acacias, the umbrella thorn, and beyond the Ndala River is a region of dense thicket and wet savanna. The strip of trees between lake and escarpment is so narrow, and the pressure on elephants in the surrounding farm country so great, that Manyara can claim the greatest elephant concentration in East Africa, an estimated twelve to the square mile. For this reason—and also because the Manyara animals are used to vehicles, and with good manners can be approached closely—it is the best place to watch elephants in the world.

In the acacia wood that descends to the lake shore, elephants were everywhere in groves and thickets. Elephants travel in matriarchal groups led by a succession of mothers and daughters—female elephants stay with their mothers all their lives—and this group may include young males which have not yet been driven off. (Elephants not fully grown are difficult to sex—their genitals are well camouflaged in the cascade of slack and wrinkles—and unless their behavior has been studied for some time, the exact composition of a cow-calf group is very difficult to determine.) Ordinarily the leader is the oldest cow, who is related to every other animal; she may be fifty years old and past the breeding age, but her great memory and experience is the herd's defense against drought and flood and man. She knows not only where good browse may be found in different seasons, but when to charge and when to flee, and it is to her that the herd turns in time of stress. When a cow is in season, bulls may join the cow-calf group; at other times, they live alone or in herds of bachelors. When I drove near, the bulls moved off after a perfunctory threat display— flared ears, brandished tusks, a swaying forefoot like a pendulum, the dismantling of the nearest tree, and perhaps a diffident scream; sometimes they ease their nervous strain by chasing a jackal or a bird. With cows, as well, aggressive behavior is usually mere threat display, though it is wiser not to count on it.

The person best acquainted with these elephants is Iain Douglas-Hamilton, who had set up a small camp on the Ndala or Buffalo River, eight miles into Lake Manyara Park. The camp is perched above a gravel bend in the Ndala, a surface stream that courses down over ancient crystalline rock in a series of lovely waterfalls and pools and empties into the lake a mile below. Though the pools are cool, and deep enough to splash in, one swims at the risk of bilharzia, an extremely disagreeable intestinal invasion by trematode larvae passed into sluggish water via hominid feces: the larvae enter a small fresh-water snail that in turn releases the cercaria life stage into the water, and the cercaria enter the pores of baboons and men. Many people have contracted bilharzia in this pool, including Douglas-Hamilton, who is not the sort to be dismayed by such ill provenance, and will almost certainly risk and receive another dose of a disease which, without long and tiresome treatment, may be debilitating and even fatal.

When I drove into camp, its proprietor was standing outside his modest research laboratory with his pretty mother, Prunella Power, who was here on a visit from England. He is a strong good-looking young man with blond hair and glasses, wearing faded green drill shorts and shirt and old black street shoes without laces or socks (he also has an excellent pair of field boots which he wears when they turn up). He took my note of introduction and stuffed it in his pocket, and I doubt if he has read it to this day. "You'll stay with us, won't you?" he said straight off. "Have you had tea? Well, do come along then, we're just off elephant-watching." I got out of my Land Rover and into his, and we set off with a turn of speed toward the lake, where Douglas-Hamilton drove straight up to an elephant herd and began taking notes. His approach was so abrupt, so lacking in finesse, that the whole herd was engaged in threat display, with much shrill screaming. "Silly old things," said Iain, scarcely looking up. "Frightful cowards, really. Silly old elephants," He gazed at them with affection.

"Oh, damn!" he said, as a big cow came blaring through the bushes. "That's Big Boadicia—she'll charge us, I expect." But Boadicia, the matriarch, held back as a younger cow charged instead. I expected Iain to drop his notebook and go for the wheel, but he merely said, "This one doesn't mean it." The young cow stopped a few yards short of the hood. Her bluff called, she backed up, forefoot swinging, and began what is known to behaviorists as displacement feeding, by way of expending her chagrin. Forefoot still swinging sideways, she wrenched at a tussock of green grass, and we were close enough to observe a trick I had never heard about—as the elephant tugs on grass, it mows it with the sharp toenails of its heavy foot, which is swinging in the rhythm of a scythe.

Iain and his mother had been asked to dinner by Jane and Hillary Hook, who were presently encamped with their safari clients in the ground-water forest near the entrance to the park; as I also knew the Hooks, I was taken along. Though not late, Iain drove like hell, slowing only to permit a puff adder to cross the road; in the headlights, the venomous thing, too fat to writhe, inched over the ground like a centipede. Rounding the bend a moment later, we found our way barred by a huge stinkbark, much too big to move, that wind had felled across the road at a point where the left side was steep uphill bank and the right a steep bank down. "I'm not missing dinner!" Iain cried, and forthwith gunned his car off the embankment into the jungle dark, in an attempt—I assume—to bypass the offending stinkbark. The undercarriage of the car struck one of several hidden stumps with an impact that drove the driver's mother into the roof, and inevitably, within seconds, the car was hung up, both front wheels spinning in the air. Iain grabbed up a monstrous jack and hoisted the transmission and axle clear of the stump. "Now I'll drive straight off the jack," he called to me. "Do catch it, will you?" I jumped away from the spinning jack as he drove off it, staring in astonishment as this inspired youth, in a series of wild spurts and caroms, bashed his way back to the road.

On the return trip, Mrs. Power was guided around the fallen tree on foot by Hillary's flashlight. Down below, also on foot, I led Iain back over the stumps, then leapt into the open rear as the car made its lunge at the steep bank. At the last moment, it altered course and proceeded into the interior of a thornbush, emerging miraculously onto the road.

"Fantastic!" said Hillary Hook. "I'd never have believed it!"

On the way home, picking thorns out of my face, I was fairly whining in annoyance, and Mrs. Power, who is resigned to Iain through love and lack of choice, said, "I rather thought you'd intercede."

"I kept hoping *you* would intercede," I told her crossly. "I have no experience of him, and anyway, you're his mother."

Early next morning, we drove south to the Endobash River. In the shallows of the lake, near a great baobab, lay a dead buffalo, and in the spreading limbs of a nearby umbrella acacia lay a lion. The tree-climbing habit evolved by the lions of Manyara is said to be a defense against the stomoxys fly, which breeds along the water edge; in time of stomoxys infestations, the Ngorongoro lions are arboreal as well, and in the summer of 1970 I saw one climb a tree in tsetse woods of the western Serengeti. But at Manyara, where there is little shelter for lions against attacks by the numerous elephants and buffalo, protection from these animals may also be a factor.

Impala, bright rust red in the early light, scampered prettily in antelope perfection, and buffalo in a herd of hundreds milled back and forth across the track. Near the Endobash were big elephants that Iain did not recognize, and these he approached with circumspection. They had come in from outside the park, where they might have been chivvied and possibly shot at by man; such elephants take offense in very short order. Also, they were browsing in the thick high brush, so that their numbers and whereabouts were still uncertain. And finally, they looked decidedly larger than the home elephants of Manyara, which tend to be small, no doubt because the population is a young one. "These are the baddies," Iain said. He sat slumped behind the wheel of his idling Land Rover, hands in pockets. "Horrible wild uncouth elephants!" he cried suddenly, as if about to shake his fist. "Turn around, you bahstards, let's have a look at you!" Here in the Endobash last year a band of strange elephants had dismantled his Land Rover around his ears while he and a girl companion cowered on the floor; the vehicle in which we rode, already battered, was its replacement.

The back of Iain's new Land Rover is open, like a short truck bed, and contained, besides spare wheel and jack, a park ranger named Mhoja whom Iain has trained to help him in his elephant surveys. Mhoja, a Nyamwezi from the great Bantu tribe of central Tanzania, was terrified at first, says Iain, but recently, for some unaccountable reason, had become more philosophical about his fate. Nevertheless, Mhoja was tapping urgently on the cab roof, for elephants were moving at us from both sides—we were caught in the middle. "They'll charge us, I expect," said Iain, and they did. He gunned his motor and we crashed between two bushes into the clear.

We went down to the Endobash River, and from there worked west up the Endobash Valley, under the cliffs of the escarpment. Last year in this place, while poking about in the thick bush, Iain and his mother surprised a rhino. Iain, run down, spent three weeks in a hospital at Arusha with a fractured vertebra. Soon after, he was a participant in the crash of a small plane, and decided to take up flying. Iain's father died in an air crash in World War II, and his mother is not happy about his new passion, but she knows better than to try to dissuade him.

One afternoon I volunteered to try Mhoja's position in the rear. As soon as possible, Iain had me surrounded with irate cows, which were menacing the car from all directions, and trying to see all ways at once, I shrank against the cab. Through his rear window, Iain said, "You'll get hardened to it, never fear." Soon a huge bull loomed alongside in threat display, and with his tusks demolished a small tree not fifteen feet from where I cowered, unable to imagine why Douglas-Hamilton was so loath to spare my life. Inching my head around to plead, I looked straight into Iain's camera; he fancied the shot of a frightened face with a big bull elephant filling the entire background. "You're going to want this picture," Iain said.

Annoyed by my annoyance, he said I had no faith: "I *know* these elephants," he complained later, "I really do." Iain was of two minds about his reputation for recklessness, which he had done nothing to discourage and which had returned to haunt him. "People seem to think I'm some sort of idiot, but I *had* to work close to elephants to do my research." To study not only elephant behavior but the effect of high numbers on the ecology of Manyara required a close record of their movements; therefore he had to know each animal's identity and position in its herd, as well as which herds were Manyara elephants and which were transient in the park. His solution was to photograph each animal with its ears flared, head-on, so that tusks and ear nicks could be used in identification, but the method demanded confrontations with four hundred and twenty agitated elephants. Iain learned the hard way which elephants were bad-tempered, and his confidence that he could distinguish a threat from an honest charge—which professional hunters who have gone out with him are unable to do—encouraged him to give visitors, as he says, "the same excitement, the same fun with elephants that I had when *I* didn't know anything." But the spreading tales of these adventures have tended to discredit the valuable research Douglas-Hamilton has done in the long days spent closer to wild elephants than anyone had ever gone before.

The elephants at Manyara are presently destroying the umbrella thorn at such a rate that regeneration cannot keep pace with the destruction, and in Iain's view, these lovely trees will be gone from the Manyara park within ten years. Those not knocked down are stripped so grievously of bark that they cannot recover; either their vascular system is destroyed or they fall prey to the boring beetle that penetrates the exposed wood. On the other hand, elephants have been destroying woodlands for thousands of years, and perhaps destruction is a part of the natural cycle of this acacia, which represses the growth of its own seedlings in its shade. In season, elephants consume great quantities of the seed pods, and as they move continually in search of the varied browse that they require, the seeds are borne elsewhere and deposited—a most auspicious start in life—in an immense warm nutritious pile of dung.

The mature umbrella thorns in the region of Ndala had been noted in transects on a chart, and as it was crucial to his studies to know what had become of them in the course of a year, Iain set out one morning to survey two transects in the forest between his camp and the lake. Since the transects were mostly covered in the kind of thick high bush favored by rhino and old solitary buffalo, he needed a gun to back him up. Mhoja carried a .470 Rigby elephant rifle and I carried a .12 gauge Greeners single shot, said to be useful in "turning" a rhino's charge. "I shouldn't load it until something happens if I were you," said Iain. "It tends to go off by itself." All morning I carried the gun broken with a shotgun shell in my right hand; if *anything* went right in an emergency, I thought, it would be pure dumb luck.

The dawn had something ominous about it, or so it seemed to me, a tinge of gloom that haunted the African morning. The swift sun of the tropics, rising, spun on the white ivory of an elephant high on the slope of the escarpment; ahead, more elephants drifted away through

134

woods that were still in shadow. Where they had forged tunnels through the brush, the brown woodland air spun with glittering webs of emerald spiders, and in a shaft of light between two trees stood a black-and-bamboo leopard tortoise, bright with dew. The sunrise fired a lizard's head, emerged from the cobra shadows of a dead tree, and glinted on a file of driver ants on the way to raid a termite nest. Sun and shadow, light and death. Through an open glade down toward the lake, impala danced.

On foot, the pulse of Africa comes through your boot. You are an animal among others, chary of the shadowed places, of sudden quiet in the air. A fine walk in the early woods turned hour by hour into a wearing trek through head-high caper and toothbrush bush, and as the sun climbed, heat settled in the woods, and colors faded, and dew dried. The thickened bush gave off coarse smells, the gun grew heavy, the step slowed. A humid pall had crossed the sun, and no bird sang. One had to concentrate to be aware, reminding oneself that this midday stillness, when dozing animals may be taken by surprise, is not the hour to walk carelessly in thickets. But a time comes when awareness goes, and one reels sweaty and heavy-legged under the sun, dulled to all signs and signals, like a laggard buffalo behind its herd. This time, for man as well as animals, is a time of danger.

"Like Endobash Plains, this," said Iain, bashing through; even Iain seemed subdued. "Let's have some gun support through here." And when at last we were in the clear again, walking homeward through the woods, he said, "Pushing through bush like that . . . a bit dicey, you know. Doesn't pay to think about it too much; you might not do it. People talk about going too near elephants, but walking these transects each month is a hell of a lot more dangerous." I was happy that the walk was over, and looked with fresh eyes on the rest of the precious day. In the afternoon, in a quiet glade, I watched striped kingfishers sing in a trio. In the urgency of their song, these woodland birds lifted bright wings like butterflies, and trembled.

In mid-February, I made a trip to southern Tanzania to look at the elephant damage in the huge new park along the Ruaha River, and Douglas-Hamilton decided to come along. He was anxious, in fact, to fly us down in his new plane, an ancient Piper with a fuel range barely adequate for the distance even if his navigation were exact. "I've just got my license," Iain said. "It will be an adventure." But the idea was discouraged by John Owen, who had us picked up in Arusha by John Savidge, the warden of Ruaha.

We flew south over the Maasai Steppe, the broad trackless central plateau of Tanzania. On the north-south line, the Maasai Steppe is located at the center of Africa, and at its western edge, Savidge picked up the Great North Road (from the Cape to Cairo; this road was pioneered in the famous five thousand-mile walk in 1898–1899 by Ewart Grogan). Here and elsewhere north of the Zambezi River, the Great North Road is mostly rude dirt track. The plane crossed a litter of tin roofs in the Kondoa-Irangi hills, where the primitive farming practices of a swelling population have caused the precious topsoil to wash down in great erosion fans onto the naked plain. In Tanzania, intensive agriculture is seen as the solution to malnutrition and unemployment, and a population increase is encouraged. But except in the highlands, the red earths of East Africa are too poor to support permanent agriculture, and where they are fertile, the soils are soon impoverished by the plow, which lays them bare to cycles of fierce sun and leaching rain. In the wet season the ground is muck, and in the dry a hard-caked dusty stone. Wind and rain erode a soil that may have taken centuries to form, and there is desert. In Ethiopia, Madagascar, and throughout East Africa one sees this fatal erosion of thin fragile lateritic soils; the rust red of the laterite comes to the surface of the African landscape like blood welling in scraped skin.

Off to the west lay Dodoma, on the old trading route from Zanzibar and Bagamoyo, on the coast, to Tabora and Lake Tanganyika; through Dodoma came the Arab and Swahili trading caravans that would emerge months later with ivory and long lines of slaves. Speke and Burton passed through here in 1857, and Speke and Grant a few years later, on their way to the discovery of the headwaters of the Nile. Traders, missionaries, and explorers were careful to avoid the country to the north, for Dodoma lies at the south end of the Maasai Steppe, the two hundred-mile southern extension of Maasai Land. Here the Maasai are alleged, on no good evidence, to have stopped the northward expansion of fierce Ngoni Zulu from southern Africa, or sometimes it is said that the Zulu stopped the southward course of the Maasai, but probably the two tribes never met. By 1840, the Ngoni had already settled in the vicinity of Lake Rukwa, in the Southern Highlands, well south of the northern edge of tsetse-infested forest that would surely have served as a barrier to the Maasai herds.

More likely the Maasai were checked by the fierce Gogo and Hehe in this region. Between 1890 and 1894, the Hehe—now demoralized, like the Maasai—were also fighting the appropriation of their lands by Germans, who refused to recognize and work with local chiefs, and levied on the tribes a repressive system of taxation and forced labor that invited incessant revolt. The Maji-Maji Rebellion, between 1905 and 1907, devastated much of the southern country, and as in the Mau-Mau Rebellion, a half-century later, it was the African who suffered; an estimated one hundred thousand died.

The great Bahi Swamp lay south and west as the plane crossed the northern boundary of the park. This west part of the park is unbroken miombo or dry forest which subsides into acacia scrub and riverain vegetation as the Great Ruaha River slides eastward toward the coast. Miombo, composed mostly of scrubby species of *Brachystegia*, extends east and west for sixteen hundred miles in a vast infertile wilderness. It is hot, dull, and oppressive, and the great emphasis in south Tanzania on bush-clearing and the slaughter of wild animals in futile attempts to eradicate the tsetse fly has made much of it more empty and monotonous than it was before.

We had a pleasant visit at Ruaha, and a good swim in a swirling pool at the edge of the river rapids. Here Iain wished to see who could swim farthest out without being swept away, and I spared one of his nine lives by declining. That evening, a spirited discussion of the elephant problem got us nowhere. Elephants have much increased along the Ruaha since the last native villages in this area were evacuated, and Savidge and his wife were upset by the elephant damage to the lovely winter thorn and baobab near park headquarters; they wanted an elephant control program set up at once. While their feelings were understandable, neither Douglas-Hamilton nor I agreed that slaughter was the solution—not, at least, until all other courses had been tried.

The Ruaha situation was discussed on the first of March at a Kenya-Tanzania elephant meeting convened at Voi, in Tsavo Park. John Owen had been kind enough to invite me to the conference, and on March 1, 1969, I flew with him to Tsavo. We left Arusha in mid-morning, passing south of black Mt. Meru and the broad back side of Kilimanjaro and its gaunt eastern peak, Mawensi, that like Mt. Kenya is the black hard core of a volcano whose sides have blown away. Straight ahead lay Kenya's Serengeti, a bare steppe with isolated rises. Beyond lay nyika, the wilderness, thousands of square miles of thorn scrub between the highland plateaus and the sea. Soon the plane's shadow was crossing Tsavo. This largest of national parks in Africa, like most, came into being because the area involved, due to tsetse or other pestilence, was considered unfit for anything else, and it is divided into eastern and western sections by the Mombasa Railroad. Surrounding the railroad is an abrupt congregation of small mountains called the Teita Hills, and under the Teita Hills lay Voi.

Our host at Voi was David Sheldrick, warden of Tsavo East and a central figure in the first flare-up in the great elephant dispute that arose in the mid-1960s. His opponent was Dr. Richard Laws, at that time head of the Tsavo Research Project and the chief proponent of elephant cropping as a means of stabilizing elephant populations to keep them in balance with contracting habitats. In a paper[5] prepared with the help of Ian Parker, whose Wildlife Services Ltd., Nairobi, did all the shooting, Laws described the elimination of four hundred elephant killed in 1965 on the south bank of the Nile at Murchison Falls, and of three hundred more destroyed at Tsavo. In effect, Laws concluded that the assumption of a general increase in elephant populations was mistaken; that what had increased was the density of elephant populations in certain protected areas, notably the parks; that this increase, at least in part, represented an immigration of elephants into the parks from unprotected areas, and a corresponding lack of places to which to emigrate, due to increasing human pressure at park boundaries; that this interruption of migration patterns, especially in the dry season, often put unnatural pressure on the habitat, which was therefore deteriorating; that one symptom of this deterioration was the rapid conversion of woodland to grassland, a process accelerated by periodic fires; that—quite apart from the progressive elimination of suitable habitat for other woodland species—the invading grassland provided inadequate nourishment for the elephants, which were exhibiting such strong evidence of nutritional deficiency as reduced fertility, increased calf mortality, retarded growth, and even such pathological symptoms of stress as deforming abscesses of the jaw (on the south bank of the Victoria Nile, these abscesses were present in thirty percent of the killed animals); that, far from increasing, many elephant populations were in the process of a "crash" that, due to elephant longevity, might extend over a half-century; and finally, that this crash, which at Murchison Falls was well advanced, had already begun at Tsavo, and because of increasing destruction of habitat, might well cause the complete extinction of elephant populations in both places. Laws concluded that these threatened populations would benefit most from an acceleration of the crash brought about by man, in order to save the remaining habitats for the animals that survived.

The Laws-Parker conclusions seemed particularly applicable to Tsavo, where the extended drought of 1960–1961, followed immediately by violent floods, had ravaged the habitat, causing the death of great numbers of elephants and rhino. Tsavo was still in poor condition in 1964, when Laws was invited by the Kenya National Parks to take a preliminary sample of three hundred elephants. Even so, further elephant slaughter on the scale recommended was resisted by Warden Sheldrick, who in the absence of more comprehensive studies felt that natural checks and balances should be permitted to take care of excess elephants. Eventually Sheldrick won the support of the Parks trustees, but meanwhile he had been attacked for the elevation of his own beliefs over trained scientific opinion. Laws spoke bitterly of "preservationists"; since man was responsible for the elephant problem, he was also responsible for its solution, no matter how abhorrent the idea of slaughter. Laws, in turn, was criticized by Sheldrick supporters for turning an honest difference of opinion into a public harangue, and anyway, these people said, Ian Parker's financial interest in cropping operations, present and future, voided the objectivity of the report, which was invalidated in any case by its inadequate attention to vegetation patterns and climatic cycles. (The ad hominem aspects of the dispute were ill-founded on both sides. Sheldrick and Laws both found support among ecologists and biologists then working in East Africa; and while Parker's interest in commercial game cropping may have lent vigor to his beliefs, he had long since demonstrated a sincere and intelligent interest in the welfare of African wildlife. As a member of the Game Department, Parker had worked on anti-poaching campaigns at Tsavo, and subsequently was made manager of the Galana River Game Management Scheme, a pioneering effort to crop wild herds for protein and profit.)

The battle raged in newspapers and journals throughout Africa and beyond, and the smoke of it has not settled to this day. "The Tsavo elephant problem is a classical example of indecision, vacillation, and mismanagement," Laws wrote in a recent paper. Still, his dire fore-

139

casts have not yet come to pass, perhaps because a series of favorable seasons have substantially restored the habitats of Tsavo. Most of the conferees at Voi were in sympathy with the anti-cropping views of David Sheldrick, although there were gradations of opinion. Tsavo ecologist Dr. Philip Glover, for example, agreed with Dr. Hugh Lamprey, head of the Serengeti Research Institute, that elephants would have to be cropped in the Serengeti unless fires there were brought under control. It was concluded that each of the parks presented a separate problem, and that in all cases more study was required before a cropping program was begun. No one agreed with the warden of Ruaha that elephants should be killed there without further ado, and no one sided publicly with the Scientific Officer of the Tanzania National Parks, who said, in effect, that no park elephants should be destroyed under any circumstances. This veteran ecologist, Mr. Vesey-FitzGerald, felt strongly that population fluctuations based on natural adjustments to inevitable ecological change within a park were part of long-range patterns not yet understood. He agreed that certain elephant populations were out of balance with their environment but felt that regulatory mechanisms such as loss of fertility would take care of this. There were no known occasions, he declared, when elephants had made their environment uninhabitable to themselves (though Laws's observations at Murchison Falls appear to refute this). While fire should certainly be controlled to lessen the impact of the animals on the habitat, he said, any artificial reduction of populations would interfere with the natural rhythms of the African land. Until a thorough study had been made of all environmental factors, and especially the regeneration of affected vegetation, the slaughter of animals in a national park was a bad mistake and a worse precedent, and probably an impertinence into the bargain.

Of all African animals, the elephant is the most difficult for man to live with, yet its passing—if this must come—seems the most tragic of all. I can watch elephants (and elephants alone) for hours at a time, for sooner or later the elephant will do something very strange such as mow grass with its toenails or draw the tusks from the rotted carcass of another elephant and carry them off into the bush. There is mystery behind that masked gray visage, an ancient life force, delicate and mighty, awesome and enchanted, commanding the silence ordinarily reserved for mountain peaks, great fires, and the sea. I remember a remark made by a girl about her father, a businessman of narrow sensibilities who, casting about for a means of self-gratification, traveled to Africa and slew an elephant. Standing there in his new hunting togs in a vast and hostile silence, staring at the huge dead bleeding thing that moments before had borne such life, he was struck for the first time in his headlong passage through his days by his own irrelevance. "Even *he*," his daughter said, "knew he'd done something stupid."

The elephant problem, still unresolved, will eventually affect conservation policies throughout East Africa, where even very honest governments may not be able to withstand political pressure to provide meat for the people. Already there is talk of systematic game-cropping in the parks on a sustained yield basis, especially since park revenues from meat and hides and tusks could be considerable, and this temptation may prove impossible to resist for the new governments. Or an outbreak of political instability might wreck the tourist industry that justifies the existence of the parks, thus removing the last barrier between the animals and a hungry populace. African schoolchildren are now taught to appreciate their wild animals and the land, but public attitudes may not change in time to spare the wildlife in the next decades, when the world must deal with the worst consequences of over-population and pollution. And a stubborn fight for animal preservation in disregard of people and their famine-haunted future would only be the culminating failure of the western civilization that, through its blind administration of vaccines and quinine, has upset the ecologies of a whole continent. Thus wildlife must be treated in terms of resource management in this new Africa which includes, besides gazelles, a growing horde of tattered humans who squat for days and weeks and months and years on end, in a seeming trance, awaiting hope. In the grotesque costumes of African roadsides—rag-wrapped heads and the wool greatcoats and steel helmets of old white man's wars are worn here in hundred-degree heat—the figures look like survivors of a cataclysm. Once, in Nanyuki, I saw a legless man, lacking all means of locomotion, who had been installed in an old auto tire in a ditch at the end of town. Fiercely, eyes bulging, oblivious of the rush of exhaust fumes spinning up the dust around his ears, he glared at an ancient newspaper, as if deciphering the news of doomsday.

*

The elephant problem is the reverse side of the problem of livestock, which are also out of balance with the environment. In small numbers, cattle were no threat to the African landscape; it is only in the past century, with the coming of the white man, that a conflict has emerged. The Europeans saw livestock as a sign of promise in the heathen: what was good for the white in Europe was good for the black in Africa, and that was that. In addition, the white encouraged a contempt for game, not only as fit food for man but as competitors of cattle and as carriers of the tsetse fly. In Uganda, Zambia, Rhodesia, Tanzania, the solution has been the destruction of the bush and a wholesale slaughter, over vast areas, of the native creatures, in a vain effort to render these regions habitable by men and cattle. Today it is known that the tsetse prefers warthog, giraffe, and buffalo, paying little attention to the antelopes, so that the vast majority of victims died in vain.

The European and his paraphernalia were all that was needed to upset the balance of man and the African land. It was clear to the simplest African that the wild animals were creatures of the past, destroying his shambas and competing with his livestock for the grass; they stood in the way of a "progress" that was very much to be desired. Game control, tsetse control, fenced water points, poaching— everywhere the wild animals made way for creatures which even from the point of view of economics seem very much less efficient than themselves. The ancestors of the wild animals have been evolving for 70 million years; the modern species, three quarters of a million years old, form the last great population of wild animals left on earth. Over their long evolutionary course, they have adapted to the heat and rain, to poor soils and coarse vegetation, and because they have had time to specialize, a dozen species can feed in the same area without competing. Rhino, giraffe, and gerenuk are browsers of leaves and shrubs, while zebra, topi, and wildebeest are grazers; buffalo, elephant, eland, impala, and most other antelope do both. Zebras will eat standing hay, and wildebeests and kongonis half-grown grass, leaving the newest growth to the gazelles; the topi has a taste for the rank meadow grass that most other antelopes avoid. Only a few wild herbivores require shade, and all have water-conserving mechanisms that permit them to go without water for days at a time; the Grant's gazelle, gerenuk, and oryx may not drink for months. Cattle, by comparison, must be brought to water every day or two, and waste coarse grasses used by the wild animals.

142

In addition, the game matures and breeds much earlier than domestic stock, and no fencing, shelter, tsetse control, or veterinary service is required. So far, game ranching experiments in Kenya and Tanzania are still experiments, having failed to anticipate the complex problems, from local politics and prejudices to the mechanics of harvesting in a hot wilderness without roads: the animals soon become so wary that systematic shooting is impossible, at least in areas accessible to service vehicles and refrigerator trucks. For this reason, the emphasis on game-cropping seems less promising than the development of semi-domesticated herds that can be harvested where needed. Whatever the solution, it seems clear that game ranching is a promising approach, all the more so since the tourists on whom East African economies count heavily do not come here to see cattle.

The eland, which mingles readily with cattle and on occasion follows herds into Maasai bomas, has been raised domestically in Southern Rhodesia, South Africa, and Russia, and recent success with buffalo and oryx at Galana River suggests that other animals may also be tamed that will yield more protein with less damage to the land than the scrub cattle. Until this is proven, however, care must be taken not to penalize the pastoral peoples for conditions caused by rain cycles and climate. Amboseli, where wildlife and the Maasai herds share a game reserve that is turning to dust, is often cited as a habitat badly damaged by too many cattle, but recent studies[6] indicate that the deteriorating vegetation is more a consequence of a raised water table with resultant high salinity than of overgrazing. Also, the contention that much of his herd is useless makes no sense to the Maasai, who knows that even the scraggiest of his cows can produce a calf in the next year. But one zebra skin is worth four times the price of such a cow, and eventually the tribe may be compelled to bring their myriad cattle into the economy by raising animals of better quality and permitting more of them to be sold and slaughtered. The population of the pastoral tribes rises between two and three percent each year, and landscape after landscape, wide open to settlement and the crude agriculture of the first comers, is ravaged by burning, subsistence farming, overgrazing, and erosion. The thin soil is cut to mud and dust by plagues of scrawny kine, following the same track to the rare waterholes, and goats scour the last nourishment from the gullied earth. Certain Turkana, after centuries as herdsmen, are reverting to the status of hunter-gatherers. Having no choice, they have given up their old taboos and will eat virtually anything, from snakes to doum palm roots; in recent years they have been seen picking through thorn trees for the eggs and young of weavers. A similar fate is threatening the Maasai, for once the earth has blown away, plague and famine are inevitable.

Tsavo East is so very vast that to get any sense of it, one must see it from the air. In two planes, we flew north over the waterhole at Mudanda Rock to the confluence of the Tsavo and Athi Rivers that together form the Galana, under the Yatta Plateau; from here, we followed the Yatta northward. This extraordinary formation, which comes south one hundred and eighty miles from the region of Thika to a point east of Mtito Andei, is capped by a great tongue of lava; all the land surrounding has eroded away. The Yatta rises like a rampart from the rivers and dry plains, yet its steep sides present no problem to the elephants, which that day were present on the heights in numbers. The elephants of Tsavo are the most celebrated in East Africa, being very large and magisterial in color, due to their habit of dusting in red desert soil. Yet they were not always common here: the great ivory hunter Arthur Neumann, traveling on foot through the Tsavo region on the way from Mombasa to Lake Rudolf in the last years of the nineteenth century, saw no elephants at all.[7] The two planes cross the high land between rivers. Somewhere here there is a rock heaped up with pebbles tossed onto it for luck by Maasai warriors on the way to raid the Giriama of the coast. Along the far side of the Yatta flows the Tiva, and beyond the Tiva the dry thorn scrub stretches eastward one hundred and fifty miles to the Tana River. Away from the rivers, the only large tree in this nyika is the great, strange baobab, but the baobab, which stores calcium in its bark, has been hammered hard by elephants, and few young trees remain in Tsavo Park. For many tribes, the baobab, being infested with such nocturnal creatures as owls, bats, bushbabies, and ghosts, is a house of spirits; the Kamba say that its weird "upside-down" appearance was its punishment for not growing where God wanted.

Kamba hunters, with a few nomadic Orma Boran and Ariangulo or "Waliangulu" have most of this hostile country to themselves. Like the Kamba, the Ariangulo, a little-known tribe of the nyika that speaks an eastern Hamitic tongue like that of the Galla, are expert trackers and bowmen and have long hunted elephants throughout this region,

144

using arrows tipped with acokanthera poison brewed by the Giriama, and selling ivory to the coastal traders. After 1948, when the Tsavo bush country, considered hopeless for all other purposes, was ordained a national park, a number of Kamba and Ariangulo hunters—or poachers, as they now were called, a matter of some indifference to them—continued in their old ways for several years. In the winter of 1950, in this burning land east of the Tiva, a band of thirty-eight Kamba, tracing a series of waterholes toward Dakadima Hill, found all of them dry. Half of the band set off for the Tiva, on the chance that the seasonal river still held water, and the rest headed south toward the Galana, which was sure to have water but was much farther away. The first group disappeared without a trace; in the second, there was one survivor.[8]

In the years of Mau-Mau, when most wardens were away in the Kenya Regiment, the elephant hunters descended upon Tsavo, but subsequent campaigns led by Sheldrick and Bill Woodley, now warden of the Aberdares National Park, compounded the excess-elephant problem by sending most of the hunters to jail. After serving sentences that were difficult for them to understand, some hunters became safari gun bearers and trackers, or scouts for the Kenya Game Department, and great credit for finding them places must go to Bill Woodley, who would later do the same for ex-Mau-Mau in the Aberdares. A few reverted to poaching, and most have joined the many other Africans whose old way of life has vanished, leaving them without heritage or hope.

I flew back to Tanzania with Douglas-Hamilton, who had brought his new plane to the elephant conference. Iain's plane is twenty years old, and looks it, but it "came with all sorts of spare parts—ailerons and wings and things. I shan't be able to use them, I suppose, unless I crump it." We took off from Voi at a very steep angle—a stalling angle, I was told later by Hugh Lamprey, a veteran flyer who once landed his plane on the stony saddle, fifteen thousand feet up, between the peaks of Kilimanjaro. Despite thunderheads and heavy rain, Iain chose a strange route through the Teita Hills, and I sat filled with gloom as the black rain smacked his windshield. There are bad air currents in the Teita Hills; it was at Voi that Karen Blixen's friend, Denys Finch-Hatton, crashed and died.

Soon I persuaded Iain to give me the wheel, and after that the flight was uneventful. We crossed the Ardai Plain beyond Arusha and the smooth Losiminguri Hills, flying westward toward the dark cliffs of the Rift. But Iain would not suffer the flight to pass without incident, for just as we reached the cliff he said, "I'll take it now." He wigwagged the tourists taking tea on the lawn of the Manyara Lodge, on the rim of the escarpment, and no doubt caused a click of cups by banking in a violent arc over the void and plunging in a power dive at the ground-water forest, a thousand feet below. He then swooped up to cliff level again, and came in to a competent landing.

A year later, when I got back to Ndala, I found Iain in a state of some chagrin. A month after my departure in the spring before, he had walked away from the wreck of his new airplane, which was far beyond the help of his spare parts. And it had scarcely been repaired when he nosed it over in soft sand while attempting to land on the sea beach at Kilifi, on the coast of Kenya. At present he was unable to accompany me on a planned climb of Ol Doinyo Lengai, having been warned by his sponsors and superiors that his reputation was outstripping his accomplishment. Nor could he go on our other planned safari to the Yaida Valley south of the Crater Highlands, where Iain's friend, a young zoologist named Peter Enderlein, was in touch with the small click-speaking Tindiga hunters. Over a whiskey, we agreed that he had done a good deal of difficult and dangerous research that more prudent students of the elephant would never attempt, and that his work or lack of it should be judged on its own merits. It often appeared that the official disapproval had less to do with deficiencies in his research than with his various mishaps, or even perhaps his domestic arrangements at Ndala, which included a friend whom he would marry a year later. Oria Rocco, whose family has a farm at Naivasha in Kenya, is a live marvelous girl with a husky laugh, fierce gentle spirit, and a natural empathy with elephants, being related to the creator of Babar, the splendid elephant of children's books. Worldly as Iain is conservative, she shares his intensity about the present and fatality about the future, and the camp was much more civilized for her presence.

I had not been in Ndala a half-hour before Iain had us in emergency. A cow-calf herd led by an old cow known as Ophelia came up the river bed to drink at a small pool at the base of the falls. The camp lies on the ascending slope of the escarpment, at the level of

146

the falls; just below, the river levels off, flowing gradually toward Lake Manyara, and downriver a short distance, Iain has a makeshift hide or blind. From here, he thought, he could get pictures of the herd with a complex camera device of his own invention which makes double images of the subject on the same negative; using parallax, animal measurements may be made with fair accuracy without destroying the animal itself. (The animal's shoulder height is a clue to its age, and the age structure of the population—the proportion of old animals to young—is an important indication of population health: despite the density of its elephant, Manyara at present has a healthy, "pyramid" population, with many young animals at the base.) Though the device works, it is so unwieldy that another person must be present with a notebook to record the data, and that other person was me.

We descended the steep bank under the camp and made our way downriver to the hide. The herd was busy at the pool, but I disliked our position very much. The animals were cut off; their only escape was straight back down the river past the hide, which was skeletal and decrepit, utterly worthless. And here we were on open ground, a hundred yards downriver from the steep bank leading up to the camp. . . . "They'll never scent us," Iain decided, setting up his apparatus, an ill-favored thing of long arms, loose parts, and prisms. But scent us they did, before he could get one picture. Ophelia, ears flared, spun around and, in dead silence, hurried her generations down the river bed in the stiff-legged elephant run that is really a walk, keeping her own impressive bulk between man and herd. We didn't move. "I don't think she's going to charge us," Iain whispered. But the moment the herd was safely past, Ophelia swung up onto the bank, and she had dispensed with threat display. There were no flared ears, no blaring, only an oncoming cow elephant, trunk held high, less than twenty yards away.

As I started to run, I recall cursing myself for having been there in the first place; my one chance was that the elephant would seize my friend instead of me. In hopelessness, or perhaps some instinct not to turn my back on a charging animal, I faced around again almost before I had set out, and was rewarded with one of the great sights of a lifetime. Douglas-Hamilton, unwilling to drop his apparatus, and knowing that flight was useless anyway, and doubtless cross that Ophelia had failed to act as he predicted, was making a last stand. As the elephant loomed over us, filling the coarse heat of noon with her dusty bulk, he flared his arms and waved his glittering contraption in her face, at the same time bellowing, "Bugger off!" Taken aback, the dazzled Ophelia flared her ears and blared, but she had sidestepped, losing the initiative, and now, thrown off course, she swung away toward the river, trumpeting angrily over her shoulder.

From high on the bank came a great peal of laughter from Oria. Iain and I trudged up to lunch; there was very damned little to say.

Another day we took a picnic to the Endobash River, which descends in a series of waterfalls that churn up a white froth in its pools. To reach it, one must push a short ways through the bush, and Iain, who has had two bad scrapes in this region, was carrying his heavy rifle. At the river, we climbed to a high pool where we stripped and swam in the cool current. Then we sat on a hot rock ledge to dry, and drank wine with Oria's fine lunch. Afterwards, like three Sunday strollers, we walked down the river bed toward the lake. In the sun and windlessness, enclosed by leafy trees, it was intimate and peaceful, with none of that vast anonymity that subdues one in the spaces of East Africa. But we had scarcely started home when the road a quarter-mile ahead was crossed by a herd of elephants. "Endobash baddies!" Iain said, grabbing his notebook. "I'll have to have a look at those! Load up the gun!" Because we would have to approach on foot to get close to these strange elephants, he needed gun support; Oria would take the pictures. We walked quickly and quietly down the river road.

The elephants were upwind of us, and before we knew it we were right among them, so close, in fact, that we dove for cover underneath the high bush beside us when it quaked with the movements of the elephant behind. A moment later, another walked out into the open a few yards ahead. It was a large cow with odd warped tusks. "Oh hell," said Iain, "it's only Jane Eyre after all." Blithely he stepped out onto the road, hailing his old friend, and there was a moment of suspense when the cow turned toward him. Then she went off sideways, ears flapping in half-hearted threat display, and her herd came out through the wall of bush and fell into step behind her.

Iain's disappointment was matched by my own relief, and Oria, who was pregnant, felt as I did: we had gotten off easily. It was a lovely late afternoon, and whirling along the lake track in the open car, exalted by wine and wind, I reveled in the buffaloes and wading birds in the bright water of the lake edge, and the great shining purple baobab that stands on the lake shore between Endobash and Ndala. But just past the Ndala crossing there were two lionesses in an acacia, and one of them lay stretched on a low limb not ten feet above the road. Oria said "I'll take her picture as we pass underneath," and Iain slowed the Land Rover on the bridge while she set her camera. At Manyara the tree-climbing lions are resigned to cars, and there is no danger in driving beneath one. But this animal was much closer to the road than most, and the car was wide open: Iain had removed the roof to feel closer to his elephants, and even the windshield was folded flat upon the hood. Lions accustomed to cameras and the faces in car windows see human beings in the open as a threat; when the car passed beneath her, the lioness and I scowled nervously, and I felt my shoulders hunch around my head.

Oria said she had missed the shot, and we passed beneath again, and then again, as she shot point-blank into the animal's mouth, which was now wide open. "Once more," she said; both Oria and Iain seemed feverish with excitement. "Christ," I said, scarcely able to speak. "You people—" But already the car had been yanked around, and seeing Iain's stubborn face, I knew that any interference short of a blunt instrument would only goad him to some ultimate stupidity that might get one of us mauled. I considered jumping out, but not for long. The lioness, extremely agitated, had risen to her feet, and a man on the ground might well invite attack. Insane as it seemed, I decided I was safer in the car, which proceeded forward.

The lioness crouched, hindquarters high, pulling her forepaws back beneath her chest, and the black tuft of her heavy tail thumped on the bark. Awaiting us, she flared her teeth, and this time I saw the muscles twitch as she hitched herself to spring: Ears back, eyes flat in an intent head sunk low upon her paws, she was shifting her bony shoulders and hind feet. Apparently Iain noticed this, for when Oria murmured, "She won't jump," he snapped at her, "Don't be so bloody sure." Nevertheless he carried on—I don't think it occurred to him to stop—and a second later we were fatally committed.

The lioness hitched her hindquarters again, snarling so loudly as the threat came close that Iain, who should have shot ahead, passing beneath her, jammed on the brakes and stalled. The front of the car stopped directly under the limb, with the cat's stiff whiskers and my whey face less than a lion's length apart; I was too paralyzed to stir. Land Rover motors spin quietly a while before they start, and while

149

we waited for that trapped lioness to explode around our ears we listened to the scrape of claws on bark and the hiss and spitting and the heavy thump of that hard tail against the wood, and watched the twitch of the black tail tassel and the leg muscles shivering in spasms under the fly-flecked hide. The intensity, the sun, the light were terrifically exciting—I hated it, but it was terrifically exciting. I felt unbearably *aware*. I think I smelled her but I can't remember; there is only a violent memory of lion-ness in all my senses. Then Iain, gone stiff in the face, was easing the car out of there, and he backed a good long way from the taut beast before turning around and proceeding homeward through the quiet woods.

Nobody spoke. When Oria pointed out more arboreal lions, we ignored her. I felt angry and depressed—angry at having our lives risked so unreasonably, and depressed because I had permitted it to happen, as if I had lacked the courage to admit fear. At camp, I said in sour tones, "Well, you got some fantastic pictures. I'll say that much." And Iain, looking cross himself, said shortly, "I'll never use them—those were for her scrapbook. I can't stand pictures of frightened animals." Two years before a friend of Iain had given him a book of mine on travels in wild parts of South America, and now he commented that I had taken a few risks myself. But calculated risks to reach a goal were quite different from risks taken for their own sake; I was thinking of George Schaller's account of his solitary camp in the grizzly tundra of Alaska, and the care he had taken, the awareness of every step on river stones, of each swing of his ax—the disciplined courage that it took to live alone in wilderness where any mistake might be the last. What we had just done, by comparison, was merely stupid.

For once, Iain failed to argue. He was silent for a while, then said abruptly that he expected to die violently, as his father had, and doubted very much that he would live to see his fortieth year. Should he maintain his present habits, this romantic prediction will doubtless be borne out. "I'd hate to die," he said on another occasion, "but I'd rather risk dying than live nine-to-five." Yet people like Iain who hurl themselves at life with such generous spirit seem to rush untouched through danger after danger, as if the embrace of death as part of life made them immortal.

Months later, when his work at Manyara had ended, Iain came with Oria to America. We discussed elephants and the fine days at

Ndala, arriving eventually at the adventure with the lioness. "Those times with the elephants weren't really dangerous," he said; he glared at Oria when she laughed. "Honestly. I knew what I was doing. But that business with the lion was absurd." He shrugged, and after a pause said quietly, "We just did it out of love of life."

At Ndala I lived happily in a thatch-roofed banda, like an African beehive hut with windows and a cement floor. The hut was perched on the high river bank just beside the falls, which washed away all noises but the clear notes of forest birds. Sometimes I climbed the stream above the falls, with its hidden rock pools and small sandy beaches shaded by figs and tamarind, and massive boulders of the ancient rock of Africa laid bare by the torrents of the rainy season. In the winter, a pair of Egyptian geese flew each day into the ravines above the falls; one watched them appear out of the sun over Manyara and vanish into the Rift wall.

In the ground-water forest, a green monitor lizard, four feet long, crosses a brook, and the speckled *Charaxes* butterflies flicker through the shades. In an open glade a fastidious impala lifts its hind leg to shed big drops of rain. At daybreak a dog baboon, taking his ease atop a termitarium, picks his breakfast from a plucked branch of red berries; finding himself observed, he cocks his head, then dismisses his fellow hominoid with a cynical nod. At evening a white-browed coucal, called the water-bottle bird, neck feathers raised, whole body shuddering, delivers that liquid falling song that only intensifies the stillness.

In the winter drought of 1961, Manyara was a pale dead place of scum froth and cracked soda; in 1969 and 1970 the water level was so high that many of the tracks behind the shore were underwater, and much of the umbrella thorn was killed. At twilight one late afternoon near the drowned forest, a herd of elephants fed on mats of dead typha sedge blown over from the far side of the lake. The animals waded to their chests in the greasy waves, trunks coiling in and out, ears blowing. Night was falling in the shadows of the Rift, which rose in a black wall behind the elephants, and from dusky woods came a solitary fluting. As the sun sank to the escarpment, the western sky took on a greenish cast, and the last light of storm caught the whiskers on the pointed lips, the torn flutings of the ears, the ragged switch of a wet tail on ancient hide. The dead forest, the doomed giants, the wild light were of another age, and made me restless, as if awakening ancestral memories of the Deluge.

8. *Great Caldron Mountains*

There is a void in the life of the African, a spiritual emptiness, divorced as he is from each world, standing in between, torn in both directions. To go forward is to abandon the past in which the roots of his being have their nourishment; to go backward is to cut himself off from the future, for there is no doubt about where the future lies. The African has been taught to abandon his old ways, yet he is not accepted in the new world even when he has mastered its ways. There seems to be no bridge, and this is the source of his terrible loneliness.

Colin Turnbull, *The Lonely African*

. . . a herd of Buffalo, one hundred and twenty-nine of them, came out of the morning mist under a copper sky, one by one, as if the dark and massive, iron-like animals with the mighty horizontally swung horns were not approaching, but were being created before my eyes and sent out as they were finished.

Isak Dinesen, *Out of Africa*

Between Kilimanjaro and Mt. Meru, off the road that winds around the side of Ngurdoto Crater, are soft ponds where hippos push and blow, and here vast beds of floating vegetation, papyrus and pale sky blue petals of nymphea drifting with the wind, may cause a pond to form or vanish before one returns along the road: I noticed this one afternoon while walking homeward to Momela. On my left as I went along, the clouds lifted from the shattered side of black Mt. Meru, revealing the jagged walls and the great cinder cone of its exploded crater. Before long, I heard the somber crack of a snapped branch, and rounding a bend, found my path barred by elephants. They were feeding on both sides, and one stood foursquare on the road, legs like stone columns. I was sorry about this, as dark was coming, and there was an elephant in this region that last year, having been approached incautiously, destroyed John Owen's friend, Baron Von Blumenthal. But Desmond Vesey-FitzGerald, who had seen these elephants earlier and anticipated the confrontation, came to fetch me. I was glad to see his Land Rover, for night came down before we reached his camp.

Vesey, who is the ecologist for Tanzania's national parks, had been kind enough to invite me to Momela, at the foot of Mt. Meru, to learn some "bush botany" from himself and his dear friend Mary Richards, a beautiful Welsh lady of eighty-three who, like Vesey himself, had transferred her botanical field work into Tanzania when the political situation in Northern Rhodesia, now Zambia, became a nuisance. ("Can't tell *what* they'll ask you at the borders anymore—doubt if they know themselves. Used to ask what sex your wife was—probably still do.") But Vesey and Mary were much too busy to bemoan the passing of the grand old days, for he was completing his work on East African grasses, while she was negotiating the purchase of a new Land Rover for a botanical safari into the remote plains behind Kilimanjaro. She had brought along from Zambia her cook Samuel, and as Vesey already had two Samuels in residence, and as these old friends are much given to good-humored shouting, their household is a lively place. Three Samuels or none might appear when one was called, whereas Vesey's cook Chilufia was apt to be there whether wanted or not, agitating in stricken silence for a chance to lay bare a calamity. The gloom of Chilufia is eternal as fire or water, and would no doubt be passed on from father to son.

"That banana pudding, Chilufia! We *don't* wish to see that again!"

And Chilufia rolls a yellow eye in resignation; one suspects Chilufia of laughter in the dark.

Toward Africans, Vesey and Mary have the good will of the earlier generations, recognizing the dignity and loyalty and courage with which Africans repay respectful treatment. Their manner is one of mixed love and exasperation, and just as the African eases his nerves with laughter at the mzungu, the European, so Vesey calms his own, when he can manage it, by laughing at the blacks. Because there is mutual loyalty in this household, blacks and whites may amuse one another in a way that is forgiven on both sides.

". . . *fright*fully smart! Stumbling about on the stones, slapping his rifle butt about—practically knocked himself down!" Vesey's cheeks, in mirth, are merry and red and round, under round glasses. "Didn't you see him? Trouble was, he'd lost his gun sling again, had his rifle all tied up with a fearful bit of string. . . ."

154

Vesey and Mary are pioneer African botanists, self-taught, and they are spirited competitors, decrying each other's botanical techniques, deploring the absence of word from "Kew" (the British Botanical Museum at Kew Gardens), fussing over each other's needs, such as proper tags and a decent supply of "polly bags" for collecting specimens. In the evening, over a stiff drink, they compare notes, recalling old times in Abercorn, and old friends like Ionides, called "Iodine," and J. A. Hunter, the hunter and game warden, and Wilfred Thesiger, the desert traveler, and Peter Greenway, the eminent botanist at the Coryndon (for their generation, Nairobi's National Museum, which acquired its new name at the time of Independence, will always be the Coryndon, just as this land will always be Tanganyika). In the back buildings of the Coryndon, I once met Dr. Greenway, a dogged bachelor in baggy plus fours and bow tie who was kind enough to sort out a crude collection I had made in the Dahlak Islands in the Red Sea; he is of the same vintage, more or less, as Mary Richards, and was greatly annoyed at young Vesey for failing to stay in touch with him. "I don't know *what* Vesey thinks he's doing down there," Dr. Greenway said, "but you may be sure it isn't botany."

I lived in a tent west of the house, which overlooks the Momela Lakes, in a saddle of green hills under Mt. Meru. Looking northeast toward Kilimanjaro, there is a broad prospect of the N'gare N'erobi region where Joseph Thomson of the Royal Geographic Society first met with the Maasai; Thomson, in 1883, was the first European to cross Maasai Land to Lake Victoria and return. "We soon set our eyes upon the dreaded warriors that had been so long the subject of my waking dreams, and I could not but involuntarily exclaim, 'What splendid fellows!' as I surveyed a band of the most peculiar race of men to be found in Africa." But soon the Maasai were behaving with the aggressive arrogance for which they are well known, and two days later, having gotten word that the Maasai in the country ahead were up in arms, Thomson felt obliged to beat a retreat around the south side of Kilimanjaro. Originally he had planned to go west over the Nguruman region to the lake, but now he was deflected, coming around by way of Loitokitok and Amboseli and heading northwest to Naivasha, Lake Baringo, and Kusumu on a route very close to today's main road from Namanga to these destinations. En route, he named

155

the Aberdare Mountains for the president of the society that had sponsored him and a lovely falls in honor of himself.

It has been said that Thomson's peril was exaggerated by the Chagga people of the foothills of Kilimanjaro, who hoped to relieve him of the trading goods intended for the Maasai. The Chagga were and are today an intelligent, ambitious tribe of Bantu-speaking cultivators who practiced irrigation in the rich highlands; like the Kikuyu, they were driven inland from the coast by northern invaders and they, too, are supposed to have displaced a small race of men with big bows and unintelligible speech, who were driven higher and higher on Mt. Kilimanjaro and eventually vanished. Subsequently the Chagga were harassed by the Maasai and displaced by Europeans, yet later became the most powerful tribe in the country. Whether the Chagga and Kikuyu got control of the best land because they are intelligent and ambitious, or whether their intelligence and ambition is a consequence of favorable environment and good nutrition would make an interesting study.

At daybreak, through the tent fly, I could see giraffe heads swaying over the small rises around camp, like giant flowers shot up overnight; the bell note of a boubou shrike distills the windless morning. Giraffes gaze raptly, one ear flicking, before moving off in that elegant slow rhythm that is tuned to the old music of the elephants. Elephants, too, convene here in the night, and sometimes buffalo, chewing their cud as they contemplate man's habitations. Below the camp, the water trails of courting coot melt the surface of Momela, and beyond the lakes, in a realm of shadow, Kilimanjaro's base forms a pedestal for its high cumulus. Birds fly from this dark world into the sunlight of Momela—a quartet of crowned cranes, wild horn note calling from across the water, and ducks that hurry down the clouds—pintail, Cape widgeon, Hottentot teal. In rain, the lakes have the monotone alpine cast of mountain lakes across the high places of the world, but here the monotone is pierced by fierce rays of African color—a rainbow in a purple sky, an emilia blossom, tropic orange, or a carmine feather, drifted down from a diadem of birds crossing the heavens in the last shreds of sunset.

His people tell of a young Bushman who came upon a rock pool in the desert. Kneeling to drink, he saw reflected in the pool a red bird more brilliant than anything he had ever seen on earth. Determined to

156

hold it in his hand, he sprang up with his bow, but there was no sign of the red bird in the sere desert sky. Wandering from place to place, inquiring after the vanished bird, he strayed farther and farther from his homeland. Days gathered into months and years, and in this way, without ever having found what he was seeking, he became old. He had hunted the land over, and talked to the few who might have glimpsed the bird as well as the many who had not, and still his heart could not give up the search. At last, on the point of turning home, he heard that the red bird had been seen from the peak of the north mountain, and he took up his bow and resumed his journey one more time. The mountain was far away across a desert, and when he reached the foothills the old hunter was mortally tired. With the end of his strength, he climbed and climbed into the sky, and on the peak he lay down upon his back, for he was dying. One last time he gazed into the distances, hoping to glimpse the splendid thing in the mountain sky. But the sky was empty, and he sighed and closed his eyes, wondering if his life had been in vain, and died with the sun upon his eyelids and a vision of the bird as he had seen it long ago, reflected in the bright pool of his childhood. And as he died, a feather of a burning red drifted down from the great sky, coming to rest in his still hand.[1]

Dark Meru is gaunt in a pearly sun that illumines the high shards of the blasted crater, and under the peaks the cotton clouds, filling with light, nudge and nestle like balloons in the corners of the dead volcano. Meru is the fifth highest mountain in all Africa, and may once have been highest of all. It is dormant, not extinct; it may have erupted as recently as 1879. An earlier explosion collapsed this eastern wall, and the glacier or crater lake cascaded down the mountain; the walls, still crumbling, raise clouds of dust on windless days.

On the northeast flank of Meru lies a mountain wilderness still relatively unexplored called the Chaperro. I went there with Vesey and John Beasley, the warden of Ngurdoto, and two askaris of the Meru tribe, Serekieli and Frank. A certain *Podocarpus* species with a finer bark pattern than the more common species occurs on Kilimanjaro, and Vesey was anxious to find out if it was native to Mt. Meru as well. *Podocarpus* belongs to a primitive group of conifers related to the yews and, with the East African cedar, forms forests of relict evergreens well over one hundred feet tall. These big trees, in East Africa, are now confined to Meru, Kilimanjaro, and Mt. Kenya.

There is a track up into the crater that crosses the fallen crater wall, and one is able to drive a vehicle with four-wheel drive to eighty-four hundred feet, where the forest opens out into a black lava tumulus, with a true montane flora of such Palearctic forms as heath, barberry, crotalaria, bracken fern, and usnea. Under the peak called Little Meru, where elephants mount stolidly to heights of eleven thousand feet, the track works around the rim to the northern face. Here we would descend through the high forest. In the silver sun of the crater mists, a dusky flycatcher, silver gray and dun, on a limb tip silvered with orchid swords and lichen, was utterly in place. This was cloud forest, with violets and buttercups, clover and geranium, and the mossy tree limbs carried ferns and yellow star flowers of stonecrop. Wild coffee and wild orange filled the clouds with scent, and here and there, like giants in the mist, stood arborescent lily and lobelia. Although animals wander high onto the mountain—the eland, klipspringer, and mountain reedbuck occur commonly at twelve thousand feet—the only antelope we saw on the descent was a lone bushbuck, and the birds were scarce: a bar-tailed trogon, red and blue, poised a moment on a limb, and John Beasley picked out an evergreen forest warbler and a broad-ringed white-eye at the edge of a sunny clearing. Meanwhile, we searched in vain for the uncommon conifer.

The forest was opening into glades where the grass, cropped short, was littered with fresh buffalo dung. "They can't be far ahead of us," John Beasley said. Last year Beasley had two ribs broken by a buffalo that caught him as he swung into a tree; he escaped the horn tip but was struck by the heavy boss. The buffalo is said to be the most aggressive animal in Africa, much more dangerous than the rhino, since that beast will often thunder past its target and keep right on going until, at some point in its course, having met with no obstacle and having forgotten what excited it in the first place, it comes to a ponderous halt. The buffalo, on the other hand, turns quickly and is diligent in its pursuit. It is keen of nose and eye and ear, and like the lion, is very difficult to stop once it attacks, often persisting in the work of destruction for some time after the object of its rage or fear is dead. It will even stalk a man, especially when wounded, coming around on its pursuer from behind, and last year near Momela a man was killed by a lurking buffalo in his own garden.

"Mbogo!"

Serekieli, in the lead, was calling back to us, and a buffalo skull, as if in sign, lay in the grass, surrounded by fresh spoor. We stood and listened. Before making their move, buffalo may lie in wait until whatever approaches them has gone past. This is customarily ascribed to malevolence or low cunning, but dull wits and slow reaction time may be an alternative explanation. "If they're good-natured, you don't see them," Vesey said crossly. "If they're not, they rush out at you. Terrific nervous tension, I must say." At sixty-two, Vesey is strong and energetic, but feels himself at a disadvantage when it comes to nipping up trees.

Then the suspense got to the buffalo, and the hidden herd rushed away down the mountainside with a heavy cracking, and a long rumbling like a mountain torrent past big boulders. Immediately, another Meru voice called out, *"Kifaru!"* and Vesey mopped his brow. The Meru were pointing at a rhino print as fresh as a black petal, and within seconds a rhino crashed into the brush off to the east. The crash started up a buffalo lying low in the wild nightshade to our left. This lone animal was the one we were afraid of, and as it was much closer than the others, its explosion through the branches caused the Wazungu to rush in all directions. Beasley sprinted past, bound for the same tree as myself, as the askari Serekieli, standing fast, fired his gun to turn the charge. The black blur whirled away, and the echo died.

On foot in Africa, one will have this experience sooner or later, and Thomson's encounter with a buffalo in this region could have described our own:

> Men were running on all sides as if the ground had yawned to swallow them up. Some were scrambling up trees, others, paralyzed, hid behind bushes, or any other object. Terror seemed to permeate the air with electric effect, and the short, quick cries of excited, panic-stricken men were heard on all sides. Almost paralyzed myself at this extraordinary but as yet unseen danger, I stood helpless till I was enlightened by one of my men screaming out to me in a warning voice, "Bwana, bwana, mboga!" (Master, a buffalo.) "Good gracious! Where?" I said, as I skipped with agility behind a tree, and peered cautiously past the side in the direction indicated—for be it known that there is not a more dangerous or dreaded animal in all Africa.[2]

The relative menace of what hunters know as "the big five"—

159

elephant, rhino, buffalo, lion, and leopard—is a popular topic of discussion in East Africa. J. A. Hunter, for example, ranked the leopard first, then lion, buffalo, elephant, and rhino, in that order. C. P. J. Ionides also thought the leopard more dangerous than the lion. This prejudice in favor of the carnivores is the prejudice of hunters who have had to finish off wounded animals, and might not be shared, say, by a farmer or field zoologist, who is more likely to be attacked by a large herbivore. In Ionides' opinion, the most dangerous animal to an unarmed person in the bush is a tuskless elephant. Lion attacks are now quite rare, but in the days of widespread game slaughter for tsetse control, a number of lions in these devastated regions turned on man in desperation, and bags of fifty, sixty, and in one case ninety human beings were recorded.[3] For people like myself who lack experience, it is purely a subjective business. I fear all five of the big five with all my heart, but I have least fear of the rhino, perhaps because one may leap aside with a reasonable hope that the rhino will keep on going. Unlike the other beasts of the big five, the rhino, with its poor vision and small powers of deduction, is only anxious to dispel an unsupportable suspense, and is probably as frightened as its foe.

In the next thousand feet of the descent there were rhino wallows and buffalo sign on every side; one kept an eye out for hospitable trees even before an emergency had been declared. In a mahogany, Meru tribesmen had placed a beehive, essentially a hollowed cedar log with a removable bottom, hung from a limb by a wooden hook. (The Dorobo add to the hive's efficiency by hailing the bees in strange high-pitched tones: "Bees, bees, all you who are in this country, come now and make honey here!")[4] In the honey harvest, the bees' wits are thickened with a smoke flare; when the hive is lowered to the ground the addled bees collect where it had hung. Easing his nerves, Vesey hypothesized the converse of the bees:

"Where the bloody hell's the hive?!"

"Right here, you idiot—it's always here."

"Well, it bloody well *isn't!*"

By the time they get through discussing it, the hive is back in place: "You see? Right there under your nose! Damned bloody fool!"

The great trees, fallen, have opened glades in a wild parkland, and silver deadwood is entwined by a climbing acanth with blossoms of light lavender. In stillness, in wind-shifted sun and shadow, a papilio butterfly, deep blue, is dancing with a Meru swallowtail, black and white, which ascends from the black and white remains of a colobus monkey, knocked from its tree by a leopard or an eagle....

"*Kifaru!*"

At six thousand feet, in a mahogany grove, a rhino digging is so fresh that it seems to breathe; we hurry past. "I must say," Vesey huffs, "on leave in England, it's nice to walk about a bit and not have some bloody ungrateful beast rush out at you." Once Vesey was chased by an irate hippopotamus that took a colossal bite out of his Land Rover.

A shy lemon dove in a pepper tree ... more spoor ...

"*Kifaru!*"

At the crash, we scatter. Horn high, tail high, a rhino lumbers forth out of the undergrowth thirty yards away. The rhino is said to hoist its tail when wishing to depart, but no one appears confident that this is so. From behind my tree, too big to climb, I see Beasley on the limb of a wild coffee, with Vesey crouched below, as the rhino, trotting heavily across the glade, emits three horrible coughing snorts. The askari Frank is somewhere out of sight, but Serekieli stands bravely, legs apart, ready to fire. There is no need—the rhino goes, and keeps on going.

The Africans permit themselves a wild sweet laughter of relief, watching the whites come down out of the trees. Vesey, treed twice in half an hour, is not amused, not yet; he will be later.

"Get on! Get on!" he says, anxious to be off this bloody mountain.

I hoped to see the white-maned Kilimanjaro bush pig, and one afternoon I went down into Ngurdoto Crater with Serekieli, accompanied by a silent boy whom we met along the road; like many people on the paths of Africa, the boy had no appointments and no destination of his own.

Ngurdoto, like the famous Ngorongoro, is extinct, and both have the graduated bowl known as a caldera, which is formed when the molten core of a volcano subsides into the earth and the steep crater sides fall inward. Ngorongoro was unknown to the outside world until 1892, and not until early in this century did the white man·find this smaller caldera to the east of Meru. Ngurdoto is larger than it appears—seen from the west rim, the farthest animals on the crater floor are two miles away—but the distance seems more temporal than spatial. Unlike Ngorongoro, there are no tracks or paths inside the crater, and as one peers down from the rim at remote creatures grazing in peace, oblivious of man, there rises from this hidden world that stillness of the early morning before man was born.

An elephant path of pressed humus and round leather-polished stones wound down among the boles of the gallery forest. The sun was high and the birds still, the forest dark and cool. Under the steep rim, out of the reach of axes, rose the great African mahogany and the elegant tropical olive, loliondo. We descended through the forest single file. The steep path leveled out into grassy glades which, being ponds in time of rain, are mostly round. We followed them eastward, under the crater rim, working our way out of the trees. Serekieli, in forest green, carried a shotgun. Like many people come lately to boots, Serekieli tends to clump, but he clumps quietly and is very surefooted; he is a lean handsome man of sad eyes and enchanted smile. Every little while he stopped to listen, giving the animals time to move away. Baboon and wart hog stared, then ran, the hominoids barking and shrieking as they scampered, the wild pigs departing the field in a stiff trot. Moments later we stood exposed in a bowl of sunlight.

Buffalo and a solitary rhino took mute note of us; the world stood still. Flat wet dung raised its reassuring smell in halos of loud flies. We turned west across wild pasture—cropped turf, cabbage butterflies, and cloven prints filled with clear rain—that rings the sedge swamp in the pit of the caldera. A hawk rose on thermals from the crater floor, and white egrets crossed the dark walls; in the marsh, a golden sedge was seeding in the swelling light of afternoon. More buffalo lay along the wood edge at the western wall, and with them rhino and an elephant. The rhinos lay still, but the elephant, a mile away, blared in alarm, and others answered from the galleries of trees, the screams echoing around the crater; the elephant's ears flared wide and closed as it passed with saintly tread into the forest. Bushbuck and waterbuck lifted carved heads to watch man's coming; their tails switched and their hind legs stamped but they did not run. Perhaps the white-maned bush pig saw us, too, raising red eyes from the snuffled dirt and scratching its raspy hide with a sharp hoof. Another time I glimpsed it from the rim at twilight, a ring of white in the dim

162

trees, and one night a year later, descending the mountain, my head-lights penned a family band, striped piglets and all, between the high sides of the road, but today it remained hidden.

The buffalo rose and split into two companies, and twelve hundred hoofs thundered at once under the walls. The thunder set off an insane screeching of baboons that spread the length and breadth of Ngurdoto, and a blue monkey dropped from a lone tree in the savanna and scampered to the forest. Some of the milling buffalo plunged off into the wood, but others turned and came straight at us, the sunlight spinning on their horns. Buffalo have good eyesight, and we expected these to veer, but a hundred yards away, they were still coming, rocking heavily across the meadow. We turned and ran. Confused by our flight, they wheeled about and fled after the rest into the thickets. There came a terrific crack and crashing, as if their companions had turned back and the two groups had collided. In the stunned silence, we headed once more for the western wall, but were scarcely in the clear when the rumbling increased again, and the wood edge quaked, swayed, and split wide as the tide of buffalo broke free onto the plain and scattered in all directions.

The hawk, clearing the crater rim, was burnt black by the western sun. From the forest, the hollow laugh of the blue monkey was answered by the froggish racketing of a turaco. Parting leaves with long shy fingers, Serekieli probed for sign of an animal trail that might climb to the western rim. We pushed through heavy growth of sage and psidia, stopping each moment to listen hard, then clap our hands. More than an hour was required to climb out of the heat and thicket to the gallery forest under the crater rim, and all the while the elephants were near, in enormous silence.

The leaves hung still. Bright on the dark humus lay a fiery fruit, white bird droppings, the blood-red feather of a turaco. When, near at hand, an elephant blared, the threat ricocheted around the walls, counterpointed by weird echoes of baboons. Serekieli offered an innocent smile and moved quietly ahead. In another hour we were on the rim, and rested on cool beds of a pink balsam. The wood smell was infused with scents of the wild orange and wild pepper trees, and of *Tabernae montana*, a white-flowered relative of frangipani. Where the western sun illumined the high leaves, a company of colobus and blue monkeys, silhouetted, leapt into the sky, careening down onto

163

the canopy of the crater's outer wall. Somewhere elephants were moving. It was near evening, and in every part the forest creaked with life.

On certain rare mornings at Momela, Mt. Kilimanjaro rises high and clear out of clouds that dissolve around it. From the north, in Kenya, it looks celestial, benign; from Momela, it is dark and looming. Such massifs as the Ruwenzoris on the Congo-Uganda border and the High Semien of Ethiopia lack the splendor of Kilimanjaro and Mt. Kenya, which stand all alone: at 19,340 feet, Kilimanjaro is the highest solitary mountain in the world. Mt. Kenya is a shard of rock thrust upward from the earth, but Kilima Njaro, the White Mountain, has ascended into the sky, a place of religious resonance for tribes all around its horizons.

The glacier glistens. A distant snow peak scours the mind, but a snow peak in the tropics draws the heart to a fine shimmering painful point of joy.

Kilimanjaro is the easternmost of the Great Caldron Mountains, which were born fifteen to twenty million years ago, in the early Pleistocene, when widespread eruptions and tectonic movements buried the ancient rock of Africa beneath volcanos, volcanic highlands, and the lava plains of what is now Maasai Land. The cones extend east and west from Kilimanjaro to the Crater Highlands, and from Shombole, just north of the Kenya border, south to Mt. Hanang. The last active volcano in the Great Caldron Mountains is Ol Doinyo Lengai, which stands by itself between the Crater Highlands and Lake Natron. One travels there by way of Mto Wa Mbu (Mosquito River), a raffish settlement on the dusty road to Lake Manyara and Ngorongoro. From Mto Wa Mbu a dirt track turns off along that part of the Rift wall formed by the Crater Highlands, arriving eventually at the village of Engaruka, thirty-five miles north; from there, it was said, a Maasai cattle path wound around the ramparts of the Highlands to Lengai.

The track to Engaruka, impassable in rain, parts the high grasses of the plain, branching and regathering according to the whims of its rare travelers, and tending always far out to the eastward, to skirt the gullies that snake down from the ravines in the Rift wall. Turning west again toward the mountains, the track arrives at the rim of Ol Kerii, where the land falls a last few hundred feet to the floor of the

Rift Valley. In East Africa, one is never far from the Great Rift, which splits the earth's crust from the Dead Sea south to the Zambezi River, and east and west in broken cracks from the Gulf of Aden to the Valley of the Congo. In places, the Rift is forty miles across, a trench of sun and tawny heat walled by plateaus. The floors that contain the Rift's long, narrow north-south lakes were created long ago when the earth sank between parallel fractures, and they are on different levels: Manyara is eleven hundred feet higher than Lake Natron, to the north.

Ol Kerii, the last great step in the descent into the Rift, has a prospect of lost mountains: Kerimasi, at the northeast corner of the Crater Highlands, and Kitumbeine, a shadow in the ancient haze beyond, and Gelai, due north, that guards the lonely sea of Natron. In every distance stand strange shrouded landscapes of the past and future. The present is wild blowing light, the sun, a bird, a baobab in heraldic isolation, like the tree where man was born.

The track descends to the riverain forests and slow swamps of the Engaruka Basin, steeping—no sign of man, no smoke nor habitation, only two giraffes still as killed trees far out in the savanna—and the sense of entering a new world is quickened by new birds. For the first time I behold the bright, marvelous mechanisms known to man as the rosy-patched shrike, white-throated bee-eater, and Fischer's widow-bird, named in honor of Thomson's rival, the German naturalist Gustav Fischer, who in 1882 discovered strange ruins at Engaruka in the course of an attempt to cross Maasai Land. But his good name only encumbers the effect of this airy thing that can draw a landscape taut with its plumed tail.

Down the track comes a loud party of Fischer's countrymen, staring bald-eyed from the windows of a white hunter's vehicle—here was one reason why game had been so scarce along the way. And seeing these tourists trundled forth to blaze away at the very last concentration of great animals left on earth, imagining the pollution of their din, the smoke and blood and shocked silence of the plain, and the wake of rotting carcasses, I stared back at them as rudely, filled with rage. Such sport made it all the harder to wean Africans away from contempt for wildlife, which is a matter of education and not culture: the British and South African soldiers stationed at Marsabit during World War II left thousands of animals to rot that had been idly shot down with automatic weapons from the backs of trucks.[5]

*

The gorges in the west Rift wall are the shadows of dead rivers that in the pluvials came rushing from the highlands, forming a lake in what is now the Engaruka Basin. For centuries, the surviving stream, thought to come from Embagai Crater in the clouds above, has attracted man to Engaruka, which is a settlement of agricultural Maasai (now known as the Arusa) as well as some Sukuma Bantu from the south. Earlier it was inhabited by people skilled in irrigation who left behind an extensive ruin of stone circles, cairns, and walled terracing for cultivation, as well as a dam one hundred feet long; the terracing on the hills above is visible from the track. The remains of another dam lie near the Ngorongoro-Olbalbal road, and some terracing near the north end of Lake Eyasi, but there is no other ruined city.

Engaruka is scarcely touched by archeologists, and its origins are presently unknown. It lies far off the traditional trading routes, an isolated stone-working community of an estimated thirty to forty thousand souls, the largest such ruin in central and south Africa except Zimbabwe in Rhodesia. Zimbabwe was constructed over centuries, beginning no later than the twelfth century and lasting until 1834, when it was overrun by tribes of Zulu, but according to preliminary investigations,[6] Engaruka may be less than three centuries old. If this is true, who were the people who constructed it, and what became of them?

The Maasai say that Engaruka was occupied by an Irakw people when they descended on this region in the eighteenth century. The Irakw tribes, which include the pit-dwelling Mbulu cultivators of the plateaus behind Lake Manyara, are that obscure group of strange archaic language that has been tentatively[7] related to those proto-Hamite hunters who were the first to invade East Africa from the north. Or perhaps the Engaruka masons, Irakw or otherwise, derive from the Neolithic Hamites who brought domestic plants and animals into the country and were scattered in the arable highlands of East Africa until a few centuries ago, when they appear to have been surrounded and absorbed by the waves of Negroids, Nilote as well as Bantu, who came after. In Kenya's Kerio Valley, for example, the Maraket people of the Nandi tribes still maintain elaborate irrigation systems, including conduits woven across the steep faces of cliffs, which they say were made by a northern people of strange language, the Sirikwa, who later died in plague: "They built the furrows, but

166

they did not teach us how to build them; we only know how to keep them as they are."[8] (The similar sound of "Sirikwa" and "Irakw" is interesting, considering the obscure history of both groups.)

There is more than a trace of a vanished race in the Bantu-speaking Sonjo, who still practice stone terracing and irrigation only sixty miles away to the northwest, above Lake Natron, and build fortified palisades around their villages that are found nowhere else south of western Ethiopia, where the Neolithic Hamites are thought to have emerged. One recalls that such non-Bantu peoples as the Hima and Tusi herdsmen of Uganda and Ruanda-Urundi have adopted the Bantu tongue, and the name Sonjo brings to mind the "Enjoe," as the Kikuyu called that vanished northern people, known to the Dorobo as the Mokwan, who built stone "hut circles" on the Uasin Gishu Plateau, and were said to have been scattered by the Maasai. These "hut circles," often mere depressions, may have served also as bomas for the long-horned cattle,[9] and are known as "Sirikwa holes": perhaps the Mokwan, Enjoe, and Sirikwa are all one.[10] Present day Sonjo stone construction cannot compare with the clean unmortared work at Engaruka, but this people have a legend of a lost city known as Belwa, and inevitably one wonders if the light-skinned Sonjo—they are even lighter than the "Nilo-Hamitic" Maasai—retreated to their remote escarpment after the fall of Engaruka.

Tribal traditions being unreliable, one cannot trust the memory of the Maasai, nor count on Belwa, but it is fine, unscientific fun to try to match the pieces of all the traditions in this region of archaic peoples, which are generally supported by the Somali belief that the stonework in the Crater Highlands region is the work of those early engineers who carved the deep wells at Wajir and Marsabit, in the Northern Frontier Province of Kenya—a race of giants, so they say, that came out of Arabia two thousand years ago, and were the ancestors of the tall Tusi. If Engaruka is more than a few centuries old, it may have been an inland settlement that like Zimbabwe traded with the coast. If so, what brought it to an end? Were the Engaruka builders the fierce il Adoru of the Maasai tradition of settlement of this region? Or did the end come before the appearance of the Maasai? According to chronicles of the Portuguese, the coastal town of Kilwa was destroyed in 1589, and three thousand of its four thousand inhabitants devoured by marauding hordes of cannibals known as the Zimba. The Zimba, who also sacked Mombasa and were finally routed at Malindi, are another mystery, since the modern Zimba are a Bantu tribe of the savannas of the lower Zambezi among whom cannibalism is not known (though they are related to cannibalistic Bantu of the central forests).[11] No one can say where the historic Zimba came from, nor what caused their locust-like advance, nor where they subsided once their rage was spent, but possibly they brought an end to Engaruka.

Engaruka today is a shady village of irrigation ditches, banana shambas, dogs and chickens, and here the last traces of good track were left behind. The cars wound down along the river, then headed off into dense thicket. The cattle track diminished in the sun and dust, and for miles the cars forced a way through tough acacia scrub with a fierce shriek of thorn on metal. Then footpath became cattle trail again, tending away from the highlands as before, and emerging eventually in a stony plain that extends to the foot of Kitumbeine. Off to the west, the rainy greens of Kerimasi loomed and passed, and then the gray cone of Lengai came into view, drifting out from behind the Crater Highlands like a moon.

In the distance were the hard white spots that in African landscapes signify far herds of cattle, but here the livestock and wild animals were still in balance, as once they were throughout Maasai Land. Everywhere along the track trailed zebra, gazelle, and wildebeest, with a few eland; outside the parks and their environs I had never seen plains game so common since leaving the Sudan nine years before. The plain was inset with fleeting pools, and a hoof-pocked track wandered from water to water. In a land so hard and flat, the pools had no more depth than mirrors, refracting the changing weathers in the sky, and but for the trees and the tramped margins, the water would have seemed a trick of light that would fade as the sun turned. Water lines of teal and dabchick cracked the mirror, and the long-stemmed silhouettes of wading birds stood still. The edges teemed with sandpipers, feeding avidly before night fell; at dark, under the moon, these Palearctic migrants would cross the equator into the Northern Hemisphere, and tomorrow might find them on Lake Rudolf or the Nile. Marabous, sitting back upon their hinges, digested some unspeakable repast, and in the new grass all around, the prosperous insects had drawn down upon their heads great companies of European storks; the tall white birds stood solemnly on every side. Storks are birds of holocaust—they dance in the heat shimmer of fires, peering down among the sparks for fleeing lizards, grass mice, snakes—and at one time, they attended locust plagues. Now the locusts can be kept under control except in those unstable regions where man has lost control over himself.[12]

At noon two days later, the stork companies rose motionless on the thermals, curling like smoke in tight flocks of many hundreds, higher and higher over Kerimasi and the Crater Highlands, until the flocks were wisps against the clouds. At the crest of a mile-high column of white birds, they set their course, blown down the sky toward the hard blue of the north horizon. The shorebirds were already gone, and of the native water birds, a solitary grebe remained. On the black margins milled thousands of small Zebu cattle, mixed with a few giant-horned Ankoles and the gaunt twist-horn kine of archaic kingdoms, all of these crowded by low pushing dung-stuck troops of sheep and goat. At the edge of the dust, in earthen robes, the herdsmen leaned upon their spears, faces in shadow. Swallows coursed the dusty herds, snatching hot insects, and the noon air danced with the drum of hoofs, wails, whistles, whoops, and tink of bells, bone clicks, bleating, and yelled laughter.

By the water's edge man squatted, worn rags pulled low over his brow against the sun. Manure smell, flies, the stamp and lowing of the herds, the heat. In the shallows a naked dancing boy darted and splashed. Then cloud shadow dimmed the water shine on his round head, and he turned black. In foreboding he paused; the water stilled, and clouds gathered in the water. He picked at his thin body, one-legged in the evanescent pool that will vanish in summer like the haze of green on this burning land.

Grasslands. Eland, swallows, clouds, and wind. A lone Maasai, stalking across the foothills of Kerimasi like a prophet, staff raised, red robe blowing.

The vehicles forsake the track and cut due west across the slopes toward Lengai. These foothills are mostly parasitic cones of the volcanoes; the cones are grassy, with neat craters. Other craters are inset in the level ground, as if the earth had fallen in, and swallows circle around the rim under the blowing grass.

Two tall Maasai rise from the grass, casting wild smiles and their few scraps of Swahili: *"Jambo! Habari gani?"* (What sort of news?) They point toward the volcano, their clubs or rungus like extensions of long bony arms: *"Kilima cha Mungu!"* they cry. Mountain of God!

I shake my head and name the mountain in Maasai: "Ol Doinyo Lengai!" And they smile and wave: "Ngai! Ngai!" In Tanzania, in 1968, the wild herdsmen were ordered to give up their airy shukas and wear pants, but the Maasai pay small attention to such laws; far from the roads, they stand exposed, like the wild people of the Sudan. Their cloth is clean and their beads bright, their ornaments of wrought copper and tin are of a quality not found in the curio shops of Arusha and Nairobi, and the holes in their ear lobes, pierced by the hard thorn of the desert date, are stretched by wooden ear plugs that, nearer the roads, are being replaced by aluminum film canisters dropped by the tourists (in a Maasai village between Makindu and Amboseli, I once found some discarded wooden plugs, silken-smooth with years of human grease). At Mto Wa Mbu, Ngorongoro, Namanga, and Narok the Maasai loiterers are much given to begging and jeering outside the Asian dukas, where they squat on their heels in vulture-like congregations and try halfheartedly to hawk to the tourists old beads and spears and milk gourds and rungus and the short double-edged simis in red scabbards. Such tribesmen bear small resemblance to the people so admired by Thomson, and in fact the suppression of their ways led very quickly to the decline of the Maasai, whose fate much resembles that of the Plains Indians of North America. A government report of 1939, hardly a half-century after Thomson saw them first, notes a decline in birth rate and a high incidence of sterility and venereal disease, as well as pervasive alcoholism, license, and general apathy. Efforts to enlist Maasai in the police or King's African Rifles were mostly a failure, and even the few who became educated often returned afterwards to the life of the grasslands, unable to put aside that fierce pride and independence that caused them to reject white settler and missionary alike. Also, in their effort to regain stability after years of plague, famine, and disruption, they clung all the more tenaciously to their old ways. "Mentally impervious to new ideas, and incapable of adapting to new conditions," they were now adjudged inferior in all respects to the peoples they had formerly ruled. But once again, like the Indians of North America, they were measured by western standards—the downfall of the Maasai had been pride, not inferiority, which was the bureaucratic way of accounting for a wild people's disdain for western values. At the same time Maasai aloofness was much romanticized and admired, since unlike the abominable Bantu, and the Kikuyu especially, who dared to resent the usurpation of their lands and were forever underfoot, the tribe kept itself out of the path of progress. "It has often been proved in other parts of the globe that the native, in the advent of the white man, alters his habits or ceases to exist, and it is to be hoped that the Maasai will choose the first of these alternatives," an observer wrote, as early as 1904.[13] The Maasai, having no choice, altered his habits, but in a spiritual sense, he has ceased to exist as well.

The plateau declines toward the pale misty vat of Natron. Around the inland sea, thirty-five miles long, rise lonely mountains: the volcano called Gelai, on the eastern shore, the dark Rift to the west, and at the northern end, in Kenya, Shombole and the Nguruman Escarpment in an horizon of half-mountain and half-cloud, and over all the Mountain of God, presiding.

It is nearly sunset, and Lengai still far away. Seasonal stream beds and ravines that carry the rain off Kerimasi trench the foothills, and time is lost scouring each gully for a place to cross. Already the motors are too hot and finally it is dark; we make camp under the highland walls, hopefully within walking distance of the great black cone that surrounds itself with stars. Two tents are pitched on the grassy slope, and a fire made. Once this is done, we have a glass of rum. Altogether we are six: besides myself, Vesey-FitzGerald and his friend George Reed and a wildlife photographer and mountaineer named Brian Hawkes, and the cook Chilufia, and the Meru ranger Frank who was with us last year on the Chaperro. Vesey is furious with Chilufia and Frank, who have brought along their water bottles as instructed—they hold them up in proof—but have neglected to put water in them. "You're a pair of idiots, do you understand that? I told you so last safari and now I'm telling you again and I expect I'll have to tell you next time, too—you're a pair of idiots!" Vesey manages to laugh before he finishes, and so do the Africans, but all know that this is not a laughing matter, since there is no good water to be found between here and Engaruka, twenty-five hard miles back. Yet two days later, when water is low, Frank fills his bottle from the jerry can in my Rover, then replaces the cap so carelessly that half of our remaining drinking water leaks away.

It is often said that Africans cannot lay straight paths or plow straight furrows, screw bottle caps, use rifle sights—in short, that they have no sense of geometric order, much less time, since there is nothing of this sort in nature to instruct them. "Have to watch these chaps every minute," white East Africans will tell you. "Can't do the first thing for themselves." But perhaps the proper word is "won't." Most Africans are so accustomed to having decisions made for them by whites, and to carrying out instructions to the letter to avoid abuse, that only rarely do they think out what they are doing, much less take initiative. Rather, they move dully through dull menial tasks—working automatically, without thought, may be all that makes such labor bearable—preferring to be thought stupid than to get in trouble, and at the same time gleeful when calamities occur. Stubborn, apathetic, and perverse, they observe the letter of their instructions, not the spirit of them (Bring your water bottles!). They are not responsible for filling the bottles unless told to do so; if the whites will treat them as children, they will act that way.

Chilufia's heart is still in Zambia, and no doubt his mind as well, but I am puzzled by Frank, who is young, ambitious, and alert. Chilufia seems indifferent to being called an idiot; such words are to be shrugged off, like rain. *Shauri ya Mungu*, he might say—this is the affair of God. But Frank dislikes it; he smiles a strange bad smile as if warning me to understand. One difference between Frank and Chilufia is the name Frank—his real name is Kessi.

Frank is anxious to communicate, though he speaks my language poorly, and I scarcely speak his at all. When Vesey isn't listening he uses my first name. The friendliness is genuine, but there is a hair of aggression in it; he scans my eyes for disapproval or rejection. Knowing this and pained by it, I respond enthusiastically, but soon we are overtaken by silence. We cannot communicate after all. Even if we could, we have little to offer but good will and our humanity. Even among white East Africans and black who converse easily in English or Swahili, the problem appears to be mutual boredom, which comes about because both find the interests of the other trivial, and their ideas therefore of small consequence.

The volcano filled the night like a great bell. Over Shombole and the Loita there was lightning, vast silent illuminations that hollowed out the heavy clouds until they glowed like fire seen through smoke. This night and the next, the lightning came every few moments, but the thunder was too distant to be heard. I listened to a solitary nightjar, fixed in the rigidity of its shrill song that under Lengai was a part of the moon silence.

With Hawkes at daybreak I set off toward the mountain. Each carried a small knapsack of tea and water, nuts and raisins, notebook and binoculars; Hawkes had a camera. Lengai was clear of clouds, and the distance to the lava fan seemed perhaps six miles. But in the bad light of the night before, we had made camp on the wrong side of a grid of steep ridges, and between the ridges lay steep bush-choked dongas. For the first two hours of the trek, we slid and clambered up and down and up and down, opposed by hidden rocks and head-high grasses. I did not expect trouble with animals, and we had none, but leopard pug marks in the sand bed of a donga were a reminder that we could not forget about them either; the giant grass that was such hard work could hide a rhino.

At eight, already hot and tired, we stopped on the crest of a ridge and stared bleakly about us. At this rate, two more hours would pass before we reached the mountain, and at least five would be required for the climb. Allowing three hours for the descent and none at all for rest or exploration, we would still face a four-hour return across these badlands after dark. Also, Lengai was gathering its clouds, which would make the climb more difficult. But we had worked too hard to give up now; the going could get easier at any moment, and from the mountainside we might perceive a better route back to the camp. Or so we persuaded each other, trudging on like pilgrims toward the magic mountain. And almost immediately we struck a Maasai cattle track over the ridges to the river of black sand that winds around the base of the volcano. From the black river, the lava plain climbed rapidly to the ridges of Lengai.

Ahead, a dark gorge cleaved the face of the volcano. The ridge that forms the west side of the gorge faces south toward the Highlands, and its lower slope, still visible beneath the clouds on the summit, looked less precipitous than the rest. We walked up the black river bed, then climbed the far bank and traversed the ash plain. Here a zebra had once wandered; into one ghostly print the wind had blown the copper shell of a large beetle. Higher still, the beetle husks were everywhere, glinting in the wind waves of the surface. The fire and ash of its last eruption, in 1967, buried Lengai in a gray lunar snow, all but these withered tips of wind-twitched grass. At the ravine edge stood the husk of a whistling-thorn on which the galls have turned to wood, yet ants inhabited the galls, subsisting, perhaps, on the dead beetles that blow across the wastes; in greener times, these ants protected the new tips of the acacia against browsers such as the giraffe. A stray lizard track excepted, the ants are the one sign of terrestrial life. Footsteps resound, for the Mountain of God is hollow; there is no sense of the present here, only the past.

In the spring of 1969, on a flight from Nairobi to Manyara, and again in the winter of 1970, coming from Seronera to Arusha, I got the pilots to circle the volcano. Buffeted by downdrafts, dodging clouds, the light planes came in over the deep furrows of the flanks and made tight circles over the sickening vat. In its brimstone smokes, dead grays, sulfurous yellows, there was no hint of green, no sign of life.

The slope had steepened. We dropped our packs beside the dead acacia, and standing there, leaning back into the hill, I became aware of butterflies and birds. The first butterfly was as orange as the sun, and the wind hurried it from east to west across the falling desert, its fire so intensified by the flat light that it was still visible where it rounded the mountain and spun away northwest toward Lake Natron. The birds were birds of high rock places—swifts, crag martins, the white Egyptian vulture—riding the drafts and currents. Then a lark came strangely near before bounding down across the deserts. On the wind this morning I had heard an elusive lark song; perhaps this solitary bird had been the singer.

I put a few nuts and raisins in my pocket and took a sip of water. The desert air of the volcano was so dry that one handled the water with the kind of reverence that the Bushman must feel for the water that he stores in ostrich eggs. Then we were off again. I concentrated on slow steady steps, a steady breath, at pains not to look down. On the narrowing ridge, there were no rocks, no sticks, no handholds of any kind, only the slick surface of the ash; it was dusty but hard, and my light boots could find no grip. Hawkes, who had climbing boots, was doing better, but he was not optimistic. Before the eruption, according to its few veterans, the conquest of Lengai had been arduous but not difficult; now, Hawkes felt, this route, at least, was a job for a four-man team with ropes and ice-axes. On our right hand, the ridge dropped sheer into the black ravine; to the left, one would roll and bounce all the way to the black river for want of something to

174

catch hold of. I stared rigorously upward, where the white vulture, stiff-winged as a kite, was suddenly sucked up into the mists.

We neared the clouds. Far below, small tornadoes or dust devils whipped ash into the air, and the wind blew it in sheets of smoke across the slopes. The mists descended, and a gathering wind nagged at the nerves; Hawkes called down that the going was getting worse. It was late morning, with the steepest rock of the volcano summit still to go, and already I was reduced to hands and knees. Again and again, my shoes lost their grip, making me throw myself belly down to avoid slipping backward and gathering speed for the ultimate descent; so steep was it where I lay flung against the mountainside that I seemed virtually upright. Breathless, heart pounding, I listened to the fate of the small debris cast loose by my desperate scrabbling—a scaling hiss, a silence, and finally from the depths of the ravine a horrid muttering, quite indescribable, the only sound I ever heard upon Lengai. And having heard it a few times, I rolled over on my back to get my breath, and drank a little water, and when I was rested, I quit.

I lay there wind-burned, scaled with sterile dust, my flask clutched in a brown hand that in this light had the fierce sinew of a talon. And my decision was the right one, for no sooner had I made it than the clouds were parted by a brilliant sun. The sun relaxed my body, and in its warmth I felt myself open outward in immense wellbeing, as if a red feather had drifted down into my hand. I lay there languid with relief, enjoying the warm wind and the touch of hair that was straying on my brow, the pure rock water from a cool spring at Manyara, the sun on my hot skin, the feel of breathing, all intensified by the wild beauty of the world. From my seat on the Mountain of God, I ruled Embagai and the green shifting shadows of the Crater Highlands, climbing away into black clouds like a mythical kingdom. The clouds guarded old volcanoes, Jaeger Summit and Loolmalassin, whose peaks I had never seen. Broad-backed, motionless on the wind, an eagle descended the black river that isolates Lengai from the Highlands. Seen from above, a bird of prey, intent on all beneath, is the very messenger of silence.

A series of small mounds, like stepping stones, emerged from the smooth surface of the ash; half-blind with effort on the climb, I had scarcely noticed them. The mounds formed a distinct line down the crest of the ridge, like rhinoceros prints elevated above the surface,

175

and as it happens this was what they were. Apparently a rhino high up on the mountain had tried to flee the last eruptions—perhaps in vain, since its tracks vanish near the edge of the ravine. There was no sign of a trail leading upward, only down. Its tread had compacted the hot ash, and afterwards the mountain winds had worn away the uncompacted ash all around, until the prints had risen above the surface.

Holding a hoofprint in my hands, I raised my eyes to where that horned lump, as if spat up by the volcano, had taken form in the poisonous clouds and rushed down the fiery ridge. What had drawn it up into the mists? Had it been blind, like the buffalo found in the snow high on Mt. Kenya? Imagine the sight of that dark thing in the smoke of the volcano; had an African seen it, the rhino might have become a beast of legend, like the hyena, for it is in such dreamlike events that myths are born.

Anxious to transfix so great a mystery, I chipped two prints clean of packed ash and wedged them into my pack. We descended the volcano, crossed the ash plains, circled dust storms. For four hours on sore feet, I carried the stone prints, but they belonged to the dead mountain, for in the journey they returned to dust.

9. Red God

Epwo m-baa pokin in-gitin' got
Everything has an end.

Maasai saying[1]

One bright day of August I went south from Nairobi on the road that crosses the Ngong Hills and descends through ever drier country, passing the site of hand-axe man at Olorgesaille, and winding down out of the hills to the magadi or soda lakes in the pit of the Rift Valley. Lake Magadi itself is a blinding white, a snowfield in the desert, but close at hand, under the stacks and litter of the soda factory, the white is somber, crusted and discolored by strange chemistries. Here a road crosses the soda lake on a narrow dike. Some thirty miles west of Magadi, beyond the Uaso Nyiro River that flows south into Lake Natron, a track turns south through long-grass thorn savanna under the Nguruman Escarpment, curving north again as it climbs onto the plateau.

In Magadi I had been joined by Lewis Hurxthal, a young biologist studying the ostrich, and his beautiful wife Nancy, an artist and designer in charge of educational material put out by the African Wildlife Leadership Foundation in Nairobi. The Hurxthals live on the edge of the Aathi Plain where his favorite birds stalk by, and it was Lew who first instructed me in the esoterica of the cock ostrich, which is unique among birds in the possession of a penis. At this time of year, the cock ostrich flushes red and tumescent in the neck and legs, and both sexes writhe and flounce and run. Careening about, they shuffle their fat wings on their backs like maids tying up apron strings while rushing to answer a bell. Once Lew interrupted a discussion of *querencia*, that territory in the bullring where the bull feels safe, acts defensively, and is therefore dangerous: "*Ostriches*"—and he emphasized the word in a soft reproachful tone, as if his great birds had been slighted—"have charisma, too."

We made camp under big sycamore figs where a clear stream coming down off the Ngurumans flows over shining stones. There

177

are few clear streams in East Africa, and we enjoyed a cool bath in its current, which washed away the danger of bilharzia. Squalls of finches—fire finches, mannikins, cutthroats, rufous-backs, queleas, cordon bleus, gray-headed social weavers, all intermixed like autumn leaves—blew in and out of a bare acacia, descending in gusts to the water's edge and whirring away again, oblivious of the human presence just across the stream. The quelea, or Sudan dioch, is known also as the plague finch, since it sometimes appears in clouds that descend like blowing smoke upon the crops, in a way of locusts. Toward evening some Maasai came down to bathe. These men were descendants of those who fled to Ngurumani, "the farms," after the disastrous civil wars of the nineteenth century; their losses made worse by cattle famine in the wake of a locust plague, they were forced to till the soil or die. Today they are found mostly in the Nguruman region, at Engaruka, and under Mt. Meru, where they are called "Warusa." In dress and customs, the agriculturalists still emulate the pastoral clans, and these arranged themselves in the middle of camp activities, so that everything might take place around their legs. "Nowhere have I met such pleasing and manly natives over the whole extent of country I have yet traversed in Africa," wrote Joseph Thomson of this people.

A pleasing and manly native, Legaturi, came along next day on an expedition up the rough track that climbs onto the higher steps of the Ngurumans, from where one has a mighty prospect of the broad green swamps of the lower Uaso Nyiro, the volcano of Shombole, and Lake Natron. Farther on, the track loses itself in tsetse bush, and the going got so rough that Nancy, who was four months pregnant, soon felt sick. While Lew tended to her beneath a tree, I went on with Legaturi up the track, which ended eventually at a safari camp set up by Philip Leakey. Beyond, the Nguruman Escarpment mounted northwestward into the wilderness of the Loita Hills.

Feeling uneasy about the Hurxthals, I turned around immediately and started back. In the hot gray day the tsetses were biting without stint; the mute oval shapes made by their overlapping wings speckled the inside of my windshield, and one smooth brute with bristled eyes lit confidingly upon my arm. Despite the thick heat I put on a shirt—Legaturi was swathed like a mummy in his red toga—though I would have been better off had the shirt been white: tsetses prefer dark animals to light, and apparently abhor the zebra, whose stripes appear to disconcert their dim perceptions.

That dipterid biting flies of the genus *Glossina* were vectors of the trypanosomes that caused nagana in cattle and sleeping sickness in man was discovered in Uganda in 1905, and two years later human beings were evacuated from Murchison Falls and many other regions, including the shores of Lake Victoria, where two hundred thousand people—two-thirds of the regional population—had been wiped out in a great epidemic. To this day, the tsetse fly, which also infests much of Kenya and the greater part of Tanzania, remains unrivaled as an impediment to human progress in East Africa. Yet there is reason to believe[2] that "fly", by eliminating susceptible animals, opened up an ecological niche for ground-dwelling primates and thereby permitted the debut of baboons and man; quite possibly it also discouraged early forms of man that had as much promise as *Homo sapiens* and very likely more. Tsetse has determined man's migration routes and settlements, and defended the interior from invasions from the coast; in regions like western Maasai Land in Kenya, where elimination of tsetse has attracted settlers of the politically powerful Luo and Kikuyu, or in Ruanda-Urundi, where the overthrow of the tall Tusi herdsmen by their Bantu serfs has permitted great areas of grassland to revert to tsetse bush, the fly still nags at the course of Africa.

I returned within the hour to the tree, where Hurxthal rose and came solemnly to meet me. Nancy, eyes wide in a face the color of magadi, was having cramps and feared she might be in labor. We were seven miles beyond our camp, and twenty miles from the Uaso Ngiro game post, which might or might not have a radio that worked; from there it was thirty miles more into Magadi. The first seven miles would be the worst, but all of this track was an ordeal for a girl who might be losing her first child. To calm her and rest her for the journey, it seemed best to make camp where we were. Lew worked unceasingly to soothe his wife and make her comfortable against the heat. Although she kept her head throughout, she was badly frightened, and with damned good reason, or so it seemed to me. Privately, I had lost hope for the child, and there was a period in the first few hours of that endless afternoon when I was very worried about Nancy, who never left the sickbed that we constructed in the back of the Land Rover. I racked my brain to make certain we understood what we would do and in what order in a crisis, at the same time marveling at our heedlessness in taking a pregnant girl so far from help. Most of all, I dreaded that my battered Land Rover would break down beyond repair at a crucial moment. In this gloomy hollow of sere thornbush, the gray rainless sky of African summer seemed to weigh upon the earth, I remembered the words of a girl born here in Tanzania: "Africa overwhelms me so, especially at twilight, that sometimes I burst into tears."

There is no wealth without children, Africans say, and children are especially precious to the Maasai. "The Kikuyu themselves told me how in the old times the Masai had thought it beneath them to intermarry with Kikuyu. But in our days the strange dying nation, to delay its final disappearance had had to come down in its pride, the Masai women have no children and the prolific young Kikuyu girls are in demand with the tribe."[3] On their fourth day of life, Maasai children are taken outside and presented to the sun, and in the days of the civil wars, so it is said, peace among the tribes was made when mothers from the opposing sides suckled one another's babies.

Legaturi, with an air of lofty detachment, was watching closely from beneath a large commiphora, the bark of which, boiled, is a Maasai medicine. His gestures made plain that Nancy's belly should be rubbed in a certain way, but unfortunately we could not understand him, and as for his commiphora infusion, we had nothing to cook with. Excepting a very light small tent and some canned food, our gear had all been left behind at the camp beside the stream.

By evening Nancy was calmer and more comfortable, despite her dread of the journey the next day. We heated some food tins in a fire, and lacking a lantern, went to bed at dark, the Hurxthals in the Land Rover, and I in their small tent under the tree. Legaturi, disdaining the offer of a place in the two-man tent, had made himself a shelter out of thorn branches, but soon he came tugging at the tent fly, murmuring excuses, and once inside, spat all over its triangular doorway of mosquito netting, to bless this transparent stuff against the passage of night animals. Near Leakey's camp, we had come upon a black-maned lion in the grass, and Legaturi, seated beside me, had hurled defiance at the king of beasts, splitting my ears with the blood-curdling whoops and chants used by the lion-killing moran of other days. The lion gazed at him, unmoved. When I drove closer, Legaturi subsided, grabbing up my binoculars and pressing them at me, imploring me to stop right there and take a picture: *"Simba! Simba mkubwa!"* (Big lion!) Closing the car window tight, he had shrunk into his blanket, glazed with fright. If Legaturi is a fair example, the agricultural Maasai have lost that aplomb with wild animals for which the tribe is so well known.

In the middle of the night, a rhino blundered into us. A rude *Chough! Chough! Chough!* at the quaking canvas brought us both upright, and Legaturi seized my knee in a famished grip as if fearful that l'Ojuju, the Hairy One, might rush out to do single combat with the huge night presence whose horn was but a few feet from our faces. He did not let go until the rhino wheeled and crashed away. "*Kifaru!*" Legaturi whispered, finding his voice at last. "*Kifaru mkubwa!*"

At daylight, slowly, the Land Rover jolted down off the Ngurumans, Nancy cradled in her husband's arms. Near our first camp we made tea, and for an hour or two she rested. Here Legaturi left us, extending a warm invitation—"*Karibu! Karibu! Karibu!*"—to visit him one day in his en-gang. Then we toiled onward, mile by slow mile, arriving at the Uaso Nyiro in the early afternoon. A professional hunter, Robert Reitnauer, camped there with clients on safari, was able to contact Nairobi by radio-telephone, and Frank Minot of the African Wildlife Leadership Foundation was waiting with an airplane at Magadi, where we arrived just before twilight. Nancy was flown out to Nairobi Hospital, and after a few days' rest was permitted to go home. (The baby was born on December 23, and on Christmas Day Nancy wrote me a letter "propped up in my Nairobi Hospital bed, plied with toast and marmalade, and just having handled and breast fed our daughter for the first time, I'm at a loss to describe my wonder and happiness. . . . She was literally my Christmas present . . . a small pink pumpkin-like creature looking remarkably like Lew.")

I made camp south of Magadi, on a ridge that rose from the white soda. In the sinking sun the flats were red and gray. I washed myself and washed my clothes and hung them from the limbs of a squat commiphora full of young skinks, and in moments the damp clothes crawled with wizened bees that came out of nowhere to suck at the precious moisture. The heat was awesome, as if the bleached grass all round had caught on fire, but the air was so dry that it was comfortable so long as one was naked and moved carefully. I made myself a cup of rum and sat on a rope camp stool under the tree, gazing out across the south end of Magadi toward the Nguruman

181

Escarpment and beyond, to the Loita Hills. Tomorrow I would walk the lunar shores of the great Lake Natron that I had seen so many times off in the distance.

Two winters before, in the Gol Mountains, Myles Turner and I had planned a foot safari over the Loita Hills, which are roadless and little known; George Schaller or Hans Kruuk and the wildlife photographer, Alan Root, might go as well. So far as Myles knew, nobody had ever attempted this trek, which he had dreamed about for many years: "One day I'll do it," he kept saying, as if forgetting that we had already made a plan. Our route would continue southward over the Ngurumans to the Sonjo villages, just across the Tanzania border, then down along the west shore of Lake Natron. A day would be taken to climb Ol Doinyo Lengai, after which we would continue into the Crater Highlands, passing by way of Embagai Crater, and coming out eventually at Nainokanoka or Ngorongoro. But this journey, potentially so much more exciting and rewarding than a shooting safari, had never come about, though Myles and I still talk about it, and hope it will.

The reasons given for the indefinite postponement of the foot safari—length of time involved, conflict of schedules, logistics, leave time, my own failure to maintain touch while away from Africa—were understandable enough, but perhaps there was a part of Myles that did not want the safari he had dreamed of for so long to be over and done with. For then some image of that epic Africa of hope and innocence that lay off there in the blue, the Africa of the ivory hunters, Selous and Neumann, Jim Sutherland and Karamoja Bell, would no longer lie safe in the past and future but in the reality of the present, and with the evaporation of the image, hope would end, and with it a sense of his own life too vital to relinquish. For Myles's tough laconic manner hides the romanticism of a man addicted fatally to the past.

A year ago, before the enterprise came all apart, I sensed that the Loita safari was a dream, and another man's dream at that, and attempted to make the journey in pieces, on my own. I went first to Lengai, for the Mountain of God was the beacon in this strangest and most beautiful of all regions that I have come across in Africa. Later, in the Crater Highlands, with a Maasai friend named Martin Mengoriki, I camped on the rim of Embagai, in the hope of going down into its crater. The rim was an alpine meadow dense with flowers, like a circlet around the cloud in the volcano, and under the cloud a crater lake lay in deep forest. All day we waited for a clearing wind, to locate a way down the steep sides, but instead the cloud overflowed onto the meadow, smothering the senses. Uneasy, Martin said: "It is so quiet," and was startled by the volume of his gentle voice: we could hear a mole rat chewing at the grass roots and the tiny wing flutter of a cisticola across the mist. In a bed of lavenders and yellows, cloud curling past the white bands of its ears, lay a big serval. The cat remained there a long moment, shifting its haunches, before sinking down into the flowers and away.

In the late afternoon, the meadows cleared. Not far off, a band of ravens connived in a dead haegenia, the lone, uncommon tree left at this altitude. Before the mists reclaimed it, I climbed the tree and with a panga chopped down dry limbs for a fire. Already, at twilight, it was very cold, but in this hour of changing weathers, odd solitary light shafts, fitful gusts, the mists were lifting, and treetops of the crater sides loomed through the cloud, then the crater floor, and finally the lake, two thousand feet below, where a herd of buffalo stood like dark outcrops on the shore. Out of the weathers fifteen miles away, the Mountain of God loomed once and withdrew; I glimpsed the ridge that I had climbed, down which that rhino had descended. Then the mists closed, and around the rim of Embagai the fire tones of aloes and red gladioli burned coldly in the cloud.

Two buffalo, tracing their old winding ruts, had ambled up into our campsite from the west. Confronted with the Land Rover, they stopped to study it a while, the last light glinting on their horns. Then they wheeled and rolled away, dropping from view; the mountain horizon, as dark came, was empty.

By morning, clouds had settled heavily into the crater, making the descent impossible. We returned south fifty miles to Ngorongoro across a waste of coarse tussock, wind and bitter cinder where the swirls of ash, puffing through each crack, burned nose and throat. In summer the moors are parched despite dark stagnant clouds that shroud the circle of old volcanoes, ten thousand feet and more, that in many trips across the Crater Highlands, summer and winter, I had never seen. The three villages here are the highest in Maasai Land, and once the car was caught in a tide of milling cattle, a maelstrom of shrouding dust and rolling eyes and a doomed bawling, as if at last the earth had tipped on end. At one time there was forest here, and water was more plentiful, but the Maasai have cut and burned the trees to make more pasture, as they have done also on the west slopes of the Mau Range, and so far they pay no heed at all to those who tell them they are ruining their country.

The three villages between volcanoes have some seventy people each, and because the moors are treeless, the villages are fenced with long split timbers brought up from the ravines; the bony staves, bent black on the barren sky, give a bleak aspect to the human habitations. But inside the stockade, out of the wind, the village called Ol Alilal is a snug place of sun-blown weeds and sheep bleats, warm manure scent, goat kids, new puppies, and grains spread upon a hide—the finger millet, eleusine, domesticated long ago in the highlands of Ethiopia. As in all Maasai villages, the corral is surrounded by low oval huts, ovens of dung stuck on a framework of bent saplings. We crouched to enter. The interiors are intricate, with small wicker-walled compartments, and the innermost chamber has a three-stone hearth and a small air vent for the smoke, with two raised beds inset in the wall, one for the father and mother and the other for children. The woman of the house was hospitable, perhaps because I was there with a Maasai; the next time we came, she said, she would prepare fresh blood-and-milk. Everyone was bold and cheerful, and though white travelers must be rare in this far place, they pretended to take no notice of me. Only the beaded infants stared through the dark circles of flies at their infected eyes. Ordinarily the eyes are never treated, so that many Maasai become blind. One pretty woman wore a necklace of lion claw and a bit of old leather that Martin said was dawa or medicine prescribed by the laibon, and a few trading cowries worn in hope of fertility, since the cowry aperture resembles the vagina.[4] In East Africa the cowry, which was brought here first from the Maldive Islands and had spread all across Africa by the fourteenth century, is used ceremonially in the first three of the great rites of passage, birth, circumcision, and marriage, the fourth rite being death.

Sun, heat, stillness were all one. The dying sun in the Ngurumans gave color to the cooking fire, and after dark came a hot wind that fanned night fires all around the horizon, and drove one tongue of flame onto the ridge above the lifeless lake. Though ready to break camp at a moment's notice, I slept poorly—the moon and wind and fire made me restless. But in a red dawn, the wind died again, and the fire sank into the grass, waiting for night.

South of Magadi the road scatters, and wandering tracks cross the white lake bed. There is water where the wading birds are mirrored, and in the liquid shimmer of the heat, a still wildebeest wavers in its own reflection. An hour later, from the west, the ghostly beast was still in sight; it had not moved.

The track winds southwest toward Shombole. Huge termitaria slouch here and there in the dry scrub, and over toward the Nguruman Escarpment, a whirlwind spins a plume of desert dust up the Rift's dark face into the smoky sky of East African summer. Eventually the track descends again, between the dead volcano and the marsh of Uaso Nyiro. In a water gleam that parts the fierce bright reeds, a woman and a man are bathing. The woman squats, her small shoulders demure, but the man stands straight as a gazelle and gazes, body shining, the archetypal man of Africa that I first saw in the Sudan.

The Shombole track comes to an end at three shacks under the volcano, where a duka serves the outlying Maasai with beads and wire for ornament, red cloth, sweet drinks, and cocoa. I gave a ride to a young morani who guided me with brusque motions through the bush to a stony cattle trail that winds between hill and marsh, around Shombole. Farther on, we picked up two Maasai women, and all four of us were squashed into the front when, in the full heat of the desert afternoon, on hot rocky ground at the mud edge of a rotting swamp in the lowest and hottest pit of the Rift Valley floor, my faithful Land Rover, thirty-five miles from Magadi and ninety-five beyond Nairobi, gave a hellish clang and, dragging its guts over the stones, lurched to a halt.

In a bad silence, the Maasai women thanked me and departed. The boy stood by, less out of expectation of reward or even curiosity, I decided, than some sense of duty toward a stranger in Maasai Land. Squatting on my heels and swatting flies, I peered dizzily at the heavy iron shaft, the sand and stone and thorn stuck to raw grease where the shaft had sheared at the universal coupling, cutting off the transmission of power to the rear wheels. In front-wheel drive, the car would move forward weakly, but my limited tools were not able to detach the revolving shaft from the transmission: dragging and clanging in an awful din of steel and rocks, it threatened to shake the car to pieces.

185

To cool my nerves, I drank a quart of Tusker beer. The Land Rover had picked a poor place to collapse, but at least it had got me to my destination, and the sun if not the heat would soon be gone. Any time now, the airplane of Douglas-Hamilton, coming to meet me, would be landing on the bare mud flats at the north end of Natron. Tomorrow we were to climb Shombole, and after that, if no repairs seemed possible, Iain could fly out to Magadi and leave word of my straits and whereabouts. But as it happened, Iain and Oria were never to appear: they had sent word to Nairobi that has not reached me to this day. Next morning I rigged a whole series of rope slings, held in place by stay lines from the side, that carried the rotating shaft just off the ground, although they burned through regularly from friction. Setting off at sunrise at three miles an hour, with the frequent stops to repair or replace the sling giving the straining car an opportunity to cool off, I arrived in two hours at the duka. A length of soft iron wire presented me by the proprietor was better than the rope, but not much better, and the last of it wore through as I reached Magadi in mid-afternoon, having made not less than fifteen trips beneath the car, in terrific heat, measuring my length in the fine volcanic ash that a hellish wind impacted in hair, lungs, and fingernails. The kind Asian manager of the Magadi Store and his driver-mechanic replaced the sheared bevel pinion with an ingenious makeshift rig that would see the car safely to Nairobi, but all of this still lay ahead as I stood there looking as stupid as I felt under the gaze of that young herdsman by the shores of Natron.

The time had come for a hard look at my old car's parts and contents. This Land Rover that has seen me so faithfully through East Africa is essentially an enclosed pickup truck with no back seats, preceded everywhere by two racks bolted to its front bumper; each rack holds four gallons of spare gasoline. The broad flat hood or bonnet is designed for a spare wheel, but as a precaution against theft I carry the spare in the back, leaving the bonnet free for pressing plants and preparing food. Inside, the steel shelves that flank the wheel hold books and maps, an adjustable wrench, screwdrivers, pliers, knife, long-beam flashlight, distilled water for the batteries, electrical tape, disinfectant, band-aids, and a roll of tissue for binocular lenses, window-wiping, oil sump dip stick, doubtful forks, and bottoms. There are three seats in the front, and a compartment under the left seat (the steering wheel is on the right) holds a foot pump,

186

tire bars, tube patches, spare fan belt, coil, spark plugs, points, distributor cap and condenser, a siphon tube, a tube of stop-leak for the radiator (raw egg white may be tried in an emergency), yellow elephant soap for fuel line leaks, lacquer thinner (emergency nostrum for failed clutch, when dumped into clutch housing), and four quarts of motor oil. Behind the seats is a large lever jack, a shovel, a long engine crank in case of battery failure, and a panga or machete, useful for meat, firewood, and chopping brush to pile under the wheels when mired.

In the days when this car belonged to the Serengeti Research Institute, the roof was fitted with two hinged viewing hatches that open upward and fall flat on the car roof, one forward and one back, for passengers standing on the truck bed. The hatches permit the entry of fresh air at night, if one is sleeping in the car, and when required a mosquito net can be suspended. Across the narrow benches on each side, which cramp the floor space, I have laid loose boards, from the front seat back to the rear door. The spare wheel is kept beneath the boards, and also rope, insecticide, and kerosene, a two-by-four used as a jack base in sand or mud, an all-purpose tin washbasin, two feet in diameter, bought for sixty cents in the Arusha marketplace, and a spare six gallons of water. On top are two mattresses with bedding and mosquito net, a tin chest of provisions, a carton containing kerosene lamp, stove, pot, pan, teapot, and utensils; a small duffel, a rope-seat stool, a plant press. At night, should space be needed, these things may be stowed beneath the car or in the front, and the two mattresses laid side by side, and when special cargo or many people must be transported, the boards are taken up and stacked, for I have carried at one time or another a whole butchered zebra, drying elephant ears, unnumerable townspeople and tribesmen, tortoises, birds, chameleons, and a diseased baboon.

In retrospect, I would recommend this additional equipment: a spare half-shaft, an asbestos filament lantern, a spare fuel pump (or a spare diaphragm, if you are a good mechanic), and a nineteenth-century tract called *Shifts and Expedients of Camp Life*, which includes such critical information as the proper method of mounting a small cannon on the hind end of a camel, to repel boarders and deal crisply with shifta or other unsavory individuals who might be gaining on one from the rear.

*

Since the disabled car was inland from the lake, it seemed best to walk the last mile to the flats, to greet Iain and Oria and to make certain that I was not overlooked; already I was listening for the droning of the motor that would draw to a point the misty distances down toward Lengai. Accompanied by the morani, I followed a cattle trail between the marsh and a thorny rock strangely swollen by thick pink blossoms of the desert rose. Near the mouth of the Uaso Nyiro, green reeds give way to open flats where the Natron leaves a crust crisscrossed by ostrich tracks. Here the young warrior, mounting the rock, made a grand sweeping gesture of his cape toward the horizons of Maasai Land, and sighed with all his being. The red and blue beads swinging from his ears stood for sun and water, but now the sun was out of balance with the rain, and the grass was thin. The Maasai speak of the benevolent Black God who brings rain, and the malevolent Red God who begrudges it, the Black God living in dark thunderheads and the Red in the merciless dry-season sun; Black God and Red are different tempers of Ngai, for God is embodied in the rain and the fierce heat, besides ruling the great pastures of the sky. Looming thunder is feared: the Red God seeks to pierce the Black God's kingdoms, in hope of bringing harm to man. But in distant thunder the Maasai hear the Black God saying, "Let man be. . . ."

From where we stood, awed by the view, white flats extended a half-mile to the water's edge, where the heat waves rose in a pink fire of thousands upon thousands of flamingos. All around the north end of the lake the color shimmered, and for some distance down both shores; on the west shore, under the dark Sonjo escarpments, an upside-down forest was reflected. Southeast, the outline of Gelai was a phantom mountain in an amorphous sky, and in the south, the lake vanished in brown vapors that shrouded Ol Doinyo Lengai.

In this somber kingdom of day shadows and dead smokes, the fresh pinks of flamingos and the desert rose appeared unnatural. What belonged here were those tracks of giant birds, like black crosses in the crystalline white soda, and this petrified white bone dung of hyena, and the hieroglyph of a gazelle in quest of salt that had followed some dim impulse far out onto the flats. I remembered the Grant's gazelles on the Chalbi Desert, and the rhino that had climbed Lengai, and the wildebeest at a dead halt for want of impulse, in the shimmer of the soda lake, at noon. What drives such animals away from life-giving conditions into the wasteland—what happens in those rigid clear-eyed heads? How did the hippopotamus find its way up into the Crater Highlands, to blunder into the waters of Ngorongoro? Today one sees them there with wonder, encircled by steep walls, and the mystery deepens when a fish eagle plummets to the springs east of the lake and rises once more against the sky, in its talons a gleam of unknown life from the volcano.

We walked out into the silence of the flats. Somewhere on the mud, our footprints crossed the border of Tanzania, for Natron lies entirely in that country. I listened for the airplane but there was nothing, only the buzzing of these birds that fed with their queer heads upside down, straining diatoms and algae from the stinking waters even as they squirted it with the guano that kept the algae reproducing—surely one of the shortest and most efficient life chains in all nature, at once exhilarating and oppressive in the mindlessness of such blind triumphal life in a place so poisonous and dead. A string of flamingos rose from the pink gases, restoring sharpness to the sky, then sank again into the oblivion of their millions.

Twilight was coming. The boy pointed to a far en-gang under Shombole. "*Aia*," he said, by way of parting—So be it—and stalked away in fear of the African night, his red cape darkening against the white. "*Aia*," I said, watching him go. Soon he vanished under the volcano. This age-set of moran may be the last, for the Maasai of Kenya, upset at being left behind by tribes they once considered worthless, voted this year to discontinue the moran system and send young Maasai to school. But in Maasai Land all change comes slowly, whether in Kenya or Tanzania. The month before, in the region of Ol Alilal, in the Crater Highlands, there was a new age-set of circumcised boys dressed in the traditional black garments bound with broad bead belts and wearing the spectral white paint around the eyes that signifies death and rebirth as a man, and on their shaved heads, arranged on a wood frame that looked from afar like an informal halo, black ostrich plumes danced in the mountain wind. When their hair grew out again, the boys would be young warriors, perhaps the last age-set of moran.

One of the Ol Alilal moran was very sick, and we took him in to the government dispensary at Nainokanoka. This tall boy of seventeen or eighteen could no longer walk; I carried his light body in my arms

189

to the dark shack where to judge from his face, he thought that he would die. Yet here at least he had a chance that he might not have had at Ol Alilal. Though the Maasai have little faith in witchcraft, they recognize ill provenance and evil spirits, and a person dying is removed outside the fences so that death will not bring the village harm. Eventually the body is taken to the westward toward the setting sun, and laid on its left side with knees drawn up, head to the north and face to the east, right arm crossing the breast and left cushioning the head. There it is left to be dealt with by hyenas. Should someone die inside a hut, then the whole village must be moved, and it is said that the people listen for the howl of the hyena, and establish the new village in that direction. The Maasai are afraid of death, though not afraid to die.

For a long time I stood motionless on the white desert, numbed by these lowering horizons so oblivious of man, understanding at last the stillness of the lone animals that stand transfixed in the distances of Africa. Perhaps because I was alone, and therefore more conscious of my own insignificance under the sky, and aware, too, that the day was dying, and that the airplane would not appear, I felt overwhelmed by the age and might of this old continent, and drained of strength: all seemed pointless in such emptiness, there was nowhere to go. I wanted to lie flat out on my back on this almighty mud, but instead I returned slowly into Kenya, pursued by the mutter of primordial birds. The flamingo sound, rising and falling with the darkening pinks of the gathering birds, was swelling again like an oncoming rush of motley wings—birds, bats, ancient flying things, thick insects.

The galumphing splosh of a pelican, gathering tilapia from the fresh-water mouth of the Uaso Nyiro, was the first sound to rise above the wind of the flamingos. Next came a shrill whooping of the herdsmen, hurrying the last cattle across delta creeks to the bomas in the foothills of Shombole. A Maasai came running from the hills to meet me, bearing tidings of two dangerous lions—"*Simba! Simba mbili!* "—that haunted this vicinity. He asked nothing of me except caution, and as soon as his warning was delivered, ran back a mile or more in the near-darkness to the shelter of his en-gang. Perhaps the earliest pioneers were greeted this way almost everywhere by the wild peoples—the thought was saddening, but his act had made me happy.

I built a fire and broiled the fresh beef I had brought for three, to keep it from going bad, and baked a potato in the coals, and fried tomatoes, and drank another beer, all the while keeping an eye out for bad lions. I also made tea and boiled two eggs for breakfast, to dispense with fire-making in the dawn. As yet I had no energy to think about tomorrow, much less attempt makeshift repairs; the cool of first light would be time enough for that. Moving slowly so as not to stir the heat, I brushed my teeth and rigged my bed roll and climbed out on the car roof, staring away over Lake Natron. I was careful to be quiet: the night has ears, as the Maasai say.

From the Crater Highlands rose the Southern Cross; the Pleiades, which the Maasai associate with rains, had waned in early June. July is the time of wind and quarrels, and now, in August, the grass was dry and dead. In August, September, and October, called the Months of Hunger, the people pin grass to their clothes in hope of rain, for grass is sign of prosperity and peace, but not until the Pleiades returned, and the southeast monsoon, would the white clouds come that bring the precious water. (The Mbugwe of the southern flats of Lake Manyara resort to rainmakers, and formerly, in time of drought, so it is said, would sacrifice an unblemished black bull, then an unblemished black man, and finally the rainmaker himself.)[5]

The light in my small camp under Shombole was the one light left in all the world. Staring up at the black cone that filled the night sky to the east, I knew I would never climb it. There was a long hard day ahead with nothing certain at the end of it, and I had no heart for the climb alone, especially here in this sullen realm that had held me at such a distance. The ascent of Lengai and the descent into Embagai Crater had both been failures, and the great volcanoes of the Crater Highlands had remained lost in the clouds. At Natron, my friends had failed to come and my transport had broken down, and tomorrow I would make a slow retreat. And perhaps this came from the pursuit of some fleeting sense of Africa, seeking to fix in time the timeless, to memorize the immemorial, instead of moving gently, in awareness, letting the sign, like the crimson bird, become manifest where it would.

From where I watched, a sentinel in the still summer, there rose and fell the night highlands of two countries, from the Loita down the length of the Ngurumans to the Sonjo scarps that overlook Lake Natron. In the Loita, so the Maasai say, lives Enenauner, a hairy giant, one side flesh, the other stone, who devours mortal men lost in the forests; Enenauner carries a great club, and is heard tokking on trees as it moves along.[6] A far hyena summoned the night feeders, and flamingos in crescents moved north across a crescent moon toward Naivasha and Nakuru. Down out of the heavens came their calls, a remote electric sound, as if in this place, in such immensities of silence, one had heard heat lightning.

Toward midnight, in the Sonjo Hills, there leapt up two sudden fires. Perhaps this was sign of the harvest festival, Mbarimbari, for these were not the grass fires that leap along the night horizons in the dry season; the twin flames shone like leopard's eyes from the black hills. At this time of year God comes to the Sonjo from Ol Doinyo Lengai, and a few of their ancient enemies, the Maasai, bring goats to be slaughtered at Mbarimbari, where they howl to Ngai for rain and children.

The Sonjo, isolated from the world, know that it is coming to an end. Quarrels and warfare will increase, and eventually the sky will be obscured by a horde of birds, then insect clouds, and finally a shroud of dust. Two suns will rise from the horizons, one in the east, one in the west, as a signal to man that the end of the world is near. At the ultimate noon, when the two suns meet at the top of the sky, the earth will shrivel like a leaf, and all will die.

10. At Gidabembe

The Abatwa are very much smaller people than all small people; they go under the grass and sleep in anthills; they go in the mist; they live in the up country in the rocks. . . . Their village is where they kill game; they consume the whole of it, and go away

an anonymous Zulu[1]

Hamana nale kui,
Nale kui.
Here we go round,
Go round.

a Hadza dance[2]

One winter day in 1969, returning to Seronera from Arusha, Myles Turner flew around the south side of the Crater Highlands, which lay hidden in its black tumulus of clouds. The light plane skirted Lake Manyara and the dusty flats of the witch-ridden Mbugwe, then crossed Mbulu Land, on the Kainam Plateau. Soon it passed over a great silent valley. "That's the Yaida," Turner told me. "That's where those Bushman people are, the Watindiga." Down there in that arid and inhospitable stillness, cut off from a changing Africa by the ramparts of the Rift, last bands of the Old People turned their heads toward the hard silver bird that crossed their sky. There was no smoke, no village to be seen, nor any sign of man.

Later that winter, at Ndala, Douglas-Hamilton had suggested a safari to Tindiga Land, where his friend Peter Enderlein had lived alone for several years, and was in touch with wild Tindiga still living in the bush. But Iain was never able to get away, and a year had passed before I crossed paths with Enderlein in Arusha, and arranged to visit his Yaida Chini game post in the summer. In July of 1970 I picked up Aaron Msindai, a young Isanzu from the Mweka College of Wildlife Management at Moshi, who had been assigned to Yaida Chini. We loaded Aaron's kit into the back of the Land Rover—a rifle and an iron bed, clothes, lantern, fuel, food for a month—and

193

headed west, spending that night at Manyara, and at seven the next morning climbing the Rift wall into the clouds of the Crater Highlands. In the dense mist, trees shifted evilly, and slow cowled figures with long staves, dark faces hidden in the gloom, moved past the ghostly fields of maize and wheat. These are the agricultural Mbulu of the so-called Irakw cluster, a group still unclassified in the ethnographic surveys, whose archaic language, related to Hamitic, suggests that they have been here in the Highlands a very long time, perhaps well before the Iron Age. Like the Hamitic tribes, the Mbulu practice circumcision and clitoridectomy, but they lack the age-set system and other customs of modern Hamites such as the Galla. Doubtless they have mingled with the waves of Bantu and Nilotic peoples who came later, but many retain a Caucasoid cast of feature: the volatile narrow faces of the men, especially, are the faces that one sees in Ethiopia. The Mbulu live in pits dug into hillsides and covered over with roofs of mud and dung; in former days these pit dwellings or tembes, like low mounds in the tall grass, are said to have hidden the people from the Maasai. Today the tembes give way gradually to tin-roofed huts.

At Karatu, a track turns south onto the fertile Kainam Plateau that forms a southern spur of the Crater Highlands. Off the main road, the Mbulu are not used to cars—in the fifty miles between Karatu and Mbulu. I met no other vehicle—and the old run disjointedly along the red sides of the road, while the young jump behind the rocks and bushes. Today was Saba Saba (Seven Seven Day, commemorating the founding of TANU, the Tanganyika African National Union Party, on the seventh day of the seventh month, 1954), and near Mbulu, the track was filled with people streaming along toward the settlement. All were hooded against wind and rain, and from behind, in their blowing shrouds, they evoked the migration of those ancestors of many centuries ago who came down out of the north into a land of Stone Age hunters, the Twa, the Small People, most of whom, like the pit-dwelling Gumba found by the Kikuyu, have vanished into the earth.

From Mbulu a rough track heads west, dropping eventually off the Kainam Plateau into the Yaida Valley. It passes a fresh lake called Tlavi, edged by papyrus and typha, a rare pretty place of swallows and blowing reeds in a landscape of sloping grain fields, meadows, and soft sheltering hills that shut away the emptiness of Africa. The

194

lake turned slowly in the lifting mists, a prism for the first rays of sun to pierce the morning clouds on the Crater Highlands. Beyond Tlavi the road rises into sun and sky and wanders along the westward scarp where highland clouds are parting; below lie the pale plains of a still valley, fifty miles long and ten across, like a world forgotten in the desert mountains. A rough rock track winding downhill is crossed by two klipspringer, yellow and gray; they bound away through low combretum woodland. Under the rim, out of the southeast wind, the air is hot. A horde of flies pours through the air vents, and Aaron strikes at them. He hisses, "Tsetse!"

In the wake of tsetse control programs that ended a few years ago, the Mbulu, already pressed for space due to population increase, overgrazing, and crude farming practices that have badly eroded the Kainam Plateau, began to move down into the Yaida Valley, while the Bantu Isanzu seeped in from the south. From the south also came fierce Barabaig herdsmen, and all of these people compete with the Tindiga and wild animals for the limited water. At the same time, the government, embarrassed that a Stone Age group should exist in the new Africa, has attempted to settle the hunters in two villages, one at Yaida Chini, the other farther west at an American Lutheran mission station called Munguli. Some three hundred now live in the settlements, and a few hundred more are still hiding in the bush.

Today, Tindiga, Mbulu, Isanzu, and Barabaig are all present at Yaida Chini, which may be the one place in East Africa where its four basic language families (Khoisan or click-speech, Hamitic, Bantu, and Nilotic) come together. Yaida Chini is a small dusty settlement strewn along under the line of giant figs by the Yaida River, and a group of Africans celebrating Saba Saba at the pombe bar milled out to greet the Land Rover as it rumbled down out of the hills. These people were mostly Isanzu, barefoot and ragtag in European shirts and pants, but to one side stood a dark thick-set pygmoid girl, and Aaron said, "Tindiga." The girl had a large head with prognathous jaw and large antelope eyes in thick black skin, and by western standards she was very ugly. Unlike the yellow-eyed peasants, who offered shouts as evidence of sophistication, she came up softly and stared seriously, mouth closed, like a shy animal. "Tindiga have a very hard tongue," Aaron told me, ignoring his pombe-drunk people. "My tongue is not the same as theirs, but when I speak, they know." It is Aaron's tribe, the Isanzu, that has assimilated most of the southern

195

Tindiga, and few are left who do not have an Isanzu parent; even "Tindiga" is an Isanzu name for a people whose true name is Hadza or Hadzapi.

Because of tsetse and the scarcity of water, the Hadza once had the Yaida to themselves, and scarcely anything was known of them before 1924, when a district officer of what had become, after World War I, the Tanganyika Territory, reported on a people who hid from Europeans and were even less affected than the Bushmen by the world beyond: . . . "a wild man, a creature of the bush, and as far as I can see he is incapable of becoming anything else. Certainly he does not desire to become anything else, for nothing will tempt him to leave his wilderness or to abandon his mode of living. He asks nothing from the rest of us but to be left alone. He interferes with no one, and does his best to insure that no one shall interfere with him."[3] A few years later, the Hadza were inspected by an authority on the Bushmen, who stated in the peremptory tones of colonial scholarship that "there must have been some connection between this black ape-like tribe and the small delicately built yellow man,"[4] whose habits, thoughts, and language structure seemed so similar.

This second authority, Miss Bleek, agrees with the first one, Mr. Bagshawe, that the typical tribesman was very black, short, thick-set, ugly and ill-smelling, with prognathous jaw and large splay feet. The blackness and the cast of jaw were most pronounced in the "purest" specimens, for even in Bleek's day, many Hadza in the south part of their range had an Isanzu parent. She does not comment on Bagshawe's contention that the Hadza is "intensely stupid and naturally deceitful" as well as "lazy," that he "does not understand why he should be investigated . . . it is more than probable that he will lie." Yet Bagshawe feels constrained to note that the Hadza "worries but little about the future and not at all about the past," that he is "happy and envies no man." Bagshawe's perplexed tone is echoed by Bleek, who observed that this unprepossessing people often danced in simple pleasure: *"Hamana nale kui,"* they sang. *"Nale kui."*

Here we go round,
Go round.

The early descriptions of the Hadza bring to mind the small men with large bows and strange speech who were driven high onto Mt. Kilimanjaro by the Chagga, and also the "people of small stature and

196

hideous features," as L. S. B. Leakey describes[5] the Gumba aborigines found by the Kikuyu in the Kenya Highlands. But in the years since they were first reported, the Hadza have mixed increasingly with the Isanzu, who may eventually absorb them as Bantu tribes have been absorbing hunter-gatherers for two millenniums. A recent student, Dr. James Woodburn, does not believe that a characteristic physical type is distinguishable any longer, nor does he accept Miss Bleek's assumption of a linguistic link between these people and the Bushmen (although the link between the click-speaking Sandawe, an acculturated tribe of south Tanzania, and the pastoral Bushman relatives known as the Hottentots is clearly established). On no evidence whatsoever, one is tempted to speculate that the Hadza may represent a relict group of pre-Bantu Negroids of the Stone Age, although there is no proof that the Hadza are a Stone Age remnant, or a remnant at all—very probably, they are as numerous as they ever were. They may even be regressive rather than primitive, a group cast out long ago from a more complex civilization, though their many affinities with the Bushmen make this unlikely. Probably we shall never come much closer to the truth than the people's own account of Hadza origins:

Man, say the Hadza, descended to earth on the neck of a giraffe, but more often they say that he climbed down from a baobab. The Hadza themselves came into being in this way: a giant ancestor named Hohole lived in Dungiko with his wife Tsikaio, in a great hall under the rocks where Haine, who is God, the Sun, was not able to follow. Hohole was a hunter of elephants, which were killed with one blow of his stick and stuck into his belt. Sometimes he walked one hundred miles and returned to the cave by evening with six elephants. One day while hunting, Hohole was bitten by a cobra in his little toe. The mighty Hohole died. Tsikaio, finding him, stayed there five days feeding on his leg, until she felt strong enough to carry the body to Masako. There she left it to be devoured by birds. Soon Tsikaio left the cave and went to live in a great baobab. After six days in the baobab, she gave birth to Konzere, and the children of Tsikaio and Konzere are the Hadza.[6] "The Hadza," as the people say, "is us."

At the west end of the settlement, downriver, Peter Enderlein has built a house. At the sound of the motor, he came out on his veranda, a tall bare-legged man in shorts, boots wide apart, hands stuck in his hip pockets. We went immediately on an inspection of the ostrich pens, where he is raising an experimental flock for plumes and skins and meat. (In the wild, there is a heavy loss of eggs and chicks to predators of all descriptions, including lions, which are fond of playing with the eggs.) With their omnivorous habits and adaptations to arid country, ostrich could be domesticated in the Yaida, where tsetse and a shortage of surface water—the annual rainfall is less than twenty inches—are serious obstacles to agriculture and livestock. Enderlein, who is employed to investigate the valley's resources, would like to try game ranching here, but he has received little support for this scheme or any other, and for the moment must content himself with shooting the animals instead. Fresh meat is sold cheaply to the local people, or dried for sale elsewhere as biltong; the valuable common animal is the zebra, and the sale of zebra hides to wholesalers is the game post's main source of income.

Pending approval of his projects, Enderlein spends most of his time supplying food for the impounded Hadza, who are not supposed to leave the settlement, much less revert to their old lives in the bush. But hunters have always made the transition to agriculture with the greatest reluctance (the Ik of the north Uganda hills are an exception), and as a rule, the people will consume immediately any livestock or maize seed that is given them, and beat their hoe blades into arrowheads. Neither the dry climate nor their temperament lends itself to tilling, and in consequence they do little but drink pombe. This enforced idleness and dependence will certainly lead to their utter disintegration. Until they can come to agriculture of their own accord, Enderlein is trying to persuade the government to establish the Yaida Valley as a game reserve in which Hadza would be hired as trackers, game scouts, and hunters in a game-cropping scheme like the one that gave work to the Ariangulo elephant hunters in the region of Tsavo. Meanwhile, settlement by outsiders would be concentrated instead of scattered at random over the landscape, destroying thousands of square miles of wildlife habitat for the sake of a few shambas that cut off the water points. The Yaida has the last important population of greater kudu in north Tanzania, in addition to all the usual trophy animals, and as a game reserve, would receive income from game-cropping and hunting fees, which at present, due to lack of roads, are negligible. There are old rock paintings in the hills, many still doubtless undiscovered, and Eyasi Man, the Rhodesioid contemporary of the Neanderthalers, was dug up near Mangoła in 1935 by

198

a German named Kohl-Larsen, who also found an Australopithecine here in 1939, two decades before the better publicized *Australopithecus* was turned up by the Leakeys at Olduvai Gorge. All that is needed to encourage tourists is a good track into the north end of the valley from the main road across the Crater Highlands.

Although he has submitted to the government a careful analysis of game numbers and potential in the valley and an imaginative program of resource management, and although Tanzania's astute president Julius Nyerere is said to agree that the Hadza might come more readily to civilization through game-cropping than agriculture, Enderlein's plans have been regularly aborted by the district politicians, who have replaced European civil servants almost everywhere, and who take care not to approve or disapprove any project of a white man lest they expose themselves to the ambitions of their peers. As in other new African nations, the government endorses the principle of conservation, since conservation seems important to those western countries which are helping it in other ways. But most educated Africans care little about wild animals, which are vectors of the tsetse fly, a threat to crops and human life, and a competitor of livestock, and are also identified emotionally with the white man, white hunters, white tourists, and a primitive past which the new Africans wish to forget. As for the Hadzapi, they are the last tribe in Tanzania that is not administered and taxed, and the sooner they vanish, the better. Like the Twa, Bushman, and Dorobo, the small hunters are looked down upon by their own countrymen, and most of those who come into the settlement soon flee back to their former life of dignity and independence.

Of the Maasai, President Nyerere has remarked quite rightly that the government cannot afford to keep part of its people as a human zoo for tourists, and the same could be said about the Hadza: the time of the hunter is past, and will never return. Yet to judge from wild peoples I have seen in South America and New Guinea, the Hadza would be better left alone until a choice that they can make naturally is provided, for this people is acknowledged by all who have met them to be healthy and happy, with no history of epidemic or famine, and able to satisfy all needs in a few hours of each day. Modern medicine, motor transport, radios, and even shoes may be crucial to the poor man, whose wants are endless, self-perpetuating, whose every acquisition means that he cannot afford something else.

199

The wants of the primitive are few, since he does not envy what he knows nothing of. Poverty and the inferior status that await the acculturated Hadza is no alternative to bush life and the serenity of the old ways, and to take this from him by exposing him to a "progress" he cannot share is to abuse his innocence and do him harm.

But Enderlein is accused of wishing to keep this people in the Stone Age "as the Americans wish for the Maasai," and told not to give game work to idle Hadza, since the government is committed to a national program of agriculture. Tsetse control is to be resumed, and the people sent out to girdle and kill the "useless" tsetse-harboring acacias that keep the valley from turning to a desert, and ever more outsiders are encouraged to settle the Yaida even though two crops out of three are lost to drought, even though the land is blowing away under the sharp hoofs of the cattle.

Enderlein showed me the hard bare flats in the grasslands that spread west to the hills called Giyeda Bárakh. "Ten years ago," he said, "the people walked a long way around the grove where my camp is now, there were so many rhino, and they still speak of the great herds of eland and elephant moving through. Ten years from now, this whole valley will be a desert." He spoke sadly of his abandoned projects, of all the potential of the Yaida, of the rock paintings and other mysteries of this region that is still so unexplored—he has never found time to go down into Isanzu Land, where there are caves containing great log drums too enormous to be moved. According to the Isanzu, the drums had been built in an older time, by an older people; one thinks of the oracle drums of the great Bantu kingdoms of the lake country. The Isanzu are superstitious about the drums and keep them hidden.

Enderlein is a handsome Swede with a young officer's moustache and a mouth broken on one side by a fist of long ago. Though tall and strong, his eyes are restless, he looks haunted and tired; the solitude and frustration of his work are wearing him down. Either he commits more time that will probably be wasted, or he abandons three years of hard lonely work and all hope, as he sees it, for the Yaida. "I think it's the loveliest place in Africa. And its almost an ecological unit, too, much more so than the Serengeti—almost all its animals are non-migratory, or would be if they'd let them get to water. I *hate* to give up, but I'm thirty-one now, and I'm getting nowhere; I just can't waste my life here."

200

The greatest present threat to the Yaida Valley is the cattle of the Barabaig, a pastoral people from the region of Mt. Hanang and the Barabaig Plain, fifty miles to the southeast. On Saba Saba, there were numbers of lean Barabaig in the settlement, drinking pombe with their traditional antagonists, the Isanzu. They are a tall, handsome people whose dress and customs resemble those of the Maasai, and on the basis of language, they are usually linked to the Nandi, who are thought to have displaced them from the region of Mt. Elgon, on the Kenya-Uganda border, about two hundred and fifty years ago. But little is known of the Barabaig, who appear to have a strong Hamitic mix; their own tradition is that they are related to the Mbulu, and that both groups came south from the shores of Lake Natron. Such names as Barabaig, Hanang, and Giyeda Barakh evoke the northern deserts, as do such habits as the cutting of trophies from the bodies of human enemies, a custom of the Danakil of Ethiopia. In any case, they display all the simplehearted ferocity of the desert nomads, and to the Maasai are known as Il-man'ati, "the Enemy," a name reserved for a worthy foe whose warriors, unlike those of the Bantu, are entitled to extend a handful of grass to the Maasai in a plea for mercy. The Mangati, as they are generally known, were once scattered by attacks of the Maasai, but more recently have withstood Maasai encroachment from the west of Lake Eyasi, and have matched them raid for raid; it is their faith that ten Barabaig will overwhelm twenty Maasai. Being farther from the reach of the authorities, their moran have retained the custom of killing a lion in sign of manhood, or a man, for that matter, and what are known as "Barabaig spear-blooding murders" have made them a great source of chagrin to government and neighbors alike. Those murdered are "enemies of the people"[7]—the real or potential thieves of Barabaig cattle, a very broad category which includes all lions and strangers, as well as the mothers of thieves as yet unborn.

One night not long ago in Yaida Chini, a young Hadza girl was pierced through the lungs by a spear hurled from behind. Since the hard-drinking Mangati are the only ones with spears and the wish to use them, it is thought here that the girl was fleeing a Mangati admirer who was unable to resist a running target. The dying girl was discovered by Enderlein's cook who, interpreting her gasps as evidence of helpless drunkenness, took speedy advantage of his opportunity and raped her; it is hard to imagine the poor creature's last conclusions

201

on the nature of her fellow man. The cook, himself drunk, got covered with blood, in which condition he was apprehended, and since no one has spoken up for him, he may stay in jail indefinitely, and perhaps be hung, for a crime of which nobody thinks him guilty.

Last September a Yaida Chini game scout, accompanied by three unarmed companions, caught some Barabaig with a dead giraffe and was unwise enough to attempt an arrest. Outraged, the moran pursued the four for three miles or more, trapping them finally in a cave, where they laid siege all night. In the morning, as the game scout came to the end of his ammunition, the warriors departed. Shortly afterwards they lost one of their number to an elephant that they had actually attacked with spears, but they were never arrested. This age-set of moran has stalked the Yaida for several years, passing through on poaching raids and raids into Maasai Land. "Their habit of killing people and cutting ears, nose, fingers, etc., off the bodies might sound exotic and interesting to somebody faraway from Mangati Land," Enderlein wrote in September, 1969, in a plea for help from the Game Department, "but for my Game Scouts and myself who have to live here and move around where these people are to be found this habit is rather disturbing. Our number is quite small already, and before it is reduced any further we would like to ask for assistance to deal with this dangerous situation."

At sunset the hot wind died, and the dust settled in the stillness; the western hills above Lake Eyasi glowed in a dusty desert sun. In Enderlein's grove the yellow-wing bats hung from the thorns in silhouette, flitted off one by one to meet the dark, while to roosts in the fat figs by the river came companies of storks and vultures, sacred ibis, a solitary pelican, sailing onto the high branches with thick wing thumps, hollow bill clack, and guttural weird protest.

At dark, the yard filled with drunken people, come to invite the white man to a party. In rural villages of East Africa, pombe-drinking consumes half the people's time and money, and the less sophisticated they are, the more hopeless they become. In his concern for the Hadza, Enderlein is trying to get the Mbulu district council to restrict the sale of pombe in this settlement: "We have seven pombe parties at Yaida Chini every week, and the men do their very best to attend all of them." But he knows perfectly well that a restriction is of small value, since anyone can brew the stuff at home.

In an Isanzu hut, we squatted on stools in the dim light and drank from a communal calabash of pombe, which at its best has a woody astringent taste and at its worst beggars description. Y-supports held up the roof beams of the flat-topped hut, and the walls were made of grass and mud caked over with dried dung. The smoke and soft voices, the hunched dark forms catching the ember light on gleaming foreheads, the eyes, the warmth, the slow hands at the hearth protected all there against the emptiness and the cold stars, night sorcery and the hyena riders. Later, the Isanzu danced to four big drums of hide and wood played by swift hands and a tin disc beaten in two-stroke rhythm with a stick, while a chanting old man was answered by fierce chorus. Here, well east of the African lakes, was the echo of the Congo and West Africa. The pounding went on and on and on, and the dry valley quaked with sound like a beaten hide, and faraway on the Giyeda Barakh the night sky glowed in a flame twenty miles long, as if the whole country would go up in fire.

Toward midnight, in a sudden silence of the drums, the yelling Africans cursed the white men, the Wazungu, who had gone to bed. One man threw something at the house that banged on the wall and fell to the veranda.

In the morning, Enderlein is exhausted. Lately he has had great trouble sleeping; his eyes twitch, and he does everything with violence. Carving a bird, he seizes the whole carcass in his hand and slings the pieces onto plates. Hunting on the plains, he yanks his car too hard, too fast, and he seems careless with his rifle though he is not. Catching himself, or realizing he has been perceived, he mutters sheepishly, "I haven't taken care of myself; I've let everything go. Perhaps I have bilharzia." He shrugs, indifferent. "When I came out here, I was so keen, but now I am not. The people I try to work with do not care, so I cannot care indefinitely. They let everything go." He nodded his head toward the kitchen. "Last night Mfupi was drunk, and didn't bother to close the gate to the duck pen, and a honey badger got all my birds but two. I ask him to set some rice aside for our safari, and he cooks my entire supply. We need two camp cots, but all twelve cots assigned to Yaida Chini are now missing. A cot that will last fifteen years is ruined in three months—the rest have been lost, or perhaps sold in Mbulu." He shrugged again. "It's the same with everything—the land, the animals. Nobody cares, and all of it is going to go." He went outside and stood on his veranda, boots spread, hands in hip pockets, glaring at an African sky shrouded in fire clouds of smoke and blowing dust. In this valley, the only land that goes unburned is land too overgrazed to carry fire.

We head north under the Yaida Escarpment. Like all mornings in the dry season, this day is born in a dusty sun and restless wind, a desert wind, or so it seems, so vast and empty is the plain from which it comes. There is an old safari track, grown over, but the Land Rover makes its own way through acacia savanna where a slender-tailed mongoose, dark and lustrous, slips like a swift fish through the fading grass. At mid-morning the lower Udahaya is crossed, a slow stream dying in the plain. Slowly we wind toward the south Sipunga Hills.

Somewhere in the Sipunga, perhaps thirty miles north of Yaida Chini, small bands of Hadza hide from the resettlement program, living as they have always lived, by hunting and gathering, a people without pottery or gardens or domestic animals other than the random dog. Probably they will hide from us, as well, unless they see that we are the Hadza whom they trust. Magandula is a game scout and the prestige of his bunduki, or rifle, entitles him to two porters, Gimbe and Giga. Magandula is loud and opinionated; Gimbe and Giga are quiet. Magandula and Gimbe have Isanzu fathers, but Giga, smaller and older, is pure Hadza, black, with heavy jaw and swollen cheek-bones and flat nose in a head too big for a small thick body which will never attain five feet in height. Until recently Giga has been living in the bush—he is one of a number of Hadza who drift back and forth between the old life and the new—and as if in sign of his transitional state he is wearing a sandal on his right foot but not on his left. Magandula, on the other hand, is an outspoken convert to the new Africa, and wears bright red socks in black street shoes with broken points.

In early afternoon, under Sipunga, Giga speaks. Off among black wrinkled trunks and silvered thorns he has glimpsed a shift of shadows, and now Magandula is speaking, too: "Tindiga!" he says in tones of triumph, choosing the Isanzu name.

There is more than one, it is a hunting party, crouching low in the golden grass to peer under the limbs; the black of their skin is the old black of acacia bark in shadow. Giga is smiling at them, and they do not run; they have seen Giga, and they have a fresh-killed zebra.

Enderlein is grinning freely for the first time since I have known him. "Oh, we are *lucky!*" he says twice; he had not thought we would find the hunters this first day.

A striped hock shines in the fork of a tree; the rest rides on the hunters' shoulders. There are ten Hadza, seven with bows and three young boys, and all are smiling. Each boy has glistening raw meat slung over his shoulders and wrapped around him, and one wears the striped hide outward, in a vest. Except for beads at neck and waist, the boys are naked. The men wear loincloths faded to an olive-earth color that blends with the tawny grass; the rags are bound at the waist by a hide thong, and some have simple necklaces of red-and-yellow berry-colored beads. All wear crude sheath knives in the center of the back, and one has a guinea fowl feather in his hair.

Shy, they await in a half-circle, much less tall than their bows. "*Tsifiaqua!*" they murmur, and our people say, "*Tsifiaqua mtana,*" and then the hunters say, "M-*taa*-na!" for warm emphasis, smiling wholeheartedly. (*Tsifiaqua* is "afternoon" as in "good afternoon," and *mtana* is "nice" as in "nice day," and *tsifiaqua m-taa-na,* as the hunters say it, may mean, "Oh beautiful day!") I am smiling wholeheartedly too, and so is Enderlein; my smile seems to travel right around my head. The encounter in the sunny wood is much too simple, too beautiful to be real, yet it is more real than anything I have known in a long time. I feel a warm flood of relief, as if I had been away all my life and had come home again—I want to embrace them all. And so both groups stand face to face, admiring each other in the sunlight, and then hands are taken all around, each man being greeted separately by all the rest. They are happy we are to visit them and delighted to pile the zebra meat into the Land Rover, for the day is hot and dry and from here to where these Hadza live, behind the Sipunga Hills, is perhaps six miles of stony walking. The eldest, Mzee Dafi, rides, and others run ahead and alongside, and others stay behind to hunt again. The runners keep pace with the car as it barges across the stones and thorn scrub and on across the south end of Sipunga through the ancestral Hadza land called T'ua. Soon Giga kicks off his remaining sandal and runs barefoot with the rest, and then Magandula, in red socks and shiny shoes, is running, too. Gimbe, a young mission boy from Munguli, sits quietly; he is not yet home.

There is no track, only an intermittent path, and here and there Enderlein heaves rocks out of the way to let us pass. Peter is happy,

205

and he works with exuberance, casting away his pent-up angers. So glad are the hunters of our coming that they hurl rocks, too, but since most of them, Giga included, have no idea what they accomplish, they struggle with rocks that are far off the route, out of pure good will. On the sky rise twin hills walled with soaring monoliths, quite unlike anything I have ever seen; the hills overlook the upper Udahaya Valley, between the Sipunga and the Mbulu Escarpment. Seeing the hills the hunters cry out, leaping rocks, and the swiftest is he with the guinea fowl feather, Salibogo.

Behind the twin portals, on a hillside, rise groves of monumental granites. Approaching this place across a meadow of pink baobabs, Dafi whispers, "Gidabembe." Still there is no sign of habitation. But bright green in the sun are two fresh gourds set out to dry on a rock shelf; the placement of the gourds gives man away. A yellow dog, the first and last such animal we saw in Hadza Land, walks stiff and silent from the bush under a tilted monolith, and from the shadows of the stone a thin smoke rises into the dry sunlight, and a crone the color of dry brush appears among the leaves. In the shadows she stands like a dead stick, observing.

At the next grove of rocks, a stone has toppled in such a way that its flat face, some fifteen feet by fifteen in dimension, is held clear of the ground by the debris of its own fall, forming an open-sided shelter five feet high; similar rock shelters at Magosi, in Uganda, have been inhabited since the Middle Stone Age.[8] Small trees at the cave's twin mouths filter the sunlight, and at the hearth is a cracked gourd, a rag, a dik-dik skin, a bone, all now abandoned, for except in time of heaviest rains, the Hadza live beneath the sky. With hand brooms of grass and twigs, Gimbe and Magandula and the hunters brush loose dust from the cave floor, while squat Giga pushes three hearthstones together and with fingertips and breath draws grass wisps into a fire and places a black pot on the points of stone to boil. Outside, an old woman has appeared, bent under a morning's harvest of orange grewia berries, which are dry and sweet and taste like nuts; offering these, she is given a strip of the zebra meat spread out across a stone. Our people take meat for ourselves, and so do others who come quietly into the glade, for the Hadza have no agonies of ownership. Soon the wild horse is gone. On sharpened sticks Gimbe skewers the red meat, laying two sticks across the fire; the rest he places in the trees to dry

206

for biltong. Our arrival at Gidabembe is celebrated with a feast of tea and zebra, ugali and the fire-colored berries.

Gidabembe, the Hadza say, has been one of their camps for a long time, longer than the oldest of them can remember. It is used mainly in the dry season, when large animals are more easily killed, and people gather into larger groups to be in the vicinity of the good hunters. The main encampment lies uphill from the cave, on a knoll overlooking the river, where four small hearths with thornbush walls are grouped among the stones. Two are backed by upright granite and a third by a fallen tree; no roofs are constructed in this season, for there is no rain. The people are invisible to the outside world, which at Gidabembe is no farther than the glint of a tin duka on the slope of the Kainam Plateau, high on the far side of the valley. Their fires are small and their voices quiet, and they are so circumspect in all their habits that no scent of human habitation is detectable, although they do not bother about the droppings of baboons, which appropriate these rocks when man is absent; the baobab seeds in the baboon droppings are sometimes gleaned for man's own use.[9] Only a rare infant's cry betrays the presence of human beings, for the children play quietly, without squalling. One is among them very suddenly, a community of small people speaking prettily in soft click-speech in the light airs of afternoon. Far below the shelter of the rocks is green forest and the brown wind-sparkled river that in July is already running dry.

Soft voices in leaf-filtered sun, and a child humming, and a warm wind off the highlands that twitches the dry trees and blows color into the embers of the hearth. The earth behind the fire has been softened with a digging stick. Here, at dark, covered only with the thin rags worn in the day, the family lies down together on the small mat of kongoni hide or hay. From the thorn walls hang gourds and arrow packets and bird skins for arrow vanes, and by one hearth is an iron pot, black and thin as a leaf cinder. In these simple arrangements is a ceremonial sense of order in which everything is in place, for the ceremony is life itself, yet these shelters last no longer than the whims of their inhabitants, who may move tomorrow to another place, nearby or far. In the rains, especially, they scatter, for game and water are widespread. Somewhere they draw a few sticks over their heads, with grass matted on top, though they are casual about the rain when food is plentiful. In the dry season, many will return to Gidabembe, by the river, for Gidabembe is permanent, although all but the oldest of its people come and go. The hunter, who must travel light, limits his family to parents and children, and the people move in ever-changing groups, with little sense of tribe. The Hadza have no chiefs, no villages, no political system; their independence is their very breath. Giga speaks of an old man who wandered off last year and was thought lost. Three months later he turned up again, well rested from the stress of human company.

In the day the men and boys remain separate from the women. The men carry a fire drill among their arrows, and wherever Hadza tarry for more than a few minutes, and tarrying occupies much of their life, a small fire will be built. One hearth overlooks the river. Here in the broken sunlight, in the odor of wood smoke, the men and boys squat on their heels, shoulder to shoulder in a warm circle around the fire. With Dafi is his son Kahunda, and Saidi the son of Chandalua, who is still hunting in the land called T'ua; both are beautiful children whose eyes are not yet red from fire smoke, nor their teeth broken and brown. Dafi and Ginawi butcher zebra with deft twists of their crude knives; at Dafi's side is an ancient sharpening stone, glinting with soft iron shavings and concave with many seasons of hard use. Knives and metal arrow points come mostly from other tribes, but sometimes they are hammered cold from soft iron acquired in trade for skins and honey. Sheaths are fashioned from two flat bits of wood bound round with hide and sinew. Until recently, a male Hadza wore the pelt of a genet cat,[10] bound on by the hide thong that holds his knife, but now almost all wear small cloth skirts. Each carries a hide pouch with shoulder strap containing scraps of skin and tendon, tobacco leaves and hemp, a disc of baobab wood, lucocuko, used in gambling, a hunk of vine tuber which, when chewed, serves as a glue for binding arrow vanes, some rag-wrapped hornet larvae medicine or dawa, useful for chest pain, and snakebite dawa, of ingredients known only to a few, which is used in trade with the Mbulu and Mangati, spare arrowheads and scraps of metal, a chisel tool made from a nail, a pipe carved from a soft stone in the river. This pipe, one of the few Hadza objects that is not obtained in barter, is no more than a tube, and the tobacco or bangi will fall from it unless it is held vertical. Both men and women, staring at the sky, smoke the

208

stone pipe with gusty sucks accompanied by harsh ritual coughing, which is followed in turn by a soft ecstatic sigh.

Dafi and Ginawi eat zebra skin after burning off the hair, and put aside strips of the thick hide to be used for the soles of sandals, which most though not all of the hunters have adopted. They are joined by a Hadza with oriental eyes, high cheekbones, and a light skin with a yellow cast who brings to mind a legend[11]—not entirely without evidence to support it—that long ago Indonesians penetrated inland from the coast; the Tatoga of this region say that their ancestors came originally from beyond the sea. This man has been to Yaida Chini, and is sorry that Enderlein does not recall his name. "Zali," he says. "It is bad of you to forget. I have told it to you at Yaida Chini."

Certain other sallow Hadza might be Bushmen but for the lack of wrinkles and steatopygous buttocks, and Enderlein says that in their attitudes and ways, the Hadza seem identical to the click-speakers of the Kalahari, whom he has read all about. Bushmanoid peoples once inhabited East Africa, and it is tempting to suppose that the two groups were related long ago. On the other hand, certain Negroid groups such as the Bergdama of southwest Africa had adopted the Bushman culture, and even the Zulu have adopted a click-speech from these Twa or Abatwa, whose old hunting lands they have appropriated. The Bushmen themselves have Negroid attributes that they may not have always possessed—it is not known what their ancestors looked like.

But the yellow-brown Hadza look not at all like Giga, and most of the tribe are of mixed appearance, despite the striking heavy-browed appearance of such individuals as Giga, and Andaranda who killed the zebra, and a man named Kargo who, in size, is a true pygmy, and the large-headed girl at Yaida Chini who was the first Hadza that I ever saw, and one identified on sight, it must be said, by my Isanzu passenger, who had never seen her in his life.

Already the hunters are tending to their arrows, long thin shafts cut from a grewia or dombeya and feathered with vanes of bustard, guinea fowl, or vulture. Bird arrows are tipped with sharpened wood, and each bundle has an arrow with a lance blade of honed iron that is used for small game like guinea fowl and dik-dik. All the rest have

209

single or double-barbed metal points dipped in black resinous poison, made ordinarily from seeds of the black strocanthus fruit or sap of the desert rose. Both poisons are heart stimulants, consumed safely in meat but fatal when received into the bloodstream. Dafi wraps the poisoned barbs in thin strips of impala hide so that the poison will not dry out; the protection of the hunter is incidental. His long stiff bow of dombeya is also wrapped with circlets of impala, though this is maridadi—decoration. Ordinarily, Hadza bow strings are of zebra tendon, while split tendons of impala are the sinew that binds the arrow vanes onto the shaft.

When not out hunting roots and tubers with their digging sticks, Hadza women remain at their own hearths. Here their children with their big bellies and small prominent behinds dusted gray with hearth ash, play a variety of games with the hard bright yellow fruits of nightshade known as Sodom apples. Gondoshabe sits with Gindu, mother of Andaranda who killed the zebra, and lank-dugged Angate with a tobacco wad behind her ear, and Hanako, young wife of the swift hunter Salibogo, threading beads on long strands of fiber from the baobab, and Giga's daughter Kabaka, who with her baby has run away from the game scout Nangai at Yaida Chini. The women wear the same three garments as the women of the Bushmen: a genital cover, skirt, and carrying bag, formerly of hide, but now of cloth. They sit flat on the ground with legs straight out, toes upright, or squat on their haunches like the men. Though the nomadic Hadza do not burden themselves with metal bracelets, most women wear single headbands of white, red, and blue beads as well as bead armlets, anklets, and knee bands, and like the men, they may have three scars cut on the cheek in decoration. Small boys wear a simple strand of beads around the waist, small girls a rag and small bead apron, while infants may wear fetishes and charms as protection against the touch of menstruating women and the night cries of hurtful birds.[12] Kabaka's baby is immobilized by strings of beads, but for all her wealth Kabaka looks disgruntled, and it is she who raises her voice against the mzungu's presence in the camp. The wild Hadza women pay her little mind; though shyer than the men, they soon disregard the visitors and go on about their business. They grind maize, gather firewood; they dry new gourds bartered from the Mbulu, for they have no pottery, and fetch water from the river in the old. The gourds of cool water stand at angles beside a calabash of bright fresh berries. In this dry place, the sparkle of precious water borne in gourds has a true splendor. Gourds and arrow shafts may be marked with cross-hatching incised between parallel lines, these pairs of lines being set at angles to each other, but otherwise the Hadza have no art besides the decoration of their persons and the simplicity of their lives.

The Gidabembe rocks fall to the river edge, two hundred feet below. On the far side of the river lies low heavy forest, and beyond the forest is acacia savanna with big trees. Mbulu people have come down off the escarpment to clear patches of savanna; their presence has brought the humble duka that glints against the hills. Already a few Mbulu have crossed the river and set up maize shambas in the region of Gidabembe, and meanwhile Mangati filter up into the Sipunga from the south. While as yet there is no sign of overgrazing, this will come. The Mbulu and Mangati have caused the wild animals to scatter, and large game has become scarce during the dry season, when the only water available, in the Udahaya, is cut off by man. Eventually the Mbulu will call upon the Game Department to destroy the last elephant and buffalo, and meanwhile the wild animals are poached relentlessly by tillers and herdsmen alike.

A very few strangers, scattered through this valley, threaten the wildlife on which the Hadza depend, yet the Hadza accept these strangers as openly and cheerfully as they accept us. They cannot know that their time is past, although hunting is much harder now, and soon may be beyond their skills. In the old days, in time of famine, people of other tribes would go into the bush to live with the hospitable Hadza, who have no memory of hunger—despite a passion for honey and meat, they depend on seeds, tubers, roots, wild cowpeas, ivy gourd, borage, and berries of toothbrush bush and grewia, in addition to certain fungi and such seasonal tree fruits as baobab, figs, desert dates (*Balanites*), and tamarind. Excess meat and honey, used formerly in trade for beads and iron and tobacco, is hard to come by, for log hives brought in by the Mbulu are attracting the wild bees, and game is scarce. When the hunting is gone, the Hadza may take to killing stock, as the Bushmen did. Already one Hadza has been speared to death near Mangola for the killing and consumption of a goat.

A few Mbulu and Mangati stroll through Gidabembe, tall and contemptuous; they grin coldly for the benefit of the white man by way of answer to the Hadza greetings. There are two Mbulu shambas within a mile of Gidabembe, and already the Hadza have adopted this Mbulu name for their ancestral place, which in their own tongue is Ugulu. Recently, a family of Mangati has built a typical figure-eight stockade close by; one of the loops of the stockade is used for cattle, and in the other is the rectangular Mangati hut, like an Mbulu tembe but built above the level of the ground. The Mbulu and the men of the Mangati wrap themselves in trade cloth, but Mangati women wear skirts of leather cured in human urine, as Maasai women did in former days. Certain warm-breasted leather-skirted girls of the Mangati, carved northern faces softened by the south, are the loveliest women, black or brown or white, that I have seen in Africa.

At dark, we go with drink onto the rock over the cave and roll a smoke, and stare out over Hadza Land, and listen. Already Peter has relaxed, though he has not slept, and I find him an excellent companion, well informed, inquiring, with an open mind and a capacity for silence, and possessed of an ironic perception that has surely spared his sanity. People who knew him from his sprees on infrequent visits to Arusha had warned me that Enderlein was "bushed," as the saying goes here, from too much time alone out in the bush; they spoke of Peter's beautiful young wife who had found bush life unbearable and had fled two years before, not to return. But a letter sent me in Nairobi gave me confidence that we would get on all right: "I think if you allow yourself two weeks here," he wrote in part, "you would be able to get a fair insight into the valley and its mysteries; if you stay longer, you might well end up at my position, knowing nothing at all. It seems the longer one stays at a place, the less one has to say about it. . . ."

For this safari we had settled on two low camp cots, without tent, a few essentials such as rice and tea and rum, and whatever tinned goods might be rattling around in the rear of my old Land Rover. For the rest we would make do as we went along. Even so, our camp was infinitely more complex than the Hadza hearths, and soon seemed littered. Both of us have a passion for traveling light, deploring the ponderous caravansary which Anglo-Saxons in particular tend to conceive of as safaris—the table, camp chairs, ice chests, private toilet tents, truckloads of provender and swarming staff that permit them to lug the colonial amenities of the Hotel Norfolk "into the blue." Like myself, Peter has often been ashamed in front of Africans by the

212

amount of equipment that his white friends required. Yet Africans admire wealth, and anyway, they do not make judgments in such matters, but accept a different culture as it is. The people at Gida-bembe, who still trust, are neither subservient nor rude. Here was the gentleness, the loving attention to the moment, that is vanishing in East Africa, as it has vanished in the western world.

Exhilarated, happy, we lie flat out on the high rocks, still warm from the hot sun of afternoon. Peter draws his finger across the sky, starting to laugh. "Fake stars have five points, isn't it true?" he says. "Now I shall try to count how many points the *real* stars have. . . ." He laughs quietly for a long time. And later he shouts suddenly, "You see? You see that constellation veering? It's like a kite! It's like a kite in that one moment just before it falls. . . ." And I turn my head to watch him bellow at the universe.

Three months after our stay at Gidabembe, Peter would write as follows from hospital in Arusha:

It seems my time in Hadza Land has come to an end. I was recently called to a meeting in Mbulu to discuss my project but I found myself the witch in a medieval witchhunt where the bonfire was built and the match already lighted. It seemed I wanted to ruin their efforts of settling the Hadza—of course everybody knows that white men like to see Africans primitive and naked only—and turn them back to the bush. I also payed them money to strip nude so that my friends could photograph them in this state—all of course to discredit the development of the country. Somebody suggested that I shoot more zebras than I account for and keep the money myself. Somebody else knew that the Hadza despised me, etc., etc., etc. So here I am, having chosen to be hospitalized for a while—how can one choose jaundice?—looking for new horizons. . . .

In a day the zebra is already gone, and Dafi and Salibogo will rejoin the hunters beyond Sipunga Hills. We go along to watch them hunt. A solitary elephant crosses a rise among great baobabs, and they cry out, but except at close range, it is hard to drive an arrow through the thick hide of an elephant. Their bows require a hundred-pound pull[13] from a hunter who weighs little more than that himself, and the poison used here is not strong enough.

On the far side of Sipunga, down toward the Yaida Plain, there are impala, and Dafi and Salibogo run through the scattered trees, moving downwind before cutting back toward the animals. Both are very small and quick, as if in hunters, this small size, like the long legs of the

213

nomadic herdsmen, was a phenomenon of natural selection. In the case of the well-fed Hadza, it would be hard to argue that small size is the consequence of life in a hostile and stunted environment; like hunter-gathers the world over, they tend to be better nourished than more settled peoples, who must struggle to subsist. Until recently there was no need to hunt hard to get all the meat they wanted, and probably the game will be all gone before they refine their skills. Enderlein once watched Ariangulo trackers brought here from the Tsavo country by white hunters. He says that the Hadza, who hunt alone except when encircling baboons, compare in neither tactics nor persistence with the Ariangulo, who have huge bows with arrows tipped in acokanthera and specialize in hunting elephants.

Magandula, grabbing a bow, trots after the hunters in his black shoes; the self-conscious leer upon his face fails to conceal an innocent excitement. Eventually Salibogo goes on by himself, running bent double over long stretches of open ground, rising and falling, crouching, peering, and snaking at last on his belly to the caper bush where he will lie. The animals drift away from Dafi, who, in the way of lions, drives them gently into ambush, but the wind shifts and the lead animal crosses Salibogo's scent. In the stillness comes the impala's blowing snort, and the bright-eyed ones are gone.

With the impala goes the last good opportunity of the day. Even when Enderlein decides to use his rifle, we come up with nothing. Zebra, impala, and wildebeest are all shy and scarce, and a wildebeest bull struck at long range fails to come down. The day is dry and very hot, and much of this landscape south and west of the Sipunga has been burned by the Mangati; on a black ground, Senegal bustards pick the burnt eggs of guinea fowl. Farther north, in a grassland with low suffocated thorn, there are no animals at all. Overhead passes a pelican, flapping and sailing on its way to distant water, but here the thorn wood and dense dusty grass is empty, and as the morning turns to afternoon, black man and white fall silent. An African landscape full of animals, even dangerous ones, does not seem hostile; life is sustained here, and somewhere there is water. But without animals, the parched grass and bitter thorn, the hard-caked earth, the old sky shrouded by smoke through which a dull sun looms like a blind eye—all seems implacable. The sun god Haine, though worshipped by the Hadza, is remote and ill disposed toward man, and is not invoked. In the dark of the moon the hunters dance all night to insure good hunting and good health, for sometimes a hunter, crouched in night ambush at a waterhole, is taken by the lion, Sesemaya.

At home, hot, tired, and oppressed, we tramp down to the Udahaya. Careless of bilharzia, we lie in the cool flow, six inches deep, that streams over fine copper-colored sand. We wash, dry off on the green bank in a cool north wind, and climb back up to Gidabembe, feeling better. There Gondoshabe and Angate are singing on their knees, breasts swinging across big flat-topped tilted stones on which maize meal is refined by being scraped by a flat rock. The meal pours onto clean impala hide below the stone.

The boy Saidi, preparing his small arrows, sits alone at a fire above the river. All Hadza boys, developing their bow strength from an early age, have weapons suitable to their size that are in constant play and practice, and the glint of a bird arrow risen through the trees of a still landscape is a sign of Hadza presence. Though some men never hunt at all, content to accept charity in return for the loss of prestige, Saidi's intensity and bearing say that he will be a hunter. Squatting on his heels, he trims his vulture plumes and binds them to a shaft with neck ligament of the impala. Four vanes are trimmed and bound on tight in as many minutes, and the binding sealed over with the glue from a chewed tuber. He sights down his new arrow shafts, then gnaws at one to soften it for straightening before fitting his arrow tips into shaft sockets dug out with a bent nail. Then he rises and goes off after dik-dik and rock hyrax, which both abound here. The hyrax looks like a sharp-nosed marmot, but on the basis of certain anatomical similarities, notably the feet, it has been determined that its nearest living kin are elephants. Perhaps as a defense against the attack of eagles, the hyrax has the astonishing ability to stare straight upward into the equatorial sun.

Watching Saidi go, Enderlein says, "Do you know what will become of him?" He scowls. "First, when all the game is gone, and the trees, too, he will be forced to go to Yaida Chini. Untrained, he can do nothing, and because he is Hadza he will be treated as inferior every-where he goes. If he is very lucky, he might become a thief in Dar es Salaam; otherwise he will be just another one of all those faces in the streets, hopeless and lost, with all the dignity that this life gives him gone." He got to his feet, disgusted, and we walked in silence toward the cave, through the beautiful rock monuments and wild still

215

twilight orchards of commiphora like old apple trees and terminalia with red pods like fruit, and figs, and fruiting grewia bushes, and a small sweet-scented acacia with recurved spines that catch hold of the unwary—the wait-a-bit thorn, from the Swahili *ngoja kidogo*, which means wait-a-little.

At the cave is the game scout Nangai, come on foot from Yaida Chini to fetch back his young wife Kabaka, daughter of Giga. "Who knows why she ran away?" Nangai shrugs, smiling shyly at his sullen wife. Giga, holding his ornamented grandchild to his cheek, rolls his eyes and croons, a love all the more affecting for the great ugliness that, as one comes to perceive this man, turns to great beauty.

Tea is served by sad-faced discreet Gimbe, who says, "*Karibu chai,*" welcome to tea, with the same sweet simplicity with which another African once said to me, "You are nicely welcomed to Samburu." With his wood ladle he stirs maize meal into boiling water to make the thick white paste called ugali that is subsistence in East Africa; ugali, eaten with the fingers, is rolled into a kind of concave ball used to mop up whatever is at hand in the way of meat, vegetables, and gravy. Soon he presents a bowl of water in which the right hand is to be dipped and rinsed prior to eating, because here in the cave our posho, or ration, is eaten from a common bowl. The Moslem washing of one hand comes up from the coast by way of the part-Arab Swahili, once the agents of the trade in slaves and ivory; so does the mbira or "marimba," called irimbako by the Hadza, who have no musical instrument of their own. The mbira, or flat-bar zither, came to East Africa centuries ago from Indonesia. It is a hollow box faced with tuned strips of stiff metal that produces soft swift wistful rhythms of time passing, and the old one here at Gidabembe is passed from hand to hand. It is Giga who plays it by the fire as we dine on ugali and delicate doves shot in the hills.

At Gidabembe Hill, among the monoliths, baboons are raving, and there comes a sudden brief strange sound that brings Giga from his cave. "*Chui,*" he whispers. Leopard. But the others shrug—how can one know? The Hadza never like to give opinions. A few days later, in this place, we find the vulture-gutted body of a young leopard on an open slope where no sick leopard would ever lie, and the grass all about has been bent and stamped by a convocation of baboons, as if the creature had been caught in the open by the huge baboon troupe, which had killed it. Yet there was no baboon fur in its mouth, nor any blood or sign of struggle in the grass.

The dark falls quiet once again. From Sipunga comes the night song of unknown birds, and the shrill ringing yip of a distant jackal, and inevitably the ululations of hyenas. The Hadza are comparatively unsuperstitious, and unfrightened of the dark: "We are ready for him," they say of Fisi, reaching out to touch their bows. "Hyena can be a bloody nuisance," Enderlein says, recalling an account, no doubt apocryphal, of a sleeping man who had his foot bitten clean off by a night hyena. He places a dim kerosene lantern near our bed rolls, for we are sleeping outside the cave. At my head is a white hyrax stain on the dark rock, and beside the stain are stacked the rifles. Mosquitoes are few and we sleep without a net, staring up through the black leaves at cruel bright stars. Gimbe is sleeping in the Land Rover, and others sleep on hides inside the cave. Magandula curls up with his bunduki, and Giga is hooked close to the embers. They murmur in their soft deep voices, which drop away one by one. Soon Giga is asleep, and all night he breathes rapidly, like a wild creature stunned and felled while running.

The Hadza see no sense in hunting hard with bow and arrow when there is a rifle in the camp. In hope of meat, people are coming in out of the hills, and there are seven hearths where there were four. The Hadza here are now no less than thirty and a buffalo would feed everyone for days.

Many buffalo, as well as rhino and elephant, live in the forest below Gidabembe. When Peter asks me if I wish to hunt, I tell him I will think about it. Enderlein is a good shot who is shooting badly, who is sleeping badly, whose every action has a trace of rage in it; he is not the companion I would choose for the pursuit of dangerous animals, and especially buffalo, toward which he seems more disrespectful than any hunter I have ever met. "He's too damned careless about buffalo; he's going to catch it one of these days," says Douglas-Hamilton, who is not known for prudence. On the other hand, though I had no wish to shoot a big animal myself, hunting dangerous game is a part of the African mystique that I did not know. And this morning is a soft green morning when death, which never seems remote in Africa, but hangs about like something half-remembered, might come almost companionably . . . be that as it may, I leave my doubts behind.

We descend to the river at daybreak, accompanied by the game scouts Magandula and Nangai, and Mugunga, who is Nangai's young porter, and two wild Hadza, Yaida and Salibogo. Magandula carries Peter's .375, which few hunters consider powerful enough to stop a buffalo, and Nangai brings a .22 for small game. Yaida and Salibogo carry bow and arrows. We ford the river where it winds around the base of Gidabembe, and enter the dense forest single file. Salibogo is in the lead, then Enderlein, Nangai, Mugunga, who carries Peter's pouch of bullets, then Magandula, then myself, and finally Yaida, who looks like a young Bushman. For the first time Magandula is shirtless, and he has a porcupine quill stuck in his hair, but he clings to his red socks and pointed shoes.

Trees in this virgin place are huge—umbrella thorn and soaring fever trees, and here and there a mighty winterthorn (*A. albida*), the noblest of all acacias, these interspersed with fat sycamore figs and sausage trees. But along the animal trails and walling the small glades is head-high thicket, hollowed out, where rhino and buffalo may stand entirely hidden. Their spoor is everywhere, and Salibogo drops behind; there is no need for a tracker. We move carefully and quietly, bending each moment to peer into the grottoes. The trick is to sight any hidden beast before it feels crowded and decides to charge, but the cover is dense, and Enderlein offers a tense grin. "Bloody dangerous bush," he murmurs. "They can see you but you can't see them." In Peter's opinion, rhino are more dangerous than buffalo, being stupid and unpredictable, a "warm-blooded dinosaur," as he says, that has outlived its time; rhinos are apt to rush out blindly where a buffalo would slip away. But I share the more common dread of the low-browed buffalo, shifting its jaws sideways as it chews its cud, light glancing from its horn.

Oblivious birdsong in the early morning wind; warm butterflies spin sunlight through the glades. The Hadza pause every little while to wring dry berries from the grewia bushes, but my own mouth is too dry, I am not hungry. There is exhilaration in the hunt, and also the quick heart of the hunted. I feel strong and light and quick, and more than a match for the nearest tree that can be climbed in haste. These are damnably few: the big trees lack low branches and the small are shrouded with thorn vine and liana. Yaida and Salibogo, like myself, keep a close watch on the trees, and we grin nervously at one another.

In a circular glade, Enderlein crouches, stiffens, and steps back, holding out his hand. Magandula gives him his rifle. In the shadows ten yards to the left, the cave of leaves is filled with a massive shape, as still as stone. A little way back there was fresh rhino track, and Peter thinks this is the rhino. He circles out a little ways, just to make sure. A slight movement may bring on a rhino charge—its poor vision cannot make out what's moving, and its nerves cannot tolerate suspense—whereas a sudden movement may put it to flight. I am considering a sudden movement, such as flight of my own, when I see a tail in a thin shaft of light, and the tail tuft in fleeting silhouette, and grunt at Peter, "Buffalo."

A sun glint on the moisture at the nostril; the animal is facing us. The tail does not move again. We stand there for long seconds, at a loss. Enderlein cannot get a fair shot in the poor light, and at such close quarters, he does not want a wounded buffalo. He starts a wide circling stalk of the entire copse, signaling his game scouts to follow. But it is the boy Mugunga who jumps forward, and the game scouts shrug, content to let him go. We follow carefully, but soon the hunters vanish in the bushes. Heat and silence. Soon the silence is intensified by a shy birdsong, incomplete, like a child's question gone unanswered.

The bird sings again, waits, sings again. Bees come and go. Soon Mugunga reappears. The beast will not be chivvied out of hiding, and there is no hope of a clear shot with the rifle. But a poisoned arrow need not be precise. The hunter had only to wait a few hours before tracking, so as not to drive the dying animal too far away, and in this time he would return to camp to find help in cutting up the meat, or if the animal was big, to move the whole camp to the carcass.

Mugunga draws on Yaida's bow, then picks the stronger bow of Salibogo. The Hadza faces fill with joy; they respect the rifle but they trust the bow. Then Mugunga vanishes once more, and the silence deepens. Leaves stir and are still.

The birdsong ceases as the buffalo crashes free, but there is no shout, no rifle shot, only more silence. When the hunters reappear, Enderlein says, "I thought the arrow might bring him out where I could get a shot at him, but Mugunga waited a split second too long, and the bloody brute pushed off, out the far side." Even so we will track this buffalo; Peter keeps the gun. The Hadza move on, bush by bush, glade by glade, checking bent grass, earth, and twigs, darting through copses where one would have thought so large an animal could not have gone. To watch such tracking is a pleasure, but this is taut work, for the buffalo is listening, it has not taken flight. Somewhere in the silent trees, the dark animal is standing still, or circling to come up behind. Wherever it is, it is too close.

In the growing heat, our nerves go dead, and we are pushing stupidly ahead, inattentive, not alert, when the spoor dies, too, and we cut away from the river in search of another animal. But the sun is climbing, and the big animals will have taken to the shade. The chance of catching one still grazing in the open is now small.

In a swampy place the Hadza fall on a tomato bush. The small fruits are warm red, intensely flavored, and we eat what we can and tie the rest into a rag to bring back to Gidabembe. Not that the hunters feel obliged to do this: men and women seek and eat food separately and quickly, to avoid the bad manners of refusing it to others, and occasional sharing between the sexes is a matter of whim. Farther on, Yaida and Salibogo locate honey in a tree, and again the hunt for buffalo is abandoned. Usually a grass torch is stuck into the hole to smoke out the bees, but the Hadza are more casual than most Africans about bee stings, and Yaida is wringing one stung hand while feeding himself with the other. The honeycomb is eaten quickly, wax, larvae, and all. The Hadza also eat hyena, cats, and jackals, though they draw the line at frogs and reptiles, and not every man will eat a vulture.

Hyena prints, and spoor of waterbuck. Nangai kicks at buffalo manure to see its freshness, and it is plain that we have passed the dark silent animals close by. Mugunga, frustrated, shoots a lance at a dik-dik half-hidden by low, intervening branches—he leans into the shot on his left foot as he shoots—and the arrow drives hard into a sapling by the dik-dik's neck. He turns to look at us, shaking his head. We circle slowly toward the Udahaya, striking it at midday far downriver. The hunt is over, and we walk barefoot in the water, shooting doves and hyrax with the .22 as we return upstream. Peter is brooding, but I am still excited by the hunt, and glad to be free of the dense bush, and so I celebrate this moment of my life, the sparkle of gold mica on my brown feet, a pair of pied kingfishers that racket from dead limb to limb, the sweet scent of the white-flowered vernonia, swarming with bees that make honey for the Hadza. And the Hadza seem happy, too: their time is now. Though there will not be nearly enough to go around, it awes them to see the doves fall to our gun. They are used to failure in the hunt, which these days occurs often, and in the future must occur more often still.

A visitor to Gidabembe comes from a small camp in the Sipunga Hills, where he helps take care of a young invalid, apparently an epileptic. Last year this boy was badly burned when he fell into a fire, and was led across the hills to the clinic in Mbulu, but after two days he ran away, back to Sipunga. This spring, left alone in camp, he fell again into the fire and was burned so drastically that he can no longer move.

Magandula has borrowed a wood comb from Giga; perched on a rock, he combs his head for a long time without discernible results. According to Magandula, it is only the influence of civilization that prevents the *Sipunganebe* from deserting the man burned, and the Hadza cheerfully agree: among nomadic hunter-gatherers, who cannot afford responsibility for others, such desertion is quite common. Only last year, Yaida says, a man in fever was abandoned in the mountains: "We left him his bow, but he could not live; surely he was eaten by lions." Magandula, scrubbing his shoes, becomes excited and speaks shrilly: "To live in the bush is bad! Hasn't the government taught us to live in houses? I want nothing to do with the bush!" In recent years the government has made of the Hadza a symbol of primitive apathy to their countrymen, who are exhorted to increase their numbers and work hard on their shambas—"Don't rot in the bush like the Watindiga!" And tillers from Mbulu come sometimes to Yaida Chini and jeer at them: "How can people be so primitive!"—just as the people of Arusha might speak of the poor peasants of Mbulu, or the people of Dar es Salaam of the provincial folk met in Arusha.

Four naked children have clambered up into a grewia bush and hunch there in the branches, knees under their chins, munching sweet berries while they watch us. Despite big bellies and thin legs, which are lost early, Hadza children are clear-eyed and energetic, and like their parents, they are cheerful. Somewhere it has been suggested that hunter-gatherers seem happier than farmers, and of necessity more versatile and alert than people who live mostly in a rut. But their good spirits may come also from their varied diet, which is far healthier than the ugali and pombe fare of the shamba dwellers they are told to emulate.

Magandula watches the white man watching the small dark naked

221

bodies in the branches. "*Kama nyani,*" he jeers, with terrific ambivalence, for Magandula is in pain—"Just like baboons!" He searches our faces for the affirmation that he feared was there before he spoke. "Look at old Mutu, and that old woman!" he bursts out again, pointing, "Life is too hard here!" And the old woman herself, coming home one day with her rag sack, speaks of berries with disdain. "Ugali is better," she declares, to show her acquaintance with maize meal paste, although ugali is woefully poor in both taste and nutrition.

Magandula's emotion is disturbing because he is angry without provocation, therefore afraid, therefore fanatic. And what can Magandula be afraid of? Unless he fears that he has lost touch with his origins, his clans, the earth and the old ways, with no real hope or promise from the new.

As if to bear witness for Magandula, old Mutu comes tottering to his hearth and sinks down in a heap against a stone. He no longer bothers with his bow and arrows, which rot in the bush behind his head; the sad old broken arrows with their tattered vanes are the home of spiders. Mutu is back from begging maize at an Mbulu shamba, and complains as ever of his feet, which are leprously cracked and horned up to the ankle bone. To my touch, his afflicted flesh feels rubbery and dead. Once Mutu walked as far east as Mbulu, where he came by his disease. "Things like *this*"—and he flicks his ruined flesh, contemptuous, lip curling around a villainous old mouthful of snag teeth—"you don't find in the bush." In proof of his corruption by the world, Mutu begs cynically for two *shillingi*—the only Hadza that ever begged at all—and is happy to accept a dove instead. Despite his misery and decrepitude, he has no wish to visit the dispensary at Yaida Chini, and waves away the offer of a ride. Already he has his stone pipe lit, tucking a red cinder into it with his bare fingers, and now he lies back laughing at some ancient joke, coughing ecstatically after the custom of his people.

Twig-legged Mutu is big-bellied as a baby, lying there in the sunlight in his swaddling. He rails at life with unholy satisfaction, and so do the two old women whose hearths adjoin his own at the base of the great tilted rock with the rounded top that might be the gravestone of God. All three worn-out souls are of separate families, and fiercely maintain their family hearths as symbols of the independence which is so vital to the Hadza, although not one has relatives at

Gidabembe who might look after him. Yet Mutu has maize and berries for his supper, and so do his two neighbors. And it was Mutu who explained the greatest mystery of life at Gidabembe: how it was, when times were hard, that a scorned people were able to beg maize and tobacco from the Mbulu, who were few and poor here, and living themselves at a subsistence level.

The Hadza claim to perform certain services for the Mbulu, helping them to dig their shambas, tend their stock, and cultivate during the wet season; also, the Mbulu come to them for honey and dawa. But these infrequent services cannot account for the munificence of the Mbulu, and it seems clear from the quantity of maize obtained that the Hadza are not begging, but go to the shambas with every expectation of reward.

For the Mbulu, death is a great disaster, and the evil effects of pollutions that they fear the most are those associated with dead bodies. In former days, bodies were left to the hyenas, as with the Maasai, but nowadays, according to Mutu, who is borne out in every particular by Giga and Nangai, the dead person is buried quickly, after which a Hadza is summoned who is of the same sex as the dead. The Hadza shaves the head of the bereaved, who then strips himself naked and presents to the Hadza his clothes and all belongings of the dead person except money, which is not thought of as polluted, and also four debes (the debe or four-gallon kerosene can is the standard container in the bush) of maize. He or she then copulates with the Hadza, who thereby inherits the disaster, and will die eventually of this act. "He may count his years," cries Magandula, who writhes at Mutu's words but does not deny them, "but it will catch him before long." Mutu is emphatic about his facts, pounding his old hand on the earth to simulate copulation. When he is finished he averts his gaze, shrugging his shoulders. Such was the penalty that his people paid for being poor; there was nothing to be done about it. But Nangai and Magandula say they would not perform such a service; it is only for these wild Hadza, who are so poor that they have no choice. (Perhaps the game scouts spread the word that there were wild Hadza at Gidabembe, for not long after our departure Enderlein sent evil news: "The people there were rounded up and taken to Yaida Chini, arriving in time for a measles epidemic in which nine Hadza children died.")

Listening politely to the shouts of Magandula, the hunters do not

223

protest. They accept the scorn of their fellow man as a part of Hadza life. On the other hand, they prefer to remain in the bush. "I have got used to it," says Chandalua, who is Yaida's older brother and the father of the boy Saidi. With Dafi, he lives ordinarily in the Giyeda Barakh, on the far side of the Yaida, overlooking Lake Eyasi: Giyeda Barakh, known in their click-speech as *Hani'abi*, "the rocks", will be a last stronghold of the Hadza. Chandalua's gentle face has the transparence of infinity. Sitting on his warm stone notching an arrow shaft, he smiles approvingly on Magandula, who still scrubs fiercely at his shoes.

A stony path of rhino, man, and elephant leads up into Sipunga, and ascending it one morning, we met four lean Mangati entering the valley armed with spears and poisoned arrows. The arrows are illegal, since only the Hadza are permitted to hunt here without restraint, but rather than kill their scraggy beasts, the meat-eating Mangati poach wherever possible.

Both groups stop at a little distance, regarding each other without pleasure. The tall sandaled Mangati, cowled and scarified with half-circles of raised welts about the eyes, are handsome remote men, with a hard cast to their gaze. They look like legendary desert bandits, and their spears have a honed shine. But our party is the stronger, with two white men and the armed game scout Nangai, as well as Salibogo, Andaranda, and Maduru; we have two rifles and three bows. When Nangai steps forward and takes hold of the poisoned arrows, the Mangati leader abandons his bad smile. He refuses to let go, and his companions, scowling, shift their feet. The youngest, a very beautiful cold-faced morani, not yet twenty, makes contemptuous remarks to Andaranda, who steps past him on his pigeon-toed bare feet and continues up the trail. To save face for both sides, it is decided that the shafts will not be taken, only the arrowheads, and the two groups part in silence, looking back over their shoulders until the others are out of sight.

The few Mangati in the region of Gidabembe are at peace with the Hadza, who have nothing worth taking away. "They do not kill us now," the Hadza say. But the hunters, who are small and peaceable and claim no territory, are neither defenseless nor lacking in courage, and their forbearance has its limits. Not long ago, near Tandusi, to the south, some Hadza caught two Mangati moran in a prized bee

224

tree, and when the Mangati defied a request that they come down, shot them out of it with lance arrows, killing both.

The Mangati, too, pay careful attention to death. An elder's funeral may last nine months, while a monument of mud, dung, and poles some twelve feet high is erected in stages on the grave; at the end of the final ceremonies, as darkness falls, two ancient men crawl naked to the deserted mound and fasten a magic vine about its base, whispering. "Don't hurry, wait for us, we will join you soon." Most women and all children are left to the hyenas, but a female elder of good repute may also be given a small mound on which her wood spoon and clay cooking pot are placed. Toward the end of a brief mourning period, a hole is poked through the clay pot, to signify that her work on earth is done.[14]

We climb steadily through the early morning, across dry open hillsides without flowers. In a broad pile of dik-dik droppings on the trail is a small hole six inches deep and six across. Though it moves in daylight with the shadows of rock and bush, the tiny antelope returns at night to these rabbity heaps out in the open; here it feels safe from stealing enemies, and waits out the long African dark. Dik-dik (so the Dorobo say) once tripped over the mighty dung pile of an elephant, and has tried ever since to reply in kind by collecting its tiny droppings in one place.[15] Man takes advantage of the habit by concealing in a hole a ring of thorns with the points facing inward and down. The dik-dik—meaning "quick-quick" in Swahili—cannot extract its delicate leg, and is killed by the first predator to come along. Whoever is hunting here is not a Hadza, for the Hadza know nothing of traps or snares of any kind.

Rhinoceros, also sedentary in their habits, follow the same trails to water, dust wallow, and browse, and on a grand scale share this custom of adding to old piles of their own droppings, which are then booted all about, perhaps as a means of marking territory but more likely as an aid to orientation in a beast whose prodigious sniff must compensate for its poor eyesight. Rhino piles are common on this path, together with wallows and the primitive three-toed print. Not far away, one or more of these beasts is listening, flicking its ears separately in the adaptation that accounts in part for its uncanny hearing, and making up its rudimentary mind whether or not to clear the air with a healthy charge.

The ridge is open, with thick trees and granite islands; a squirrel sways among strange star-shaped fruits of a sterculia. Andaranda on his short bent legs, a hyrax swinging from his waist, views all about him with a smile. His bare feet, impervious to burrs and stones, thump steadily against the earth, and his hands, too, are tough as stumps, as they must be in a life so close to bees and thorns and fire. The trail arrives at a water point, Halanogamai, which Mbulu or Mangati have fenced off with thorn brush to keep out wild animals. Enderlein attacks the fence without a word, hurling it into high piles for a bonfire, and the Hadza drag wood to the fire that has nothing to do with the thorn fence, the threat of which to their way of life they have not grasped. Maduru gets a thorn branch stuck to his back, and I pick him free. One day, emerging from beneath the Land Rover, I was picked free by Salibogo, and another day by Gimbe; no African would expect thanks for this basic courtesy, and Maduru did not pause to thank me now.

On the far side of the Sipunga, the track turns north, skirting the heads of narrow gorges; the gorges open out on a broad prospect of the Yaida Plain, pale in the desert sun of summer. All along the rim rise granite monoliths, and at one of these vast rocks known as Maseiba there lived until a few years ago an old Hadza named Seira and his wife Nyaiga. One day, says Maduru, Seira was out hunting hyrax, and had killed five with his bow, but the sixth fell into a dark crevice which hid a snake. Seira, three times bitten—Maduru slaps his arm, then chest, then side—ran home and applied strong snakebite dawa. Feeling better, he lay down to rest. But unlike most hunters, who avoid encumbrance, Seira had two wives, and Nyaiga was very jealous of the second wife, even though she lived at Gidabembe. Nyaiga rubbed arrow poison into Seira's bites and he shortly died.

The Hadza leave the elephant trail, circling west through windy glades toward high rocks bright with orange, blue-gray, and crusting gray-green lichens. Below, a cleft between two portals forms a window on the Yaida plain, and nestled in the cleft, entirely hidden from the world except from the spot on which we stand, is a small ledge shaded by a grove of three commiphora. The myrrh trees stand in heraldic triangles, and set against their scaly trunks are three shelters so well camouflaged by cut branches that the trees appear to grow out of a thicket. In seasons when the commiphora is in leaf, the shelters would not be visible at all.

226

We descend quietly, watched from hiding by the inhabitants. This place is Sangwe, Maduru whispers, and eight Hadza live here. They are very shy and hide behind the huts, though they have recognized Maduru, and been greeted. All three huts are roofed and lined with grass. The wall of one sustains the next, and the tight interiors are spare and orderly as new bird nests. As at Gidabembe, there is no scent of human waste and no notice taken of the seedy feces of baboons. Between the huts and the ledge rim where the cleft falls away into the canyon is a place scarcely large enough for the cooking fire, and beside the fire, on a kongoni hide, lies a strongly built young Hadza with a twisted eye and a stiff right hand bent back toward his wrist by the burnt hide. Healed flesh on his deformed left foot is a bare pink, but the crust on a hand-sized wound over his heel is oozing. This is Magawa, in whose wild eyes I see the choking struggle in the fire, and the thrashing on his rock of pain in the weeks afterward, under the far, unforgiving eye of the sun god, Haine.

Magawa says that he fled the clinic at Mbulu because he could not live so far from Sangwe, and like Mutu, he has no wish to go to Yaida Chini even though here he must remain a helpless cripple. Maduru decides to go to Yaida Chini in Magawa's place, and instead of remaining behind at Sangwe, he comes with us. The others watch Maduru go, and Magandula would say that in time they, too, will depart, leaving Magawa to the lions.

Nangai and Maduru know of a great rock with red paintings, which in this land may be thousands of years old; more recent drawings, usually abstract, are done in white and gray. Earlier this morning, off the trail, we found a large cave almost hidden in the thicket that had overgrown its mouth; Maduru had not known about this cave, which is occupied at present by bats and hornets but also contains an ancient hearth and vertical red stripes. The Hadza have no special curiosity about red markings, since every tree and boulder in this land which gives them life has its own portent and significations.

We descend the ridge, moving southeast along Sipunga. Maduru points out the holes of bees into which he has wedged stones. If the entrance to a hive must be enlarged to reach the honey, and if stones are handy, one or more may be stuck into the hole until the entrance is reduced again to the size approved by bees. "We put stones here," Salibogo says, "so that the honey will come back." Stones stuck in trees are one of the few signs of the presence of Hadza, who unlike the Mbulu and Mangati are invisible in their environment; they have no idea of wilderness, for they are part of it. At the foot of a ravine a bird comes to the trees with urgent trilling, then flies off again, pursued by Salibogo and Andaranda, who are trilling urgently themselves. This bird is the black-throated honey guide, which has evolved the astonishing habit of leading honey badger and man to the hives of bees and feasting upon the leavings of the raid; if no honey is left for the honey guide, Africans say, it will lead the next man to a snake or lion. But this bird is soon back again, still trilling, having left the Hadza far away under the hill.

Southeastward, under the soaring rock, we follow in the noble paths of elephant. Maduru points at an overhanging wall, like a wave of granite on the yellow sky: Darashagan. A hot climb brings us out at last onto a ledge under the overhang, well hidden by the tops of trees that rise from the slopes below; the ledge looks south down the whole length of the Yaida Valley. There is a hearth here, still in use, and on the wall behind the hearth, sheltered by the overhang, are strong paintings in a faded red of a buffalo and a giraffe. We stand before them in a line, in respectful silence. One day another man, all nerves and blood and hope just like ourselves, drew these emblems of existence with a sharpened bird bone spatula, a twist of fur, a feather, and others squatted here to watch, much as the Hadza are squatting now. The Mbulu and Barabaig have no tradition of rock painting, whereas the Bushmen, before they became fugitives, made paintings very similar to these. The only other red paintings in this country are found in the region of Kondoa-Irangi, in the land of the click-speaking Sandawe.

Andaranda makes a fire and broils hyrax and a guinea fowl. When we have eaten, he picks grewia leaves, and the Hadza trim the leaves and roll tobacco from their pouches. I try Nangai's uncultivated weed, and the Hadza giggle at my coughs. Of the drawings they say shyly, "How can we know?" Pressed, they ascribe them to the Old People or to Mungu (God), searching our faces in the hope of learning which one we prefer: our need to *understand* makes them uncomfortable. For people who must live from day to day, past and future have small relevance, and their grasp of it is fleeting; they live in the moment, a very precious gift that we have lost.

Lying back against these ancient rocks of Africa, I am content. The great stillness in these landscapes that once made me restless seeps into me day by day, and with it the unreasonable feeling that I have found what I was searching for without ever having discovered what it was. In the ash of the old hearth, ant lions have countersunk their traps and wait in the loose dust for their prey; far overhead a falcon—and today I do not really care whether it is a peregrine or lanner—sails out over the rim of rock and on across the valley. The day is beautiful, my belly full, and returning to the cave this afternoon will be returning home. For the first time, I am in Africa among Africans. We understand almost nothing of one another, yet we are sharing the same water flask, our fingers touching in the common bowl. At Halanogamai there is a spring, and at Darashagan are red rock paintings—that is all.

In a few swift days of a dry summer this ancient cave in central Africa, blackened by centuries of smoke, has become for me my own ancestral place where fifty millenniums ago, a creature not so different from myself hunched close to the first fire. The striped swallow that nests under the arch was here before man's upright troupes came through the silent baobabs, and so were the geckos, hornets, and small mice that go about their bright-eyed business undisturbed.

Giga and Gimbe mind the cave, which stays cool in the dry heat of the day, and one or the other is always by the fire, playing delicately on an mbira. Meals are at random in the African way, and we have no wish to give them order. We eat before going on a hunt and after we return, and on some days there are two meals and on others four or five. When least expected and most wanted, Gimbe will come with a basin of fresh water—karibu—and then he will stir our posho into his charred pot with his wood spoon and present this warming stuff with a fine stew of whatever wild meat is at hand. In the afternoons, we bathe in the river and stand on the cool banks to dry, and toward twilight almost every night we climb onto the toppled monolith that forms the roof over the cave, and smoke, and watch the sun go down over Sipunga.

To the rock cast like a gravestone, the oldest woman, muttering, comes home each twilight with a bundle of sticks for her night fire. When, out of happiness, I greet her, she gives me the cold cheerless stare of ancient women—Why do you greet me, idiot? Can't you see the way that the world goes?—and totters past me to her hearth without a word. At darkness, in wind, three fires light the rock face, with leaping shadows of the three small human forms, clattering and cawing under the skeleton of their lone tree. But the dance of shadows dies as the fires dim and the three panakwetepi, the "old children," fall silent. The eldest draws bat-colored rags about her, hunched and nodding, and subsides into a little heap of dim mortality. I wonder if she hears hyenas howling.

An Mbulu donkey gives its maniacal cry, and far away on the escarpment, probing slowly across the mountain darkness, shine the hard eyes of a truck, bringing in cheap trade goods for the duka. From the Seven Hearths, the Hadza see the outside world, but the world cannot see them. "This valley, this people—it is a tragedy we are watching!" Enderlein cries. "And it is a sign of what is happening everywhere in this country, in the whole world! Sometimes I really don't think it is bearable to watch it, I have not the heart for it, I will have to leave. And other times, especially when I am drunk, I can see myself as a spectator at the greatest comedy there ever was, the obliteration of mankind by our own hand."

When the air grows cold we come down off the rock. In the cave, Hadza are gathered at the fire, shoulder to shoulder like the swallows, clicking endlessly in their warm tongue, with big sighs and little groans of emphasis and soft *n* and *anh* and *m* sounds, hands moving in and out among the embers, the scraping of a knife blade on a stone, a cough, a whiff of bangi, until finally the people of the Seven Hearths depart. The last man squatting, Magandula, crawls off to his sleep with a loud self-conscious sigh that tells the white men, stretched silent as two dead beneath the stars, that the worldly Magandula, although patient to a fault, has no place among such simple folk. Already Giga the fire tender is breathing his night breath that sounds like a man pulled down in flight; I watch his face, asleep, and feel a tingling at the temples. Giga has been in Africa forever, he is the prototypic model of a man, the clay, and one loves not Giga but this being who is mortal, a kind humorous fellow of great presence and no small intelligence who will die. And Gimbe, too, singing his songs and playing his sweet irimbako, and even the brash Magandula, donning his magic street shoes for his flight from the old ways: to perceive them in their sleep—Enderlein, too—is to perceive and to make peace with one's own self.

Toward dawn, Giga hurls faggots on the fire and rolls himself a fat and lumpy smoke and coughs and coughs and coughs to his heart's content, and one forgives him even this. Soon the cricket stops its singing, and after a silence there is birdsong, the bell note of the slate-colored boubou, the doves and turacos, a hornbill. At sun-up comes an electric screeching that signals the passage of swift petal-colored lovebirds.

The Hadza hunch close to their fires, getting warm; when the sun has heat in it, the day begins. Soon the akwetepi, the "little people," come past the cave, first boys with bows, then younger children seeking berries—"*Shai-yaamo!*" they call. And the answer is *Shai-yamo mtana*, to which they echo a soft *m-taa-na*. They pull berry branches down and strip them, laughing. At the fire, long-legged in shorts and boots, the restless white men sip their tea and listen, warming cold hands on their tin cups. In the next days we will go away without the game scout Magandula, who is muttering about poachers in the region, and asks if he might linger in the bush.

The last day at the cave is slow and peaceful. The hunters come down from the Seven Hearths to a discreet fire from where they can spy politely on the visitors; they carve and chew and soften and sight new arrow shafts, bracing them by inserting them between the toes, or cut pipe holes into new pieces of stone found in the river.

"*Dong-go-ko.*" One man sings softly of zebras and lions. "*Dong-go-ko gogosala . . .*"

Zebra, zebra, running fast . . .

The women are out gathering roots and tubers, and also the silken green nut of the baobab which, pounded on a stone and cooked a little, provides food for five months of the year. The still air of the hillside quakes with the pound of rock on rock, and in this place so distant from the world, the steady sound is an echo of the Stone Age. Sometimes the seeds are left inside the hull to make a baby's rattle, or a half shell may be kept to make a drinking cup. In the rains, the baobab gives shelter, and in drought, the water that it stores in its soft hollows, and always fiber thread and sometimes honey. Perhaps the greatest baobab were already full grown when man made red rock paintings at Darashagan. Today young baobab are killed by fires, set by the strangers who clear the country for their herds and gardens, and the tree where man was born is dying out in Hadza Land.

231

From a grove off in the western light, an arrow rises, piercing the sun poised on the dark massif of the Sipunga; the shaft glints, balances, and drops to earth. Soon the young hunters, returning homeward, come in single file between the trees, skins black against black silhouetted thorn. One has an mbira, and in wistful monotony, in hesitation step, the naked forms with their small bows pass one by one in a slow dance of childhood. The figures wind in and out among black thorn and tawny twilight grass and vanish. Once more as in a dream, like a band of the Old People, the small Gumba, who long ago went into hiding in the earth.

Acknowledgments

For encouraging the making of this book I am particularly grateful to John Owen, whose vision and dedication in a crucial time helped to save African wildlife for the future.

I thank Martha Gellhorn and Truman Capote for recommending me so generously to Dr. Owen, and also William Shawn of *The New Yorker* magazine for the unfailing support that has made my travels possible for years.

Frank Minot and his staff at the African Wildlife Leadership Foundation in Nairobi (a branch of the Conservation Foundation in Washington, dedicated to the vital task of turning young Africans toward conservation), and also his wife, Mary, were helpful in innumerable ways that made an important contribution, not least of which was the warmth and hospitality of their lovely house in Langata. Other good friends who took me in with unfailing hospitality were Iain Douglas-Hamilton (Manyara), Peter Enderlein (Yaida Chini), Nancy and Lewis Hurxthal (Embakasi), Patricia and John Owen (Arusha), Ruth and Hugh Russell (Arusha), and Desmond Vesey-FitzGerald (Momela). At Seronera, where I had my own quarters, the parks staff and the scientists of the Serengeti Research Institute were most hospitable, in particular Kay and George Schaller and Kay and Myles Turner. Prince Sadruddin Aga Khan kindly invited me to join his safari in the Ngorongoro Crater in 1970, and another safari there later that year was greatly assisted by the generosity of Mr. Solomon Ole Saibull, then conservator of the Crater, who made available his private tent.

In gratitude for kindnesses, information, and assistance, I mention the following in the knowledge that the names of others no less helpful will occur to me when it is too late; those I thank, too, with my apologies:

Terence Adamson (Samburu)
Jock Anderson (NFD)*
Ir. Hubert Braun (SRI)**
M. K. Chauhar (Magadi)
Mervyn Cowie (Nairobi) (1961)
Dr. Harvey Croze (SRI)**
Mme. Leo d'Erlanger (Seronera)
Reggie Destro (Ngorongoro)

 * Northern Frontier District
** Serengeti Research Institute

Iain Douglas-Hamilton (Ndala)
Badru Eboo (Nairobi)
Dr. G. Eckhart (Njombe)
Ulla Ekblad (Nairobi) (1961)
Peter Enderlein (Yaida Chini)
Luis Fernandes (Nairobi)
P. A. G. "Sandy" Field (Seronera)
Martha Gellhorn (Naivasha)
J. B. Gillett (East African Herbarium)
Giga (Gidabembe)
Gimbe (Gidabembe)
Aleicester Graham (Langata)
Dr. Peter Greenway, O.B.E. (East African Herbarium)
Dr. Bernhard Grzimek (Seronera)
Patrick Hemingway (Arusha) (1961)
Jane and Hillary Hook (Kiganjo)
Nancy and Lewis Hurxthal (Embakasi—Ngurumans)
Dr. Alan Jacobs (Inst. African Studies—Nairobi)
E. P. K. Kayu (East African Herbarium)
Kessi (Frank) (Mt. Meru—Ol Doinyo Lengai)
Prince Sadruddin Aga Khan (Ngorongoro)
Kimunginye (Derati)
Dr. Hans Kruuk (SRI)**
John Kufunguo (Ngorongoro)
Dr. Hugh Lamprey (SRI)**
Richard Leakey (National Museum)
Leite (Gol Mountains)
Adrian Luckhurst (NFD)*
Sir Malcolm MacDonald (Seronera)
Magandula (Gidabembe)
Martin ole Mengoriki (Embagai)
Mary and Frank Minot (Langata)
Jonathan Muhanga (Manyara)
M. Nawaz (Seronera)
Perez Olindo (Nairobi)
Patricia and John Owen (Arusha)
David Ommaney (Nairobi)
Ian S. C. Parker (Nairobi)
Eliot Porter (NFD)*
Sandy Price (National Museum)
Robert Reitnauer (Ngurumans)
Mary Richards (Momela)

234

Oria Rocco (Ndala)
Alan Root (Nairobi)
Hilary and Monty Ruben (Nairobi)
Ruth and Hugh Russell (Arusha)
Solomon ole Saibull (Ngorongoro)
Yvonne and John Savidge (Ruaha)
Kay and George Schaller (Seronera)
Serekieli (Mt. Meru—Ngurdoto)
David Stevens (Manyara)
Simon Trevor (Nairobi)
Kay and Myles Turner (Seronera)
Desmond Vesey-FitzGerald (Momela)
David Western (Nairobi)
Dr. James Woodburn (London)

Finally, I am much indebted to the people who checked the manuscript for mistakes; they are, of course, in no way responsible for errors that may remain.

Most or all of the book was read by Dr. John S. Owen and Myles Turner, by ecologists Desmond Vesey-FitzGerald and David Western, and by Hugh Russell, who paid particular attention to the use and spelling of Swahili. In addition, particular chapters benefited greatly from the attentions of the following:

Chapter I	John S. Owen
Chapter II	Mary and Frank Minot, Hugh Russell
Chapter III	Jock Anderson, Richard Leakey
Chapter IV	Dr. George Schaller, Myles Turner
Chapter V	Myles Turner
Chapter VI	Dr. George Schaller, Myles Turner
Chapter VIII	Desmond Vesey-FitzGerald
Chapter IX	Nancy and Lewis Hurxthal
Chapter X	Peter Enderlein, Dr. James Woodburn (conversation in London)
Glossary	Hugh Russell

Peter Matthiessen

Glossary

(All words are Swahili where not otherwise indicated)

askari   soldier, warden, guard
banda   shed, thatched hut, rondavel
bangi   from Indian *bhang*: (*Cannabis*) hemp, narcotic
bao   ancient pebble game
biltong   dried strips of wild meat
boma   stock corral, thorn-walled shelter
dawa   medicine, charm, talisman
debe   4–gallon kerosene can
donga   gully, ravine, dry except in rains
duka   trading post or general store
en-gang   Maasai: home village
kanga   shawl (of East Indian print batik)
karibu   welcome to . . .
kikoi   (see shuka)
korongo   small stream, drainage line
laibon   Maasai: medicine man
magadi   soda, soda lake
mbira   marimba
miombo   dry forest, mostly *Brachystegia*
morani   Maasai; pl. il-moran: warrior
mswaki   toothbrush bush (*Salvadora*)
mzungu   pl. wazungu: white person, European wilderness (especially dry
nyika   thorn scrub waste between highlands and the sea)
ol duvai   Maasai: bayonet aloe (*Sansevieria*)
panga   cane- or brush-cutting machete
pombe   local beer (usually from maize)
posho   ration (especially ugali)
shamba   farm plot
shifta   Somali: bandit (literally "wanderer")
shuka   rectangular piece of cloth, printed or dyed, worn as herdsman's
cape or toga; also, as kikoi, or man's "skirt" (on the East African
Coast)
ugali   maize meal, porridge

Notes

Chapter 1

1. Willard Trask, ed., *The Unwritten Song*, Macmillan, 1966.
2. A. J. Arkell, *A History of the Sudan*, Oxford, 1961.
3. Godfrey Lienhardt, "The Shilluk of the Upper Nile," in *African Worlds*, ed. by Daryll Forde, Oxford, 1954.
4. Trask, *op. cit.*
5. Mary Douglas, *Purity and Danger*, Routledge, 1966.
6. E. E. Evans-Pritchard, *The Nuer*, Oxford, 1940.
7. Geoffrey Parrinder, *African Mythology*, Hamlyn, 1967.

Chapter 2

1. Marjorie Perham, in Preface to *Mau Mau Detainee* by J. M. Kariuki, Penguin, 1964.
2. J. M. Kariuki, *Mau Mau Detainee*, Penguin, 1964.
3. Patrice Lumumba, quoted in *The Horizon History of Africa* by Horizon Editors, McGraw-Hill, 1971.
4. G. P. Murdock, *Africa: Its Peoples and Their Culture History*, McGraw-Hill, 1959.
5. K. R. Dundas, "Notes on the Origin and History of the Kikuyu and Dorobo Tribes," *Man*, no. 78, 1908.
6. Joseph Thomson, *Through Masai Land*, Cass, 1968.
7. Ludwig R. von Hohnel, *Discovery by Count Teleki of Lakes Rudolf and Stephanie*, Cass, 1968.
8. J. H. Patterson, *The Man-Eaters of Tsavo*, Macmillan, 1963.
9. R. Oliver and G. Matthew, *History of East Africa*, vol. 1, Oxford, 1963, p. 417.
10. Jomo Kenyatta, *Facing Mt. Kenya*, Secker, 1938.
11. Peter Beard, *The End of the Game*, Viking, 1965.
12. Placide Tempels in Basil Davidson, *The African Past*, Grosset & Dunlap, 1964.
13. Peter Beard, *op. cit.*
14. Karen Blixen, *Out of Africa*, Putnam, 1937.
15. Peter Beard, *op. cit.*

Chapter 3

1. Gerhard Lindblom, *The Akamba in British East Africa*, Uppsala, 1920.
2. Elspeth Huxley, *The Flame Trees of Thika*, Penguin, 1962.
3. Dundas, *op. cit.*
4. G. W. B. Huntingford, *The Southern Nilo-Hamites*, Internat. African Inst., 1953.
5. Paul Spencer, *The Samburu*, University of California Press, 1965.
6. J. A. Hunter, *Hunter*, Hamish Hamilton, 1952.
7. Dr. Alan Jacobs, correspondence.
8. Spencer, *op. cit.*
9. John G. Williams, *Field Guide to Birds of Central and East Africa*, Houghton, 1964; idem., *Field Guide to the National Parks of East Africa*, Collins, 1968.
10. M. Posnansky, ed., *Prelude to East African History*, Oxford, 1966.
11. Sonia Cole, *The Prehistory of East Africa*, Macmillan, 1965.
12. R. Oliver and G. Matthew, *History of East Africa*, vol. I. Oxford, 1963.
13. *Ibid.*
14. G. P. Murdock, *op. cit.*
15. *Ibid.*
16. Lindblom, *op. cit.*
17. Jacobs, correspondence.
18. von Hohnel, *op. cit.*
19. Joy Adamson, *The Peoples of Kenya*, Collins, 1967.
20. Kariuki, *op. cit.*
21. Spencer, *op. cit.*
22. Thomson, *op. cit.*

Chapter 4

1. Huntingford, *op. cit.*
2. Murdock, *op. cit.*
3. George B. Schaller, *The Serengeti Lion*, Univ. Chicago Press, 1972 (uncorrected proofs).
4. Frederick C. Selous, *A Hunter's Wanderings in Africa*, London, 1881.
5. Parrinder, *op. cit.*
6. George B. Schaller and Gordon R. Lowther, "The Relevance of Carnivore Behavior to the Study of Early Hominids," *Southwestern Jour. Anthrop.*, vol. 25, no. 4, 1969.
7. Hugh Russell, conversations and correspondence.

Chapter 5

1. C. W. Hobley, "Notes on the Dorobo," *Man,* no. 76, 1906.
2. H. A. Fosbrooke, "An Administrative Record of the Masai Social System." *Tanganyika Notes and Records,* no. 26, 1948 (hereafter cited as *TNR*).
3. *Ibid.*
4. Joseph H. Greenberg, *The Languages of Africa,* University of Indiana Press, 1963.
5. Karl Peters, quoted in Fosbrooke, *op. cit.*
6. G. W. B. Huntingford, "The Peopling of East Africa by Its Modern Inhabitants," from *History of East Africa* by R. Oliver and G. Matthew, Oxford, 1963.
7. Robert F. Gray, *The Sonjo of Tanganyika,* Oxford, 1963.
8. Ian Henderson (with Philip Goodhart), *The Hunt for Kimathi,* Hamish Hamilton, 1958.
9. A. Wykes, *Snake Man,* Simon and Schuster, 1961.
10. C. P. J. Ionides, "Southern Province Native Superstitions," *TNR,* no. 29, 1950.
11. Russell, *op. cit.*
12. Colin Turnbull, *The Lonely African,* Chatto, 1963.
13. H. K. Schneider, "The Lion-Men of Singida: A Reappraisal," *TNR,* no. 58, 1962.
14. Elspeth Huxley, *With Forks and Hope,* Morrow, 1964.
15. Parrinder, *op. cit.*
16. Blixen, *op. cit.*
17. Robert F. Gray, "Structural Aspects of Mbugwe Witchcraft," from *Witchcraft and Sorcery in East Africa,* ed. by John Middleton and E. H. Winter, Routledge, 1963.

Chapter 6

1. D. M. Sindiyo, "Game Department Field Experience in Public Education." *E. African Agric. & Forestry Journal,* Vol. XXXIII, 1968.
2. George B. Schaller, conversations.
3. George B. Schaller, *The Serengeti Lion.*
4. *Ibid.*

Chapter 7

1. J. A. Hunter, *op. cit.*
2. Henri Junod, from *Life in a South African Tribe,* Macmillan, 1912, quoted in *Technicians of the Sacred* by J. Rothenburg, Doubleday, 1968.

3. Stewart Edward White, *The Rediscovered Country*, Doubleday, 1915.
4. R. M. Laws and I. S. C. Parker, "Recent Studies on Elephant Populations in East Africa," *Symp. Zool. Soc.*, 1968.
5. *Ibid.*
6. David Western, conversations.
7. Arthur Neumann, *Elephant Hunting in East Equatorial Africa*, London, 1898.
8. Dennis Holman, *The Elephant People*, Murray, 1967.

Chapter 8

1. Adapted from Colin Turnbull, *Tradition and Change in African Life*, Barmerlea, 1967.
2. Thomson, *op cit*.
3. Ionides, in Wykes, *op. cit.*
4. G. W. B. Huntingford, "The Social Organisation of the Dorobo," *African Studies*, no. 1, 1942.
5. Huxley, *With Forks and Hope*.
6. L. S. B. Leakey, "Preliminary Report on ... Engaruka Ruins," *TNR*, no. 1, 1936.
7. Murdock, *op. cit.*
8. Elspeth Huxley, *A New Earth*, Chatto, 1960.
9. Posnansky, *op cit*.
10. Gray, *The Sonjo of Tanganyika*.
11. Murdock, *op. cit.*
12. Leslie Brown, *Africa: A Natural History*, Hamish Hamilton, 1965.
13. Sir A. Claud Hollis, *The Masai*, Oxford, 1935.

Chapter 9

1. Hollis, *op. cit.*
2. Frank Lambrecht, "Aspects of the Evolution and Ecology of Tsetse Flies ... ," from *Papers in African Prehistory* by J. D. Fage and R. A. Oliver, Cambridge, 1970.
3. Blixen, *op. cit.*
4. Adamson, *op. cit.*
5. Gray, *The Sonjo of Tanganyika*.
6. Myles Turner, conversations and correspondence.

Chapter 10

1. From Olivia Vlahos, *African Beginnings*, Viking, 1967.

2. Dorothea Bleek, "The Hadzapi or Watindega of Tanganyika Territory," *Africa*, no. 3, 1931.

3. F. J. Bagshawe, "The Peoples of the Happy Valley," *Jour. of the African Society*, Part II, no. 24, 1925.

4. Dorothea Bleek, "Traces of Former Bushman Occupation in Tanganyika Territory," *South African Jour. Sci.*, no. 28, 1931.

5. L. S. B. Leakey, *Stone Age Cultures of Kenya Colony*, Cambridge, 1931.

6. Peter Enderlein, conversations and correspondence.

7. George J. Klima, *The Barabaig*, Holt, Rinehart and Winston, 1970.

8. Posnansky, *op. cit.*

9. James C. Woodburn, "Hunters and Gatherers," Brit. Mus. brochure, 1970. See also Selected Bibliography.

10. *Ibid.*

11. G. M. Wilson, "The Tatoga of Tanganyika," *TNR*, no. 33, 1952.

12. Woodburn, *op. cit.*

13. B. Cooper, "The Kindiga," *TNR*, no. 27, 1949.

14. Klima, *op. cit.*

15. R. A. J. Maguire, "Il-Torobo," *TNR*, no. 25, 1948.

Selected Bibliography

Abrahamson, H. *The Origin of Death.* Kegan Paul, 1952.

Adamson, Joy. *The Peoples of Kenya.* Collins, 1967.

Arkell, A. J. *A History of the Sudan,* Oxford, 1961.

Bagshawe, F. J. "The Peoples of the Happy Valley," *Jour. of the African Society,* Part II, no. 24, 1925.

Beard, Peter. *The End of the Game.* Viking, 1965.

Bleek, Dorothea. "The Hadzapi or Watindega of Tanganyika Territory," *Africa,* no. 3, 1931; *idem,* "Traces of Former Bushman Occupation in Tanganyika Territory," *South African Jour. Sci.,* no. 28, 1931.

Blixen, Karen. *Out of Africa.* Putnam, 1937; Cape, 1964.

Brown, Leslie. *Africa: A Natural History.* Hamish Hamilton, 1965.

Carrington, Richard. *Elephants.* Chatto, 1958.

Cave, F. O., and James D. MacDonald. *Birds of the Sudan.* Oliver & Boyd, 1955.

Clark, J. Desmond. *The Prehistory of Africa.* Praeger, 1970.

Cole, Sonia. *The Prehistory of East Africa.* Weidenfeld & Nicolson, 1964.

Cooper, B. "The Kindiga," *Tanganyika Notes and Records* (hereafter *TNR*), no. 27, 1949.

Davidson, Basil. *The African Past.* Longmans, 1964.

Douglas, Mary. *Purity and Danger.* Routledge, 1966.

Douglas-Hamilton, Iain. "The Lake Manyara Elephant Problem," unpub. ms., 1969.

Dundas, K. R. "Notes on the Origin and History of the Kikuyu and Dorobo Tribes," *Man,* no. 78, 1908.

Dyson, W. S., and V. E. Fuchs. "The Elmolo," *Jour. Royal African Inst.,* no. 67, 1937.

Enderlein, Peter. "The Yaida Valley," unpub. ms.

Evans-Pritchard, E. E. *The Nuer.* Oxford, 1940.

Fage, J. D., and R. A. Oliver. *Papers in African Prehistory.* Cambridge, 1970.

Fordham, Paul. *The Geography of African Affairs.* Penguin, 1965.

Fosbrooke, H. A. "An Administrative Record of the Masai Social System," *TNR,* no. 26, 1948; *idem.* "A Stone Age Tribe in Tanganyika," *South African Arch. Bull.,* no. 11, 1956.

Graham, Aleicester. "The Lake Rudolf Crocodile," unpub. ms.

Gray, Robert F. *The Sonjo of Tanganyika.* Oxford, 1963; *idem,* "Structural

242

Aspects of Mbugwe Witchcraft," in Middleton and Winter, *Witchcraft and Sorcery in East Africa.* Routledge, 1963.

Greenberg, Joseph H. *The Languages of Africa.* University of Indiana, 1963.

Gregory, J. W. *The Rift Valley and the Geology of East Africa.* Seeley, Service, 1910.

Gulliver, P., and P. H. Gulliver. *The Central Nilo-Hamites.* Internat. African Inst., 1953.

Henderson, Ian (with Philip Goodhart). *The Hunt for Kimathi.* Hamish Hamilton, 1958.

Hobley, C. W. "Notes on the Dorobo." *Man,* no. 76, 1906.

Hollis, Sir A. Claud. *The Masai.* Oxford, 1935.

Holmon, Dennis. *The Elephant People.* Murray, 1967.

Horizon Editors. *The Horizon History of Africa.* McGraw-Hill, 1971.

Hunter, J. A. *Hunter.* Hamish Hamilton, 1952.

Huntingford, G. W. B. "The Peopling of East Africa by Its Modern Inhabitants," in Oliver and Matthew, *History of East Africa,* vol. 1, Oxford, 1963; *idem,* "The Social Organisation of the Dorobo," *African Studies,* no. 1, 1942; *idem, The Southern Nilo-Hamites.* Internat. African Inst., 1953.

Huxley, Elspeth. *The Flame Trees of Thika.* Penguin, 1962; *idem, A New Earth.* Chatto, 1960; *idem, With Forks and Hope,* Chatto, 1964.

Ionides, C. P. J. "Southern Province Native Superstitions," *TNR,* no. 29, 1950.

Junod, Henri. *Life in a South African Tribe.* Macmillan, 1912, quoted in *Technicians of the Sacred* by J. Rothenburg, Doubleday, 1968.

Kariuki, J. M. *Mau Mau Detainee.* Penguin, 1964.

Kenyatta, Jomo. *Facing Mt. Kenya.* Secker, 1938.

Klima, George J. *The Barabaig.* Holt, Rinehart and Winston, 1970.

Laws, R. M., and I. S. C. Parker. "Recent Studies on Elephant Populations in East Africa," *Symp. Zool. Soc.,* 1968.

Leakey, L. S. B. *Adam's Ancestors.* Harper (Torch-books), 1960; *idem,* "Preliminary Report on an Examination of the Engaruka Ruins," *TNR,* no. 1, 1936; *idem, Stone Age Cultures of Kenya Colony,* Cambridge, 1931.

Leakey, Richard. "In Search of Man's Past at Lake Rudolf," *Nat. Geog.,* 1969.

Lee, Richard, and I. Devore, eds. *Man the Hunter.* Aldine, 1968.

Lienhardt, Godfrey. "The Shilluk of the Upper Nile," in *African Worlds,* ed. Daryll Forde, Oxford, 1954.

Lindblom, Gerhard. *The Akamba in British East Africa.* Uppsala, 1920.

Maguire, R. A. J. "Il-Torobo," *TNR,* no. 25, 1948.

el Mahdi, Mandour. *A Short History of the Sudan.* Oxford, 1965.

Meinertzhagen, Col. Richard. *Kenya Diary: 1902–1906.* Oliver & Boyd, 1957.

Middleton, John, and E. H. Winter, eds. *Witchcraft and Sorcery in East Africa.* Routledge, 1963.

Murdock, G. P. *Africa: Its Peoples and Their Culture History.* McGraw-Hill, 1959.

Neumann, Arthur. *Elephant Hunting in East Equatorial Africa.* London, 1898.

Oliver, R., and J. D. Fage. *A Short History of Africa.* Penguin, 1962.

Oliver, R., and G. Matthew. *History of East Africa,* vol. 1, Oxford, 1963.

Parrinder, Geoffrey. *African Mythology.* Hamlyn, 1967.

Patterson, J. H. *The Man-Eaters of Tsavo.* Macmillan, 1963.

Posnansky, M., ed. *Prelude to East African History.* Oxford, 1966.

Praed, C. W. Mackworth, and Capt. C. H. B. Grant, *Birds of East and North East Africa.* Longmans, 1952.

Radin, Paul. *African Folktales.* Bollingen, 1952.

Ricciardi, Mireilla. *Vanishing Africa.* Reynal, 1971.

Schaller, George B. *The Serengeti Lion.* Univ. Chicago Press, 1972 (uncorrected proofs).

Schaller, George B., and Gordon R. Lowther. "The Relevance of Carnivore Behavior to the Study of Early Hominids," *Southwestern Jour. Anthrop.*, vol. 25, no. 4, 1969.

Schneider, H. K. "The Lion-Men of Singida: A Reappraisal," *TNR,* no. 58, 1962.

Selous, Frederick C. *A Hunter's Wanderings in Africa.* London, 1881.

Sindiyo, D. M. "Game Department Field Experience in Public Education," *E. African Agric. and Forestry Journal,* vol. XXXIII, 1968.

Spencer, Paul. *The Samburu.* University of California Press, 1965.

Thomas, Elizabeth Marshall. *The Harmless People.* Secker, 1959.

Thomson, Joseph. *Through Masai Land.* Cass, 1968.

Trask, Willard, ed. *The Unwritten Song.* Macmillan, 1966.

Turnbull, Colin. *The Forest People.* Chatto, 1961; *idem, The Lonely African.* Chatto, 1963; *idem, Tradition and Change in African Tribal Life.* Barmerlea, 1967.

Van der Post, Laurens. *The Lost World of the Kalahari.* Hogarth Press, 1958.

Vesey-FitzGerald, Desmond. "Elephants in National Parks: A Problem of the Environment," unpub. ms., 1969.

Vlahos, Olivia. *African Beginnings.* Viking, 1967.

von Hohnel, Ludwig R. *Discovery by Count Teleki of Lakes Rudolf and Stephanie.* Cass, 1968.

White, Stewart Edward. *The Rediscovered Country.* Doubleday, 1915.

Williams, John. *Field Guide to the Birds of Central and East Africa.* Houghton, 1964; *idem, Field Guide to the National Parks of East Africa.* Collins, 1968.

Wilson, G. M. "The Tatoga of Tanganyika," *TNR,* no. 33, 1952.

Woodburn, James C. "The Future of the Tindiga," *TNR*, no. 58, 1962; *idem*, "Hunters and Gatherers," British Museum brochure, 1970.

Wykes, A. *Snake Man*. Simon and Schuster, 1961.

Index

247

251